TAXMANN'S

BHARATIYA SAKSHYA ADHINIYAM 2023

TAXMANN®'S

Bharatiya Sakshya Adhiniyam 2023

With Comparative Study of Bharatiya Sakshya Adhiniyam 2023 & Indian Evidence Act 1872

© Taxmann

Price : ₹ 495

Published by :
Taxmann Publications (P.) Ltd.

Sales & Marketing :
59/32, New Rohtak Road, New Delhi-110 005 India
Phone : +91-11-45562222
Website : www.taxmann.com
E-mail : sales@taxmann.com

Regd. Office :
21/35, West Punjabi Bagh, New Delhi-110 026 India

Printed at :
Tan Prints (India) Pvt. Ltd.
44 Km. Mile Stone, National Highway, Rohtak Road
Village Rohad, Distt. Jhajjar (Haryana) India
E-mail : sales@tanprints.com

9 789364 551380

Disclaimer

CONTENTS

1

TABLE SHOWING SECTIONS OF INDIAN EVIDENCE ACT, 1872 AND CORRESPONDING SECTIONS OF BHARATIYA SAKSHYA ADHINIYAM, 2023

INDIAN EVIDENCE ACT, 1872		BHARATIYA SAKSHYA ADHINIYAM, 2023	
SEC.	***HEADING***	***SEC.***	***HEADING***
1	Short title, extent and commencement	**1**	Short title, application and commencement
2	Repeal of enactments [Repealed]	**170**	Repeal and savings
3	Interpretation clause	**2**	Definitions
3, para 1	"Court"	**2(*1*)(*a*)**	"Court"
3, para 2	"Fact"	**2(*1*)(*f*)**	"fact"
3, para 3	"Relevant"	**2(*1*)(*k*)**	"relevant"
3, para 4	"Facts in issue"	**2(*1*)(*g*)**	"facts in issue"
3, para 5	"Document"	**2(*1*)(*d*)**	"document"
3, para 6	"Evidence"	**2(*1*)(*e*)**	"evidence"
3, para 7	"Proved"	**2(*1*)(*j*)**	"proved"

INDIAN EVIDENCE ACT, 1872		BHARATIYA SAKSHYA ADHINIYAM, 2023	
SEC.	*HEADING*	*SEC.*	*HEADING*
3, para 8	"Disproved"	**2(*1*)(*c*)**	"disproved"
3, para 9	"Not proved"	**2(*1*)(*i*)**	"not proved"
3, para 10	"India"	—	—
4, para 1	"may presume"	**2(*1*)(*h*)**	"may presume"
4, para 2	"Shall presume"	**2(*1*)(*l*)**	"shall presume"
4, para 3	"Conclusive proof"	**2(*1*)(*b*)**	"conclusive proof"
5	Evidence may be given of facts in issue and relevant facts	**3**	Evidence may be given of facts in issue and relevant facts
6	Relevancy of facts forming part of same transaction	**4**	Relevancy of facts forming part of same transaction
7	Facts which are the occasion, cause or effect of facts in issue	**5**	Facts which are the occasion, cause or effect of facts in issue or relevant facts
8	Motive, preparation and previous or subsequent conduct	**6**	Motive, preparation and previous or subsequent conduct
9	Facts necessary to explain or introduce relevant facts	**7**	Facts necessary to explain or introduce fact in issue or relevant facts
10	Things said or done by conspirator in reference to common design	**8**	Things said or done by conspirator in reference to common design
11	When facts not otherwise relevant become relevant	**9**	When facts not otherwise relevant become relevant

INDIAN EVIDENCE ACT, 1872		BHARATIYA SAKSHYA ADHINIYAM, 2023	
SEC.	***HEADING***	***SEC.***	***HEADING***
12	In suits for damages, facts tending to enable Court to determine amount are relevant	**10**	Facts tending to enable Court to determine amount are relevant in suits for damages
13	Facts relevant when right or custom is in question	**11**	Facts relevant when right or custom is in question
14	Facts showing existence of state of mind, or of body or bodily feeling	**12**	Facts showing existence of state of mind, or of body or bodily feeling
15	Facts bearing on question whether act was accidental or intentional	**13**	Facts bearing on question whether act was accidental or intentional
16	Existence of course of business when relevant	**14**	Existence of course of business when relevant
17	Admission defined	**15**	Admission defined
18	Admission by party to proceeding or his agent	**16**	Admission by party to proceeding or his agent
19	Admissions by persons whose position must be proved as against party to suit	**17**	Admissions by persons whose position must be proved as against party to suit
20	Admissions by persons expressly referred to by party to suit	**18**	Admissions by persons expressly referred to by party to suit

INDIAN EVIDENCE ACT, 1872		BHARATIYA SAKSHYA ADHINIYAM, 2023	
SEC.	***HEADING***	***SEC.***	***HEADING***
21	Proof of admissions against persons making them, and by or on their behalf	**19**	Proof of admissions against persons making them, and by or on their behalf
22	When oral admissions as to contents of documents are relevant	**20**	When oral admissions as to contents of documents are relevant
22A	When oral admissions as to contents of electronic records are relevant	—	—
23	Admissions in civil cases, when relevant	**21**	Admissions in civil cases when relevant
24	Confession caused by inducement, threat or promise, when irrelevant in criminal proceeding	**22(1)**	Confession caused by inducement, threat, coercion or promise, when irrelevant in criminal proceeding
25	Confession to police officer not to be proved	**23(1)**	Confession to police officer
26	Confession by accused while in custody of police not to be proved against him	**23(2)**	Confession to police officer
27	How much of information received from accused may be proved	**23(2)**	Confession to police officer

INDIAN EVIDENCE ACT, 1872		BHARATIYA SAKSHYA ADHINIYAM, 2023	
SEC.	***HEADING***	***SEC.***	***HEADING***
28	Confession made after removal of impression caused by inducement, threat or promise, relevant	**22(1)**	Confession caused by inducement, threat, coercion or promise, when irrelevant in criminal proceeding
29	Confession otherwise relevant not to become irrelevant because of promise of secrecy, etc.	**22(2)**	Confession caused by inducement, threat, coercion or promise, when irrelevant in criminal proceeding
30	Consideration of proved confession affecting person making it and others jointly under trial for same offence	**24**	Consideration of proved confession affecting person making it and others jointly under trial for same offence
31	Admissions not conclusive proof, but may estop	**25**	Admissions not conclusive proof, but may estop
32	Cases in which statement of relevant fact by person who is dead or cannot be found, etc., is relevant	**26**	Cases in which statement of relevant fact by person who is dead or cannot be found, etc., is relevant
33	Relevancy of certain evidence for proving, in subsequent proceeding, the truth of facts therein stated	**27**	Relevancy of certain evidence for proving, in subsequent proceeding, truth of facts therein stated

INDIAN EVIDENCE ACT, 1872		BHARATIYA SAKSHYA ADHINIYAM, 2023	
SEC.	**HEADING**	**SEC.**	**HEADING**
34	Entries in books of account including those maintained in an electronic form when relevant	**28**	Entries in books of account when relevant
35	Relevancy of entry in public record or an electronic record made in performance of duty	**29**	Relevancy of entry in public record or an electronic record made in performance of duty
36	Relevancy of statements in maps, charts and plans	**30**	Relevancy of statements in maps, charts and plans
37	Relevancy of statement as to fact of public nature, contained in certain Acts or notifications	**31**	Relevancy of statement as to fact of public nature contained in certain Acts or notifications
38	Relevancy of statements as to any law contained in law books	**32**	Relevancy of statements as to any law contained in law books including electronic or digital form
39	What evidence to be given when statement forms part of a conversation, document, electronic record, book or series of letters or papers	**33**	What evidence to be given when statement forms part of a conversation, document, electronic record, book or series of letters or papers

I-12.1 TABLE SHOWING SECS. OF IEA, 1872 & BSA, 2023

INDIAN EVIDENCE ACT, 1872		BHARATIYA SAKSHYA ADHINIYAM, 2023	
SEC.	***HEADING***	***SEC.***	***HEADING***
40	Previous judgments relevant to bar a second suit or trial	**34**	Previous judgments relevant to bar a second suit or trial
41	Relevancy of certain judgments in probate, etc., jurisdiction	**35**	Relevancy of certain judgments in probate, etc., jurisdiction
42	Relevancy and effect of judgments, orders or decrees, other than those mentioned in section 41	**36**	Relevancy and effect of judgments, orders or decrees, other than those mentioned in section 35
43	Judgments, etc., other than those mentioned in sections 40 to 42, when relevant	**37**	Judgments, etc., other than those mentioned in sections 34, 35 and 36 when relevant
44	Fraud or collusion in obtaining judgment, or incompetency of Court, may be proved	**38**	Fraud or collusion in obtaining judgment, or incompetency of Court, may be proved
45	Opinions of experts	**39(1)**	Opinions of experts
45A	Opinion of Examiner of Electronic Evidence	**39(2)**	Opinions of experts
46	Facts bearing upon opinions of experts	**40**	Facts bearing upon opinions of experts
47	Opinion as to handwriting, when relevant	**41(1)**	Opinion as to handwriting and signature, when relevant

INDIAN EVIDENCE ACT, 1872		BHARATIYA SAKSHYA ADHINIYAM, 2023	
SEC.	*HEADING*	*SEC.*	*HEADING*
47A	Opinion as to electronic signature when relevant	**41(2)**	Opinion as to handwriting and signature, when relevant
48	Opinion as to existence of right or custom, when relevant	**42**	Opinion as to existence of general custom or right, when relevant
49	Opinions as to usages, tenets, etc., when relevant	**43**	Opinion as to usages, tenets, etc., when relevant
50	Opinion on relationship, when relevant	**44**	Opinion on relationship, when relevant
51	Grounds of opinion, when relevant	**45**	Grounds of opinion, when relevant
52	In civil cases character to prove conduct imputed, irrelevant	**46**	In civil cases character to prove conduct imputed, irrelevant
53	In criminal cases, previous good character relevant	**47**	In criminal cases previous good character relevant
53A	Evidence of character or previous sexual experience not relevant in certain cases	**48**	Evidence of character or previous sexual experience not relevant in certain cases
54	Previous bad character not relevant, except in reply	**49**	Previous bad character not relevant, except in reply
55	Character as affecting damages	**50**	Character as affecting damages

I-12.3 TABLE SHOWING SECS. OF IEA, 1872 & BSA, 2023

INDIAN EVIDENCE ACT, 1872		BHARATIYA SAKSHYA ADHINIYAM, 2023	
SEC.	***HEADING***	***SEC.***	***HEADING***
56	Fact judicially noticeable need not be proved	**51**	Fact judicially noticeable need not be proved
57	Facts of which Court must take judicial notice	**52**	Facts of which Court shall take judicial notice
58	Facts admitted need not be proved	**53**	Facts admitted need not be proved
59	Proof of facts by oral evidence	**54**	Proof of facts by oral evidence
60	Oral evidence must be direct	**55**	Oral evidence to be direct
61	Proof of contents of documents	**56**	Proof of contents of documents
62	Primary evidence	**57**	Primary evidence
63	Secondary evidence	**58**	Secondary evidence
64	Proof of documents by primary evidence	**59**	Proof of documents by primary evidence
65	Cases in which secondary evidence relating to documents may be given	**60**	Cases in which secondary evidence relating to documents may be given
65A	Special provisions as to evidence relating to electronic record	**62**	Special provisions as to evidence relating to electronic record
65B	Admissibility of electronic records	**63**	Admissibility of electronic records
66	Rules as to notice to produce	**64**	Rules as to notice to produce

INDIAN EVIDENCE ACT, 1872		BHARATIYA SAKSHYA ADHINIYAM, 2023	
SEC.	***HEADING***	***SEC.***	***HEADING***
67	Proof of signature and handwriting of person alleged to have signed or written document produced	**65**	Proof of signature and handwriting of person alleged to have signed or written document produced
67A	Proof as to electronic signature	**66**	Proof as to electronic signature
68	Proof of execution of document required by law to be attested	**67**	Proof of execution of document required by law to be attested
69	Proof where no attesting witness found	**68**	Proof where no attesting witness found
70	Admission of execution by party to attested document	**69**	Admission of execution by party to attested document
71	Proof when attesting witness denies the execution	**70**	Proof when attesting witness denies execution
72	Proof of document not required by law to be attested	**71**	Proof of document not required by law to be attested
73	Comparison of signature, writing or seal with others admitted or proved	**72**	Comparison of signature, writing or seal with others admitted or proved
73A	Proof as to verification of digital signature	**73**	Proof as to verification of digital signature

INDIAN EVIDENCE ACT, 1872		BHARATIYA SAKSHYA ADHINIYAM, 2023	
SEC.	***HEADING***	***SEC.***	***HEADING***
74	Public documents	**74(1)**	Public and private documents
75	Private documents	**74(2)**	Public and private documents
76	Certified copies of public documents	**75**	Certified copies of public documents
77	Proof of documents by production of certified copies	**76**	Proof of documents by production of certified copies
78	Proof of other official documents	**77**	Proof of other official documents
79	Presumption as to genuineness of certified copies	**78**	Presumption as to genuineness of certified copies
80	Presumption as to documents produced as record of evidence	**79**	Presumption as to documents produced as record of evidence, etc.
81	Presumption as to Gazettes, newspapers, private Acts of Parliament and other documents	**80**	Presumption as to Gazettes, newspapers, and other documents
81A	Presumption as to Gazettes in electronic forms	**81**	Presumption as to Gazettes in electronic or digital record
82	Presumption as to document admissible in England without proof of seal or signature	—	—

INDIAN EVIDENCE ACT, 1872		BHARATIYA SAKSHYA ADHINIYAM, 2023	
SEC.	***HEADING***	***SEC.***	***HEADING***
83	Presumption as to maps or plans made by authority of Government	**82**	Presumption as to maps or plans made by authority of Government
84	Presumption as to collections of laws and reports of decisions	**83**	Presumption as to collections of laws and reports of decisions
85	Presumption as to powers of attorney	**84**	Presumption as to powers of attorney
85A	Presumption as to electronic agreements	**85**	Presumption as to electronic agreements
85B	Presumptions as to electronic records and electronic signatures	**86**	Presumption as to electronic records and electronic signatures
85C	Presumption as to Electronic Signature Certificates	**87**	Presumption as to Electronic Signature Certificates
86	Presumption as to certified copies of foreign judicial records	**88**	Presumption as to certified copies of foreign judicial records
87	Presumption as to books, maps and charts	**89**	Presumption as to books, maps and charts
88	Presumption as to telegraphic messages	—	—
88A	Presumption as to electronic messages	**90**	Presumption as to electronic messages

INDIAN EVIDENCE ACT, 1872		BHARATIYA SAKSHYA ADHINIYAM, 2023	
SEC.	***HEADING***	***SEC.***	***HEADING***
89	Presumption as to due execution, etc., of documents, not produced	**91**	Presumption as to due execution, etc., of documents not produced
90	Presumption as to documents thirty years old	**92**	Presumption as to documents thirty years old
90A	Presumption as to electronic records five years old	**93**	Presumption as to electronic records five years old
91	Evidence of terms of contracts, grants and other dispositions of property reduced to form of document	**94**	Evidence of terms of contracts, grants and other dispositions of property reduced to form of document
92	Exclusion of evidence of oral agreement	**95**	Exclusion of evidence of oral agreement
93	Exclusion of evidence to explain or amend ambiguous document	**96**	Exclusion of evidence to explain or amend ambiguous document
94	Exclusion of evidence against application of document to existing facts	**97**	Exclusion of evidence against application of document to existing facts
95	Evidence as to document unmeaning in reference to existing facts	**98**	Evidence as to document unmeaning in reference to existing facts

INDIAN EVIDENCE ACT, 1872		BHARATIYA SAKSHYA ADHINIYAM, 2023	
SEC.	***HEADING***	***SEC.***	***HEADING***
96	Evidence as to application of language which can apply to one only of several persons	**99**	Evidence as to application of language which can apply to one only of several persons
97	Evidence as to application of language to one of two sets of facts, to neither of which the whole correctly applies	**100**	Evidence as to application of language to one of two sets of facts, to neither of which the whole correctly applies
98	Evidence as to meaning of illegible characters, etc.	**101**	Evidence as to meaning of illegible characters, etc.
99	Who may give evidence of agreement varying terms of document	**102**	Who may give evidence of agreement varying terms of document
100	Saving of provisions of Indian Succession Act relating to wills	**103**	Saving of provisions of Indian Succession Act relating to wills
101	Burden of proof	**104**	Burden of proof
102	On whom burden of proof lies	**105**	On whom burden of proof lies
103	Burden of proof as to particular fact	**106**	Burden of proof as to particular fact
104	Burden of proving fact to be proved to make evidence admissible	**107**	Burden of proving fact to be proved to make evidence admissible

INDIAN EVIDENCE ACT, 1872		BHARATIYA SAKSHYA ADHINIYAM, 2023	
SEC.	***HEADING***	***SEC.***	***HEADING***
105	Burden of proving that case of accused comes within exceptions	**108**	Burden of proving that case of accused comes within exceptions
106	Burden of proving fact especially within knowledge	**109**	Burden of proving fact especially within knowledge
107	Burden of proving death of person known to have been alive within thirty years	**110**	Burden of proving death of person known to have been alive within thirty years
108	Burden of proving that person is alive who has not been heard of for seven years	**111**	Burden of proving that person is alive who has not been heard of for seven years
109	Burden of proof as to relationship in the cases of partners, landlord and tenant, principal and agent	**112**	Burden of proof as to relationship in the cases of partners, landlord and tenant, principal and agent
110	Burden of proof as to ownership	**113**	Burden of proof as to ownership
111	Proof of good faith in transactions where one party is in relation of active confidence	**114**	Proof of good faith in transactions where one party is in relation of active confidence
111A	Presumption as to certain offences	**115**	Presumption as to certain offences

INDIAN EVIDENCE ACT, 1872		BHARATIYA SAKSHYA ADHINIYAM, 2023	
SEC.	***HEADING***	***SEC.***	***HEADING***
112	Birth during marriage, conclusive proof of legitimacy	**116**	Birth during marriage, conclusive proof of legitimacy
113	Proof of cession of territory	—	—
113A	Presumption as to abetment of suicide by a married woman	**117**	Presumption as to abetment of suicide by a married woman
113B	Presumption as to dowry death	**118**	Presumption as to dowry death
114	Court may presume existence of certain facts	**119**	Court may presume existence of certain facts
114A	Presumption as to absence of consent in certain prosecution for rape	**120**	Presumption as to absence of consent in certain prosecution for rape
115	Estoppel	**121**	Estoppel
116	Estoppel of tenant; and of licensee of person in possession	**122**	Estoppel of tenants and of licensee of person in possession
117	Estoppel of acceptor of bill of exchange, bailee or licensee	**123**	Estoppel of acceptor of bill of exchange, bailee or licensee
118	Whom may testify	**124**	Whom may testify
119	Witness unable to communicate verbally	**125**	Witness unable to communicate verbally

INDIAN EVIDENCE ACT, 1872		BHARATIYA SAKSHYA ADHINIYAM, 2023	
SEC.	***HEADING***	***SEC.***	***HEADING***
120	Parties to civil suit, and their wives or husbands - Husband or wife of person under criminal trial	**126**	Competency of husband and wife as witnesses in certain cases
121	Judges and Magistrates	**127**	Judges and Magistrates
122	Communications during marriage	**128**	Communications during marriage
123	Evidence as to affairs of State	**129**	Evidence as to affairs of State
124	Official communications	**130**	Official communications
125	Information as to commission of offences	**131**	Information as to commission of offences
126	Professional communications	**132(1)/(2)**	Professional communications
127	Section 126 to apply to interpreters, etc.	**132(3)**	Professional communications
128	Privilege not waived by volunteering evidence	**133**	Privilege not waived by volunteering evidence
129	Confidential communications with legal advisers	**134**	Confidential communication with legal advisers
130	Production of title-deeds of witness not a party	**135**	Production of title-deeds of witness not a party

INDIAN EVIDENCE ACT, 1872		BHARATIYA SAKSHYA ADHINIYAM, 2023	
SEC.	***HEADING***	***SEC.***	***HEADING***
131	Production of documents or electronic records which another person, having possession, could refuse to produce	**136**	Production of documents or electronic records which another person, having possession, would refuse to produce
132	Witness not excused from answering on ground that answer will criminate	**137**	Witness not excused from answering on ground that answer will criminate
133	Accomplice	**138**	Accomplice
134	Number of witnesses	**139**	Number of witnesses
135	Order of production and examination of witnesses	**140**	Order of production and examination of witnesses
136	Judge to decide as to admissibility of evidence	**141**	Judge to decide as to admissibility of evidence
137	Examination-in-chief	**142**	Examination of witnesses
138	Order of examinations	**143**	Order of examinations
139	Cross-examination of person called to produce a document	**144**	Cross-examination of person called to produce a document
140	Witnesses to character	**145**	Witnesses to character
141	Leading questions	**146(1)**	Leading questions

I-12.13 TABLE SHOWING SECS. OF IEA, 1872 & BSA, 2023

INDIAN EVIDENCE ACT, 1872		BHARATIYA SAKSHYA ADHINIYAM, 2023	
SEC.	***HEADING***	***SEC.***	***HEADING***
142	When they must not be asked	**146(2)/(3)**	Leading questions
143	When they may be asked	**146(4)**	Leading questions
144	Evidence as to matters in writing	**147**	Evidence as to matters in writing
145	Cross-examination as to previous statements in writing	**148**	Cross-examination as to previous statements in writing
146	Questions lawful in cross-examination	**149**	Questions lawful in cross-examination
147	When witness to be compelled to answer	**150**	When witness to be compelled to answer
148	Court to decide when question shall be asked and when witness compelled to answer	**151**	Court to decide when question shall be asked and when witness compelled to answer
149	Question not to be asked without reasonable grounds	**152**	Question not to be asked without reasonable grounds
150	Procedure of Court in case of question being asked without reasonable grounds	**153**	Procedure of Court in case of question being asked without reasonable grounds
151	Indecent and scandalous questions	**154**	Indecent and scandalous questions

INDIAN EVIDENCE ACT, 1872		BHARATIYA SAKSHYA ADHINIYAM, 2023	
SEC.	***HEADING***	***SEC.***	***HEADING***
152	Questions intended to insult or annoy	**155**	Questions intended to insult or annoy
153	Exclusion of evidence to contradict answers to questions testing veracity	**156**	Exclusion of evidence to contradict answers to questions testing veracity
154	Question by party to his own witness	**157**	Question by party to his own witness
155	Impeaching credit of witness	**158**	Impeaching credit of witness
156	Questions tending to corroborate evidence of relevant fact, admissible	**159**	Questions tending to corroborate evidence of relevant fact, admissible
157	Former statements of witness may be proved to corroborate later testimony as to same fact	**160**	Former statements of witness may be proved to corroborate later testimony as to same fact
158	What matters may be proved in connection with proved statement relevant under section 32 or 33	**161**	What matters may be proved in connection with proved statement relevant under section 26 or 27
159	Refreshing memory	**162**	Refreshing memory
160	Testimony to facts stated in document mentioned in section 159	**163**	Testimony to facts stated in document mentioned in section 162

I-12.15 TABLE SHOWING SECS. OF IEA, 1872 & BSA, 2023

INDIAN EVIDENCE ACT, 1872		BHARATIYA SAKSHYA ADHINIYAM, 2023	
SEC.	*HEADING*	*SEC.*	*HEADING*
161	Right of adverse party as to writing used to refresh memory	**164**	Right of adverse party as to writing used to refresh memory
162	Production of documents	**165**	Production of documents
163	Giving, as evidence, of document called for and produced on notice	**166**	Giving, as evidence, of document called for and produced on notice
164	Using, as evidence, of document, production of which was refused on notice	**167**	Using, as evidence, of document production of which was refused on notice
165	Judge's power to put questions or order production	**168**	Judge's power to put questions or order production
166	Power of jury or assessors to put questions	—	—
167	No new trial for improper admission or rejection of evidence	**169**	No new trial for improper admission or rejection of evidence

2

TABLE SHOWING NEW SECTIONS OF BHARATIYA SAKSHYA ADHINIYAM, 2023

BHARATIYA SAKSHYA ADHINIYAM, 2023	
SECTION	***HEADING***
2(2)	Words and expressions
61	Electronic or digital record

3

TABLE SHOWING SECTIONS OF INDIAN EVIDENCE ACT REPEALED BY BHARATIYA SAKSHYA ADHINIYAM, 2023

INDIAN EVIDENCE ACT, 1872	
SECTION	***HEADING***
3, para 10	"India"
22A	When oral admissions as to contents of electronic records are relevant
82	Presumption as to document admissible in England without proof of seal or signature
88	Presumption as to telegraphic messages
113	Proof of cession of territory
166	Power of jury or assessors to put questions

4

COMPARATIVE STUDY OF BHARATIYA SAKSHYA ADHINIYAM, 2023 (BSA) & INDIAN EVIDENCE ACT, 1872

AIMS AND OBJECTS OF BHARATIYA SAKSHYA ADHINIYAM, 2023 (BSA)

- The avowed aims and objects of the Indian Evidence Act, 1872 (Evidence Act), as per its long title, were to consolidate, define and amend the law of evidence.
- The avowed aims and objects of the Bharatiya Sakshya Adhiniyam, 2023 (BSA), as per its long title, are to consolidate and to provide for general rules and principles of evidence for fair trial.
- The BSA recognizes that enunciating the rules and principles of evidence is not an end in itself. The aim for providing for general rules and principles of evidence is to ensure a fair trial.
- It is submitted that the provisions of the BSA should be interpreted in the light of the avowed aim expressed in long title to achieve a fair trial.

Statement of Objects and Reasons to the BSA, 2023 are as under:

"2. .... The law of evidence (not being substantive or procedural law), falls in the category of 'adjective law', that defines the pleading and methodology by which the substantive or procedural laws are operationalised. The existing law does not address the technological advancement undergone in the country during the last few decades.

** ** **

4. The proposed legislation, namely "Bharatiya Sakshya Adhiniyam", *inter alia*, provides as under:—

(*i*) it provides that 'evidence' includes any information given electronically, which would permit appearance of witnesses, accused, experts and victims through electronic means;

(*ii*) it provides for admissibility of an electronic or digital record as evidence having the same legal effect, validity and enforceability as any other document;

(*iii*) it seeks to expand the scope of secondary evidence to include copies made from original by mechanical processes, copies made from or compared with the original, counterparts of documents as against the parties who did not execute them and oral accounts of the contents of a document given by some person who has himself seen it and giving matching hash value of original record will be admissible as proof of evidence in the form of secondary evidence;

(*iv*) it seeks to put limits on the facts which are admissible and its certification as such in the courts. The proposed Bill introduces more precise and uniform rules of practice of courts in dealing with facts and circumstances of the case by means of evidence.

** ** **

6. The Bill seeks to achieve the above objectives."

SECTION 1 OF BSA : SHORT TITLE, APPLICATION AND COMMENCEMENT

Corresponding provision

- Section 1 of the BSA corresponds to section 1 of the Evidence Act

Territorial extent of the legislation

- Section 1 of the Evidence Act provided that it extended to the whole of India. Section 1 of the BSA omits this provision on territorial extent. It also omits the definition of "India" given in section 3 of the Evidence Act.
- The possible reason for such omission is that any stipulation that the BSA extends to the whole of India would call into question the admissibility of evidence digitally generated outside the borders of India.

Applicability to Courts-martial

- Section 1 of the Evidence Act provided that the said Act did not apply to Courts-martial convened under the Army Act, the Naval Discipline Act or the Indian Navy (Discipline) Act or the Air Force Act.
- Section 1(2) of the BSA omits the words "convened under the Army Act, the Naval Discipline Act or the Indian Navy (Discipline) Act or the Air Force Act".
- Thus, unlike the Evidence Act, the BSA shall also apply to courts-martial convened under the Army Act, the Naval Discipline Act or the Indian Navy (Discipline) Act or the Air Force Act.

SECTION 2 OF BSA : DEFINITIONS

Corresponding provision

- Section 2(*1*) of the BSA corresponds to section 3 of the Evidence Act
- There are no changes

SECTION 2(*1*)(*a*) OF BSA : COURT

Corresponding provision

- Section 2(*1*)(*a*) of the BSA corresponds to section 3, para 1, of the Evidence Act
- There are no changes

SECTION 2(*1*)(*b*) OF BSA : CONCLUSIVE PROOF

Corresponding provision

- Section 2(*1*)(*b*) of the BSA corresponds to section 4, para 3, of the Evidence Act
- There are no changes

SECTION 2(*1*)(*c*) OF BSA : DISPROVED

Corresponding provision

- Section 2(*1*)(*c*) of the BSA corresponds to section 3, para 8, of the Evidence Act
- There are no changes

SECTION 2(*1*)(*d*) OF BSA : DOCUMENT

Corresponding provision

- Section 2(*1*)(*d*) of the BSA corresponds to section 3, para 5, of the Evidence Act

Electronic & digital records

- Section 2(*1*)(*d*) of BSA gives a new definition of the word "document" which is compatible with the modern digital era.
- The new definition specifically includes electronic and *digital* records within the scope of the term "document".
- The five statutory illustrations in old definition have been retained. The new definition gives a sixth statutory illustration No. (*vi*) which clarifies that "An electronic record on emails, server logs, documents on computers, laptop or smartphone,

messages, websites, locational evidence and voice mail messages stored on digital devices are documents".

- Under the new definition, to qualify as "document" or "documentary evidence", it is not necessary that matter be expressed or described upon any substance by means of letters, figures or marks only.
- Any matter which is "otherwise recorded" upon any substance "by any other means" will also qualify as "document" or "documentary evidence".

  It appears that video recording on mobile phone would qualify as "documentary evidence" as it is "otherwise recorded" upon any substance "by any other means".

SECTION 2(*1*)(*e*) OF BSA : EVIDENCE

Corresponding provision

- Section 2(*1*)(*e*) of the BSA corresponds to section 3, para 6, of the Evidence Act

Electronic/Digital records

- Under the new definition of "evidence" in section 2(*1*)(*e*) of the BSA, 'statements including statements given electronically' are to be treated as evidence as well as oral evidence. This is a logical corollary to section 530 of Bharatiya Nagarik Suraksha Sanhita, 2023 (BNSS) providing for examination of complainant and witnesses in electronic mode by use of electronic communication or by audio-video electronic means.
- Under Evidence Act, only electronic records were treated as documentary evidence and there was no express mention of digital records in definition of 'evidence' under Evidence Act.
- Section 2(*1*)(*e*) of BSA specifically includes electronic or *digital* records as documentary evidence.

SECTION 2(1)(f) OF BSA : FACT

Corresponding provision

- Section 2(*1*)(*f*) of the BSA corresponds to section 3, para 2, of the Evidence Act

Illustration

- Illustration (*e*) in section 3 (2nd para) of Evidence Act which states that "(*e*) That a man has a certain reputation, is a fact." is omitted in new definition of "fact" in section 2(*1*)(*f*)

SECTION 2(1)(g) OF BSA : FACTS IN ISSUE

Corresponding provision

- Section 2(*1*)(*g*) of the BSA corresponds to section 3, para 4, of the Evidence Act
- There are no changes

SECTION 2(1)(h) OF BSA : MAY PRESUME

Corresponding provision

- Section 2(*1*)(*h*) of the BSA corresponds to section 4, para 1, of the Evidence Act
- There are no changes

SECTION 2(1)(i) OF BSA : NOT PROVED

Corresponding provision

- Section 2(*1*)(*i*) of the BSA corresponds to section 3, para 9, of the Evidence Act
- There are no changes

SECTION 2(1)(j) OF BSA : PROVED

Corresponding provision

- Section 2(*1*)(*j*) of the BSA corresponds to section 3, para 7, of the Evidence Act
- There are no changes

SECTION 2(*1*)(*k*) OF BSA : RELEVANT

Corresponding provision

- Section 2(*1*)(*k*) of the BSA corresponds to section 3, para 3, of the Evidence Act
- There are no changes

SECTION 2(*1*)(*l*) OF BSA : SHALL PRESUME

Corresponding provision

- Section 2(*1*)(*l*) of the BSA corresponds to section 4, para 2, of the Evidence Act
- There are no changes

SECTION 2(2) OF BSA : WORDS AND EXPRESSIONS

Corresponding provision

- No corresponding provision in Evidence Act
- ***This is a new provision***

Words not defined

- Sub-section (2) of section 2 of BSA provides that words and expressions used herein and not defined but defined in the Information Technology Act, 2000, Bharatiya Nagarik Suraksha Sanhita, 2023 and Bharatiya Nyaya Sanhita, 2023 shall have the same meanings as assigned to them in the said Act and Sanhita.

SECTION 3 OF BSA : EVIDENCE MAY BE GIVEN OF FACTS IN ISSUE AND RELEVANT FACTS

Corresponding provision

- Section 3 of the BSA corresponds to section 5 of the Evidence Act
- There are no changes

SECTION 4 OF BSA : RELEVANCY OF FACTS FORMING PART OF SAME TRANSACTION

Corresponding provision

- Section 4 of the BSA corresponds to section 6 of the Evidence Act

Facts not in issue

- Section 6 of Evidence Act provided that facts which, though not in issue, but which are so connected with a fact in issue as to form part of the same transaction, are relevant.
- In addition, section 4 of the BSA also provides that facts though not in issue are so connected with a relevant fact as to form part of the same transaction, are relevant.

SECTION 5 OF BSA : FACTS WHICH ARE OCCASION, CAUSE OR EFFECT OF FACTS IN ISSUE OR RELEVANT FACTS

Corresponding provision

- Section 5 of the BSA corresponds to section 7 of the Evidence Act
- There are no changes

SECTION 6 OF BSA : MOTIVE, PREPARATION AND PREVIOUS OR SUBSEQUENT CONDUCT

Corresponding provision

- Section 6 of the BSA corresponds to section 8 of the Evidence Act
- The first para in section 8 of Evidence Act is now sub-section (1) of section 6 in the BSA
- The second para in section 8 of Evidence Act is now sub-section (2) of section 6 in the BSA

Illustrations

- In Statutory Illustration (*d*) to section 8 of Evidence Act, reference to "vakils" is replaced with "advocates"
- In Statutory Illustration (*e*) to section 8 of Evidence Act, typographical error of "proved" corrected by making it "provided"

- In Statutory Illustration (*f*) to section 8 of Evidence Act, word "man" is replaced with "person" to make it gender neutral
- In Statutory Illustration (*j*), word "ravished" has been replaced with the word "raped"

SECTION 7 OF BSA : FACTS NECESSARY TO EXPLAIN OR INTRODUCE FACT IN ISSUE OR RELEVANT FACTS

Corresponding provision

- Section 7 of the BSA corresponds to section 9 of the Evidence Act
- There are no changes

SECTION 8 OF BSA : THINGS SAID OR DONE BY CONSPIRATOR IN REFERENCE TO COMMON DESIGN

Corresponding provision

- Section 8 of the BSA corresponds to section 10 of the Evidence Act
- There are no changes

SECTION 9 OF BSA : WHEN FACTS NOT OTHERWISE RELEVANT BECOME RELEVANT

Corresponding provision

- Section 9 of the BSA corresponds to section 11 of the Evidence Act
- There are no changes

SECTION 10 OF BSA : FACTS TENDING TO ENABLE COURT TO DETERMINE AMOUNT ARE RELEVANT IN SUITS FOR DAMAGES

Corresponding provision

- Section 10 of the BSA corresponds to section 12 of the Evidence Act
- There are no changes

SECTION 11 OF BSA : FACTS RELEVANT WHEN RIGHT OR CUSTOM IS IN QUESTION

Corresponding provision

- Section 11 of the BSA corresponds to section 13 of the Evidence Act
- There are no changes

SECTION 12 OF BSA : FACTS SHOWING EXISTENCE OF STATE OF MIND, OR OF BODY OR BODILY FEELING

Corresponding provision

- Section 12 of the BSA corresponds to section 14 of the Evidence Act
- There are no changes

SECTION 13 OF BSA : FACTS BEARING ON QUESTION WHETHER ACT WAS ACCIDENTAL OR INTENTIONAL

Corresponding provision

- Section 13 of the BSA corresponds to section 15 of the Evidence Act
- There are no changes

SECTION 14 OF BSA : EXISTENCE OF COURSE OF BUSINESS WHEN RELEVANT

Corresponding provision

- Section 14 of the BSA corresponds to section 16 of the Evidence Act
- There are no changes

SECTION 15 OF BSA : ADMISSION DEFINED

Corresponding provision

- Section 15 of the BSA corresponds to section 17 of the Evidence Act
- There are no changes

SECTION 16 OF BSA : ADMISSION BY PARTY TO PROCEEDING OR HIS AGENT

Corresponding provision

- Section 16 of the BSA corresponds to section 18 of the Evidence Act
- There are no changes

SECTION 17 OF BSA : ADMISSIONS BY PERSONS WHOSE POSITION MUST BE PROVED AS AGAINST PARTY TO SUIT

Corresponding provision

- Section 17 of the BSA corresponds to section 19 of the Evidence Act
- There are no changes

SECTION 18 OF BSA : ADMISSIONS BY PERSONS EXPRESSLY REFERRED TO BY PARTY TO SUIT

Corresponding provision

- Section 18 of the BSA corresponds to section 20 of the Evidence Act
- There are no changes

SECTION 19 OF BSA : PROOF OF ADMISSIONS AGAINST PERSONS MAKING THEM, AND BY OR ON THEIR BEHALF

Corresponding provision

- Section 19 of the BSA corresponds to section 21 of the Evidence Act
- There are no changes

SECTION 20 OF BSA : WHEN ORAL ADMISSIONS AS TO CONTENTS OF DOCUMENTS ARE RELEVANT

Corresponding provision

- Section 20 of the BSA corresponds to section 22 of the Evidence Act
- There are no changes

SECTION 21 OF BSA : ADMISSIONS IN CIVIL CASES WHEN RELEVANT

Corresponding provision

- Section 21 of the BSA corresponds to section 23 of the Evidence Act

Advocate

- "Advocate" is replaced for "barrister, pleader, attorney or vakil"

SECTION 22 OF BSA : CONFESSION CAUSED BY INDUCEMENT, THREAT, COERCION OR PROMISE, WHEN IRRELEVANT IN CRIMINAL PROCEEDING

Corresponding provision

- Section 22 of the BSA corresponds to sections 24, 28 and 29 of the Evidence Act
- Section 22(1) of BSA corresponds to section 24 of IPC
- Section 22(1), first proviso of BSA corresponds to section 28 of IPC
- Section 22(2), second proviso of BSA corresponds to section 29 of IPC

Coercion

- Words "coercion" are inserted in section 22 of BSA, which was not there in section 24 of Evidence Act

SECTION 23 OF BSA : CONFESSION TO POLICE OFFICER

Corresponding provision

- Section 23(1) of the BSA corresponds to section 25 of the Evidence Act
- Section 23(2) of the BSA corresponds to sections 26 and 27 of the Evidence Act

Magistrate

- *Explanation* to section 26 of the Evidence Act providing that "Magistrate" does not include head of a village, etc., is omitted

SECTION 24 OF BSA : CONSIDERATION OF PROVED CONFESSION AFFECTING PERSON MAKING IT AND OTHERS JOINTLY UNDER TRIAL FOR SAME OFFENCE

Corresponding provision

- Section 24 of the BSA corresponds to section 30 of the Evidence Act

Joint Trial

- *Explanation* to section 30 of Evidence Act incorporated in section 24 of BSA is renumbered as *Explanation I*
- New *Explanation II* is added in section 24 of BSA so as to clarify that "A trial of more persons than one held in the absence of the accused who has absconded or who fails to comply with a proclamation issued under section 84 of the Bharatiya Nagarik Suraksha Sanhita, 2023 shall be deemed to be a joint trial for the purpose of this section."

SECTION 25 OF BSA : ADMISSIONS NOT CONCLUSIVE PROOF, BUT MAY ESTOP

Corresponding provision

- Section 25 of the BSA corresponds to section 31 of the Evidence Act
- There are no changes

SECTION 26 OF BSA : CASES IN WHICH STATEMENT OF RELEVANT FACT BY PERSON WHO IS DEAD OR CANNOT BE FOUND, ETC., IS RELEVANT

Corresponding provision

- Section 26 of the BSA corresponds to section 32 of the Evidence Act
- There are no changes

SECTION 27 OF BSA : RELEVANCY OF CERTAIN EVIDENCE FOR PROVING, IN SUBSEQUENT PROCEEDING, TRUTH OF FACTS THEREIN STATED

Corresponding provision

- Section 27 of the BSA corresponds to section 33 of the Evidence Act
- There are no changes

SECTION 28 OF BSA : ENTRIES IN BOOKS OF ACCOUNT WHEN RELEVANT

Corresponding provision

- Section 28 of the BSA corresponds to section 34 of the Evidence Act
- There are no changes

SECTION 29 OF BSA : RELEVANCY OF ENTRY IN PUBLIC RECORD OR AN ELECTRONIC RECORD MADE IN PERFORMANCE OF DUTY

Corresponding provision

- Section 29 of the BSA corresponds to section 35 of the Evidence Act
- There are no changes

SECTION 30 OF BSA : RELEVANCY OF STATEMENTS IN MAPS, CHARTS AND PLANS

Corresponding provision

- Section 30 of the BSA corresponds to section 36 of the Evidence Act
- There are no changes

SECTION 31 OF BSA : RELEVANCY OF STATEMENT AS TO FACT OF PUBLIC NATURE CONTAINED IN CERTAIN ACTS OR NOTIFICATIONS

Corresponding provision

- Section 31 of the BSA corresponds to section 37 of the Evidence Act

Official Gazette in electronic or digital form

- Electronic or digital form of Official Gazette is made admissible evidence by section 31 of BSA

SECTION 32 OF BSA : RELEVANCY OF STATEMENTS AS TO ANY LAW CONTAINED IN LAW BOOKS INCLUDING ELECTRONIC OR DIGITAL FORM

Corresponding provision

- Section 32 of the BSA corresponds to section 38 of the Evidence Act

E-books/Websites

- In certain circumstances electronic or digital form of law books as well as Court's rulings in electronic or digital form are now made admissible in evidence by section 32 of BSA
- Section 32 of BSA provides that when the Court has to form an opinion as to a law of any country, any statement of such law contained in a book purporting to be printed or published including in electronic or digital form under the authority of the Government of such country and to contain any such law, and any report of a ruling of the Courts of such country contained in a book including in electronic or digital form purporting to be a report of such rulings, is relevant.

SECTION 33 OF BSA : WHAT EVIDENCE TO BE GIVEN WHEN STATEMENT FORMS PART OF A CONVERSATION, DOCUMENT, ELECTRONIC RECORD, BOOK OR SERIES OF LETTERS OR PAPERS

Corresponding provision

- Section 33 of the BSA corresponds to section 39 of the Evidence Act
- There are no changes

SECTION 34 OF BSA : PREVIOUS JUDGMENTS RELEVANT TO BAR A SECOND SUIT OR TRIAL

Corresponding provision

- Section 34 of the BSA corresponds to section 40 of the Evidence Act
- There are no changes

SECTION 35 OF BSA : RELEVANCY OF CERTAIN JUDGMENTS IN PROBATE, ETC., JURISDICTION

Corresponding provision

- Section 35 of the BSA corresponds to section 41 of the Evidence Act

Tribunal's Orders

- Tribunal's orders are now also covered in section 35 of BSA

SECTION 36 OF BSA : RELEVANCY AND EFFECT OF JUDGMENTS, ORDERS OR DECREES, OTHER THAN THOSE MENTIONED IN SECTION 35

Corresponding provision

- Section 36 of the BSA corresponds to section 42 of the Evidence Act
- There are no changes

SECTION 37 OF BSA : JUDGMENTS, ETC., OTHER THAN THOSE MENTIONED IN SECTIONS 34, 35 AND 36 WHEN RELEVANT

Corresponding provision

- Section 37 of the BSA corresponds to section 43 of the Evidence Act
- There are no changes

SECTION 38 OF BSA : FRAUD OR COLLUSION IN OBTAINING JUDGMENT, OR INCOMPETENCY OF COURT, MAY BE PROVED

Corresponding provision

- Section 38 of the BSA corresponds to section 44 of the Evidence Act
- There are no changes

SECTION 39 OF BSA : OPINIONS OF EXPERTS

Corresponding provision

- Section 39(1) of the BSA corresponds to section 45 of the Evidence Act
- Section 39(2) of the BSA corresponds to section 45A of the Evidence Act

Experts in 'other' fields

- Section 45 of Evidence Act provided that when the Court has to form an opinion upon a point of foreign law, or of science, or art, the opinions upon that point of persons specially skilled in such foreign law, science or art are relevant facts. Such specially skilled persons are "experts".
- Section 39 of BSA incorporates provisions of section 45 of Evidence Act and provides that opinions of experts in a field other than foreign law, or of science, or art are also relevant facts when Court has to form to an opinion upon a point in that field.

SECTION 40 OF BSA : FACTS BEARING UPON OPINIONS OF EXPERTS

Corresponding provision

- Section 40 of the BSA corresponds to section 46 of the Evidence Act
- There are no changes

SECTION 41 OF BSA : OPINION AS TO HAND-WRITING AND SIGNATURE, WHEN RELEVANT

Corresponding provision

- Section 41(1) of the BSA corresponds to section 47 of the Evidence Act
- Section 41(2) of the BSA corresponds to section 47A of the Evidence Act
- There are no changes

SECTION 42 OF BSA : OPINION AS TO EXISTENCE OF GENERAL CUSTOM OR RIGHT, WHEN RELEVANT

Corresponding provision

- Section 42 of the BSA corresponds to section 48 of the Evidence Act
- There are no changes

SECTION 43 OF BSA : OPINION AS TO USAGES, TENETS, ETC., WHEN RELEVANT

Corresponding provision

- Section 43 of the BSA corresponds to section 49 of the Evidence Act
- There are no changes

SECTION 44 OF BSA : OPINION ON RELATIONSHIP, WHEN RELEVANT

Corresponding provision

- Section 44 of the BSA corresponds to section 50 of the Evidence Act
- There are no changes

SECTION 45 OF BSA : GROUNDS OF OPINION, WHEN RELEVANT

Corresponding provision

- Section 45 of the BSA corresponds to section 51 of the Evidence Act
- There are no changes

SECTION 46 OF BSA : IN CIVIL CASES CHARACTER TO PROVE CONDUCT IMPUTED, IRRELEVANT

Corresponding provision

- Section 46 of the BSA corresponds to section 52 of the Evidence Act
- There are no changes

SECTION 47 OF BSA : IN CRIMINAL CASES PREVIOUS GOOD CHARACTER RELEVANT

Corresponding provision

- Section 47 of the BSA corresponds to section 53 of the Evidence Act
- There are no changes

SECTION 48 OF BSA : EVIDENCE OF CHARACTER OR PREVIOUS SEXUAL EXPERIENCE NOT RELEVANT IN CERTAIN CASES

Corresponding provision

- Section 48 of the BSA corresponds to section 53A of the Evidence Act
- There are no changes

SECTION 49 OF BSA : PREVIOUS BAD CHARACTER NOT RELEVANT, EXCEPT IN REPLY

Corresponding provision

- Section 49 of the BSA corresponds to section 54 of the Evidence Act
- There are no changes

SECTION 50 OF BSA : CHARACTER AS AFFECTING DAMAGES

Corresponding provision

- Section 50 of the BSA corresponds to section 55 of the Evidence Act
- There are no changes

SECTION 51 OF BSA : FACT JUDICIALLY NOTICEABLE NEED NOT BE PROVED

Corresponding provision

- Section 51 of the BSA corresponds to section 56 of the Evidence Act
- There are no changes

SECTION 52 OF BSA : FACTS OF WHICH COURT SHALL TAKE JUDICIAL NOTICE

Corresponding provision

- Section 52 of the BSA corresponds to section 57 of the Evidence Act

Scope of provisions

- Section 52(*a*) of the BSA requires Courts to take judicial notice of all laws in force in the territory of India including laws having extra-territorial operation. Section 57(1) of Evidence Act referred to 'all laws in force in territory of India'.
- Section 52(*b*) of the BSA requires Courts to take judicial notice of international treaty, agreement or convention with country or countries by India, or decisions made by India at the international associations or other bodies.
- Section 52 of the BSA omits reference to all public Acts passed or hereafter to be passed by Parliament of the United Kingdom, and all local and personal Acts directed by Parliament of the United Kingdom. Courts in India will not be required to take judicial notice of Acts passed by Parliament of UK since India ceased to be a UK colony in 1947.
- Section 52 of the BSA omits reference to "The course of proceeding of Parliament of the United Kingdom". No judicial notice will be required to be taken of 'course of proceedings of UK Parliament'.
- Section 52 of the BSA also omits reference to "The accession and the sign manual of the Sovereign for the time being of the United Kingdom of Great

Britain and Ireland" and to "All seals of which English Courts take judicial notice" and "all seals which any person is authorised to use by the Constitution or an Act of Parliament of the United Kingdom or an Act".

- Reference to "The territories under the dominion of the Government of India" have been replaced with "the territory of India".
- Reference to "articles of war for Indian Army, Navy or Air Force" are omitted.

SECTION 53 OF BSA : FACTS ADMITTED NEED NOT BE PROVED

Corresponding provision

- Section 53 of the BSA corresponds to section 58 of the Evidence Act
- There are no changes

SECTION 54 OF BSA : PROOF OF FACTS BY ORAL EVIDENCE

Corresponding provision

- Section 54 of the BSA corresponds to section 59 of the Evidence Act

Electronic records

- Though section 54 of BSA omits reference to "electronic records" which words were there in section 59 of Evidence Act, it makes no substantive change as section 2(*1*)(*c*) of BSA defines 'documents' to include electronic records.

SECTION 55 OF BSA : ORAL EVIDENCE TO BE DIRECT

Corresponding provision

- Section 55 of the BSA corresponds to section 60 of the Evidence Act
- There are no changes

SECTION 56 OF BSA : PROOF OF CONTENTS OF DOCUMENTS

Corresponding provision

- Section 56 of the BSA corresponds to section 61 of the Evidence Act
- There are no changes

SECTION 57 OF BSA : PRIMARY EVIDENCE

Corresponding provision

- Section 57 of the BSA corresponds to section 62 of the Evidence Act

Electronic record

- New *Explanations* (*Explanation 4* to *Explanation 7*) are inserted in section 57 of BSA.
- New *Explanation 4* clarifies that where an electronic or digital record is created or stored, and such storage occurs simultaneously or sequentially in multiple files, each such file is primary evidence.
- New *Explanation 5* clarifies that where an electronic or digital record is produced from proper custody, such electronic and digital record is primary evidence unless it is disputed.
- New *Explanation 6* clarifies that where a video recording is simultaneously stored in electronic form and transmitted or broadcast or transferred to another, each of the stored recordings is primary evidence.
- New *Explanation 7* clarifies that where an electronic or digital record is stored in multiple storage spaces in a computer resource, each such automated storage, including temporary files, is primary evidence.

SECTION 58 OF BSA : SECONDARY EVIDENCE

Corresponding provision

- Section 58 of the BSA corresponds to section 63 of the Evidence Act

Secondary evidence

- Under section 58 of BSA Secondary evidence also includes
  - oral admissions.
  - written admissions.
  - evidence of a person who has examined a document, the original of which consists of numerous accounts or other documents which cannot conveniently be examined in Court, and who is skilled in the examination of such documents.

SECTION 59 OF BSA : PROOF OF DOCUMENTS BY PRIMARY EVIDENCE

Corresponding provision

- Section 59 of the BSA corresponds to section 64 of the Evidence Act
- There are no changes

SECTION 60 OF BSA : CASES IN WHICH SECONDARY EVIDENCE RELATING TO DOCUMENTS MAY BE GIVEN

Corresponding provision

- Section 60 of the BSA corresponds to section 65 of the Evidence Act
- There are no changes

SECTION 61 OF BSA : ELECTRONIC OR DIGITAL RECORD

Corresponding provision

- Section 61 of BSA is a new provision. There was no corresponding provision in Evidence Act.

Electronic records

- Section 61 of BSA provides that electronic or digital record shall have the same legal effect, validity and enforceability as paper records.

- Section 61 of BSA provides that nothing in the Adhiniyam shall apply to deny the admissibility of an electronic or digital record in the evidence on the ground that it is an electronic or digital record and such record (subject to section 63 of BSA) shall have the same legal effect, validity and enforceability as other documents.

SECTION 62 OF BSA : SPECIAL PROVISIONS AS TO EVIDENCE RELATING TO ELECTRONIC RECORD

Corresponding provision

- Section 62 of the BSA corresponds to section 65A of the Evidence Act
- There are no changes

SECTION 63 OF BSA : ADMISSIBILITY OF ELECTRONIC RECORDS

Corresponding provision

- Section 63 of the BSA corresponds to section 65B of the Evidence Act

Scope of provision

- Section 63 of BSA uses the words "computer or any communication device" for words "computer"
- Section 65B(1) of Evidence Act provided that any information contained in an electronic record which is printed on a paper, stored, recorded or copied in optical or magnetic media produced by a computer (the computer output) shall be deemed to be also a document, if the specified conditions are satisfied in relation to the information and computer in question and shall be admissible in any proceedings, without further proof or production of the original, as evidence of any contents of the original or of any fact stated therein of which direct evidence would be admissible.

  Section 63(1) of BSA extends the scope of above provision to make it applicable also to any information contained in semiconductor memory or in any communication device (*e.g.* smartphone) or otherwise stored, recorded or copied in any electronic form.

Section 63 of BSA provides that notwithstanding anything contained in this Adhiniyam, any information contained in an electronic record which is printed on paper, stored, recorded or copied in optical or magnetic media or semiconductor memory which is produced by a computer or any communication device or otherwise stored, recorded or copied in any electronic form (hereinafter referred to as the computer output) shall be deemed to be also a document, if the conditions mentioned in this section are satisfied in relation to the information and computer in question and shall be admissible in any proceedings, without further proof or production of the original, as evidence or any contents of the original or of any fact stated therein of which direct evidence would be admissible.

◆ Section 65B(3) of Evidence Act provides that where over any period, the function of storing or processing information for the purposes of any activities regularly carried on over that period as mentioned in clause (*a*) of sub-section (2) was regularly performed by computer, whether—

(*a*) by a combination of computers operating over that period; or

(*b*) by different computers operating in succession over that period; or

(*c*) by different combinations of computers operating in succession over that period; or

(*d*) in any other manner involving the successive operation over that period, in whatever order, of one or more computers and one or more combinations of computers,

all the computers used for that purpose during that period shall be treated for the purposes of this section as constituting a single computer; and references in this section to a computer shall be construed accordingly.

- Section 63(3) of BSA provides that where over any period, the function of creating, storing or processing information for the purposes of any activity regularly carried on over that period as mentioned in clause (*a*) of sub-section (2) was regularly performed by means of one or more computers or communication device, whether—

  (*a*) in standalone mode; or

  (*b*) on a computer system; or

  (*c*) on a computer network; or

  (*d*) on a computer resource enabling information creation or providing information processing and storage; or

  (*e*) through an intermediary,

  all the computers or communication devices used for that purpose during that period shall be treated for the purposes of this section as constituting a single computer or communication device; and references in this section to a computer or communication device shall be construed accordingly.

- Sub-sections (4) and (5) of section 65B of Evidence Act provides that in any proceedings where it is desired to give a statement in evidence by virtue of this section, a certificate doing any of the following things, that is to say,—

  (*a*) identifying the electronic record containing the statement and describing the manner in which it was produced;

  (*b*) giving such particulars of any device involved in the production of that electronic record as may be appropriate for the purpose of showing that the electronic record was produced by a computer;

  (*c*) dealing with any of the matters to which the conditions mentioned in sub-section (2) relate,

  and purporting to be signed by a person occupying a responsible official position in relation to the operation of the relevant device or the management of the relevant activities (whichever is appropriate) shall be evidence of any matter stated in the certificate; and for the purposes of this sub-section it shall be sufficient for a matter to be stated to the best of the knowledge and belief of the person stating it.

For the purposes of this section,—

(*a*) information shall be taken to be supplied to a computer if it is supplied thereto in any appropriate form and whether it is so supplied directly or (with or without human intervention) by means of any appropriate equipment;

(*b*) whether in the course of activities carried on by any official, information is supplied with a view to its being stored or processed for the purposes of those activities by a computer operated otherwise than in the course of those activities, that information, if duly supplied to that computer, shall be taken to be supplied to it in the course of those activities;

(*c*) a computer output shall be taken to have been produced by a computer whether it was produced by it directly or (with or without human intervention) by means of any appropriate equipment.

For the purposes of this section, any reference to information being derived from other information, shall be a reference to its being derived therefrom by calculation, comparison or any other process.

- Sub-sections (4) and (5) of section 63 of BSA provides that in any proceeding where it is desired to give a statement in evidence by virtue of this section, a certificate doing any of the following things shall be submitted along with the electronic record at each instance where it is being submitted for admission, namely:—

(*a*) identifying the electronic record containing the statement and describing the manner in which it was produced;

(*b*) giving such particulars of any device involved in the production of that electronic record as may be appropriate for the purpose of showing that the electronic record was produced by a computer or a communication device referred to in clauses (*a*) to (*e*) of sub-section (3);

(*c*) dealing with any of the matters to which the conditions mentioned in sub-section (2) relate,

and purporting to be signed by a person in charge of the computer or communication device or the management of the relevant activities (whichever is appropriate) and an expert shall be evidence of any matter stated in the certificate; and for the purposes of this sub-section it shall be sufficient for a matter to be stated to the best of the knowledge and belief of the person stating it in the certificate specified in the Schedule.

For the purposes of this section,—

(*a*) information shall be taken to be supplied to a computer or communication device if it is supplied thereto in any appropriate form and whether it is so supplied directly or (with or without human intervention) by means of any appropriate equipment;

(*b*) a computer output shall be taken to have been produced by a computer or communication device whether it was produced by it directly or (with or without human intervention) by means of any appropriate equipment or by other electronic means as referred to in clauses (*a*) to (*e*) of sub-section (3).

- Format of certificate under section 63(4) which is to accompany electronic record evidence is specified in Schedule to BSA. There was no such format specified in Evidence Act for certificate in section 65B(4).

SECTION 64 OF BSA : RULES AS TO NOTICE TO PRODUCE

Corresponding provision

- Section 64 of the BSA corresponds to section 66 of the Evidence Act

Advocate

- Reference to "attorney or pleader" is replaced with reference to "advocate or representative"

SECTION 65 OF BSA : PROOF OF SIGNATURE AND HANDWRITING OF PERSON ALLEGED TO HAVE SIGNED OR WRITTEN DOCUMENT PRODUCED

Corresponding provision

- Section 65 of the BSA corresponds to section 67 of the Evidence Act
- There are no changes

SECTION 66 OF BSA : PROOF AS TO ELECTRONIC SIGNATURE

Corresponding provision

- Section 66 of the BSA corresponds to section 67A of the Evidence Act
- There are no changes

SECTION 67 OF BSA : PROOF OF EXECUTION OF DOCUMENT REQUIRED BY LAW TO BE ATTESTED

Corresponding provision

- Section 67 of the BSA corresponds to section 68 of the Evidence Act
- There are no changes

SECTION 68 OF BSA : PROOF WHERE NO ATTESTING WITNESS FOUND

Corresponding provision

- Section 68 of the BSA corresponds to section 69 of the Evidence Act

Outdated references omitted

- Reference to "or if the document purports to have been executed in the United Kingdom" are omitted from section 69 of Evidence Act

SECTION 69 OF BSA : ADMISSION OF EXECUTION BY PARTY TO ATTESTED DOCUMENT

Corresponding provision

- Section 69 of the BSA corresponds to section 70 of the Evidence Act
- There are no changes

SECTION 70 OF BSA : PROOF WHEN ATTESTING WITNESS DENIES EXECUTION

Corresponding provision

- Section 70 of the BSA corresponds to section 71 of the Evidence Act
- There are no changes

SECTION 71 OF BSA : PROOF OF DOCUMENT NOT REQUIRED BY LAW TO BE ATTESTED

Corresponding provision

- Section 71 of the BSA corresponds to section 72 of the Evidence Act
- There are no changes

SECTION 72 OF BSA : COMPARISON OF SIGNATURE, WRITING OR SEAL WITH OTHERS ADMITTED OR PROVED

Corresponding provision

- Section 72 of the BSA corresponds to section 73 of the Evidence Act
- There are no changes

SECTION 73 OF BSA : PROOF AS TO VERIFICATION OF DIGITAL SIGNATURE

Corresponding provision

- Section 73 of the BSA corresponds to section 73A of the Evidence Act

Controller

- Definition of 'controller' in *Explanation* to section 73A of Evidence Act is omitted in view of section 2(2) of BSA.

SECTION 74 OF BSA : PUBLIC AND PRIVATE DOCUMENTS

Corresponding provision

- Section 74(1) of the BSA corresponds to section 74 of the Evidence Act
- Section 74(2) of BSA corresponds to section 75 of the Evidence Act

Outdated references

- Reference to "of the Commonwealth" is omitted from section 74 of BSA

Union Territory

- Words "Union Territory" is added after "State"

SECTION 75 OF BSA : CERTIFIED COPIES OF PUBLIC DOCUMENTS

Corresponding provision

- Section 75 of the BSA corresponds to section 76 of the Evidence Act
- There are no changes

SECTION 76 OF BSA : PROOF OF DOCUMENTS BY PRODUCTION OF CERTIFIED COPIES

Corresponding provision

- Section 76 of the BSA corresponds to section 77 of the Evidence Act
- There are no changes

SECTION 77 OF BSA : PROOF OF OTHER OFFICIAL DOCUMENTS

Corresponding provision

- Section 77 of the BSA corresponds to section 78 of the Evidence Act

Omission of outdated referencer

- Section 77 of BSA omits references to "Crown Representative", "Her Majesty", "Privy Council", "Her Majesty's Government", "London Gazette" and "Queen's Printer" contained in section 78(1) of Evidence Act.
- Section 77 of BSA omits the provision that proclamations, orders or regulations issued by her Majesty or by the Privy Council, or by any department of her Majesty's Government may be proved by copies or extracts contained in the London Gazette, or purporting to be printed by the Queen's Printer. [Section 78(3) of Evidence Act].
- Section 77(*c*) of BSA provides that proclamations, orders or regulations issued by the President of India or the Governor of a State or the Administrator or Lieutenant Governor of a Union territory, may be proved by copies or extracts contained in the Official Gazette.

SECTION 78 OF BSA : PRESUMPTION AS TO GENUINENESS OF CERTIFIED COPIES

Corresponding provision

- Section 78 of the BSA corresponds to section 79 of the Evidence Act

Jammu & Kashmir

- References to "State of Jammu and Kashmir" omitted since that legal entity ceased to exist with effect from 31-10-2019 and what exist now are UT of Jammu and Kashmir and UT of Ladakh.

SECTION 79 OF BSA : PRESUMPTION AS TO DOCUMENTS PRODUCED AS RECORD OF EVIDENCE, ETC.

Corresponding provision

- Section 79 of the BSA corresponds to section 80 of the Evidence Act
- There are no changes

SECTION 80 OF BSA : PRESUMPTION AS TO GAZETTES, NEWSPAPERS, AND OTHER DOCUMENTS

Corresponding provision

- Section 80 of the BSA corresponds to section 81 of the Evidence Act

Official Gazette

- Section 80 of BSA omits references to "the London Gazette or any Official Gazette, or the Government Gazette of any colony, dependency or possession of the British Crown" and "a copy of a private Act of Parliament of the United Kingdom printed by the Queen's Printer". Courts in India are not anymore required to presume the genuineness of these documents.
- Section 80 of BSA requires that Court shall presume genuineness only of every document purporting to be the Official Gazette, or to be a newspaper or journal. Section 80 of BSA provides that the Court shall presume the genuineness of every document purporting to be the Official Gazette, or to be a newspaper or journal, and of every document purporting to be a document directed by any law to be kept by any person, if such document is kept substantially in the form required by law and is produced from proper custody.

British Private Acts

- Reference to private Acts of Parliament in marginal note of section 81 of Evidence Act are omitted from marginal note of section 80 of BSA.

Custody of documents

- Section 81 of Evidence Act provided that the Court shall presume the genuineness of every document purporting to be a document directed by any law to be kept by any person, if such document is kept substantially in the form required by law and is produced from proper custody. However, section 81 did not define what is proper custody.
- *Explanation* to section 80 clarifies that for the purposes of sections 80 and 92 of BSA, document is said to be in proper custody if it is in the place in which, and looked after by the person with whom such document is required to be kept; but no custody is improper if it is proved to have had a legitimate origin, or if the circumstances of the particular case are such as to render that origin probable.

SECTION 81 OF BSA : PRESUMPTION AS TO GAZETTES IN ELECTRONIC OR DIGITAL RECORD

Corresponding provision

- Section 81 of the BSA corresponds to section 81A of the Evidence Act

Digital records

- Section 81A of Evidence Act provided that the Court shall presume the genuineness of every *electronic* record purporting to be the Official Gazette. Section 81 of BSA provides that the Court shall presume the genuineness of every *electronic or digital* record purporting to be the Official Gazette.

Keeping of records

- Section 81A of Evidence Act provided that the Court shall presume the genuineness of every electronic record purporting to be electronic record directed by any law to be kept by any person, if such electronic record is kept substantially in the form required by law and is produced from proper custody. However, section 81A did not clarify as to what is proper custody.

- Section 81 of BSA provides that the Court shall presume the genuineness of every electronic or digital record purporting to be electronic or digital record directed by any law to be kept by any person, if such electronic or digital record is kept substantially in the form required by law and is produced from proper custody. Further, new *Explanation* in section 81 of BSA clarifies that "For the purposes of this section and section 96 electronic records are said to be in proper custody if they are in the place in which, and looked after by the person with whom such document is required to be kept; but no custody is improper if it is proved to have had a legitimate origin, or the circumstances of the particular case are such as to render that origin probable.".

SECTION 82 OF BSA : PRESUMPTION AS TO MAPS OR PLANS MADE BY AUTHORITY OF GOVERNMENT

Corresponding provision

- Section 82 of the BSA corresponds to section 83 of the Evidence Act
- There are no changes

SECTION 83 OF BSA : PRESUMPTION AS TO COLLECTIONS OF LAWS AND REPORTS OF DECISIONS

Corresponding provision

- Section 83 of the BSA corresponds to section 84 of the Evidence Act
- There are no changes

SECTION 84 OF BSA : PRESUMPTION AS TO POWERS-OF-ATTORNEY

Corresponding provision

- Section 84 of the BSA corresponds to section 85 of the Evidence Act
- There are no changes

SECTION 85 OF BSA : PRESUMPTION AS TO ELECTRONIC AGREEMENTS

Corresponding provision

- Section 85 of the BSA corresponds to section 85A of the Evidence Act

Digital signature

- Section 85A of Evidence Act provided that the Court shall presume that every electronic record purporting to be an agreement containing the *electronic signatures* of the parties was so concluded by affixing the electronic signature of the parties.
- Section 85 of BSA provides that the Court shall presume that every electronic record purporting to be an agreement containing the electronic or *digital* signature of the parties was so concluded by affixing the electronic or *digital* signature of the parties.

SECTION 86 OF BSA : PRESUMPTION AS TO ELECTRONIC RECORDS AND ELECTRONIC SIGNATURES

Corresponding provision

- Section 86 of the BSA corresponds to section 85B of the Evidence Act
- There are no changes

Electronic signature

- In section 85 of BSA words 'electronic or digital signature' are used. However, in section 86 words 'electronic signature' alone are used.

SECTION 87 OF BSA : PRESUMPTION AS TO ELECTRONIC SIGNATURE CERTIFICATES

Corresponding provision

- Section 87 of the BSA corresponds to section 85C of the Evidence Act
- There are no changes

SECTION 88 OF BSA : PRESUMPTION AS TO CERTIFIED COPIES OF FOREIGN JUDICIAL RECORDS

Corresponding provision

- Section 88 of the BSA corresponds to section 86 of the Evidence Act

Outdated reference

- References to "Her Majesty's Dominions" have been omitted

Place outside India

- For words "place not forming part of India", words "place outside India" are used
- For words 'any country and not forming part of India', words 'any country beyond India' are used

SECTION 89 OF BSA : PRESUMPTION AS TO BOOKS, MAPS AND CHARTS

Corresponding provision

- Section 89 of the BSA corresponds to section 87 of the Evidence Act
- There are no changes

SECTION 90 OF BSA : PRESUMPTION AS TO ELECTRONIC MESSAGES

Corresponding provision

- Section 90 of the BSA corresponds to section 88A of the Evidence Act

Definition of "addressee" and "originator"

- *Explanation* to section 88A has been omitted. The said *Explanation* clarified that the expressions "addressee" and "originator" shall have the same meanings respectively assigned to them in clauses (*b*) and (*za*) of sub-section (1) of section 2 of the Information Technology Act, 2000.
- *Explanation* has been omitted since it has become redundant in view of section 2(*2*) of BSA providing that words used but not defined in BSA shall have

the meanings assigned to them in the Information Technology Act, 2000 if defined in that Act. The definitions of "addressee" and "originator" in clauses (*b*) and (*za*) of sub-section (1) of section 2 of the Information Technology Act, 2000 will apply to section 90 of BSA in view of section 2(*2*) of BSA.

SECTION 91 OF BSA : PRESUMPTION AS TO DUE EXECUTION, ETC., OF DOCUMENTS NOT PRODUCED

Corresponding provision

- Section 91 of the BSA corresponds to section 89 of the Evidence Act
- There are no changes

SECTION 92 OF BSA : PRESUMPTION AS TO DOCUMENTS THIRTY YEARS OLD

Corresponding provision

- Section 92 of the BSA corresponds to section 90 of the Evidence Act

Custody of documents

- *Explanation* to section 90/90A of Evidence Act dealing with custody of documents is omitted
- *Explanation* to section 92 of BSA refers to section 80 of BSA which refers to custody of documents

SECTION 93 OF BSA : PRESUMPTION AS TO ELECTRONIC RECORDS FIVE YEARS OLD

Corresponding provision

- Section 93 of the BSA corresponds to section 90A of the Evidence Act

Custody of documents

- *Explanation* to section 90/90A of Evidence Act dealing with custody of documents is omitted
- Section 93 of BSA now refers to section 81 of BSA which deals with custody of documents

SECTION 94 OF BSA : EVIDENCE OF TERMS OF CONTRACTS, GRANTS AND OTHER DISPOSITIONS OF PROPERTY REDUCED TO FORM OF DOCUMENT

Corresponding provision

- Section 94 of the BSA corresponds to section 91 of the Evidence Act
- There are no changes

SECTION 95 OF BSA : EXCLUSION OF EVIDENCE OF ORAL AGREEMENT

Corresponding provision

- Section 95 of the BSA corresponds to section 92 of the Evidence Act
- There are no changes

SECTION 96 OF BSA : EXCLUSION OF EVIDENCE TO EXPLAIN OR AMEND AMBIGUOUS DOCUMENT

Corresponding provision

- Section 96 of the BSA corresponds to section 93 of the Evidence Act
- There are no changes

SECTION 97 OF BSA : EXCLUSION OF EVIDENCE AGAINST APPLICATION OF DOCUMENT TO EXISTING FACTS

Corresponding provision

- Section 97 of the BSA corresponds to section 94 of the Evidence Act
- There are no changes

SECTION 98 OF BSA : EVIDENCE AS TO DOCUMENT UNMEANING IN REFERENCE TO EXISTING FACTS

Corresponding provision

- Section 98 of the BSA corresponds to section 95 of the Evidence Act
- There are no changes

SECTION 99 OF BSA : EVIDENCE AS TO APPLICATION OF LANGUAGE WHICH CAN APPLY TO ONE ONLY OF SEVERAL PERSONS

Corresponding provision

- Section 99 of the BSA corresponds to section 96 of the Evidence Act
- There are no changes

SECTION 100 OF BSA : EVIDENCE AS TO APPLICATION OF LANGUAGE TO ONE OF TWO SETS OF FACTS, TO NEITHER OF WHICH THE WHOLE CORRECTLY APPLIES

Corresponding provision

- Section 100 of the BSA corresponds to section 97 of the Evidence Act
- There are no changes

SECTION 101 OF BSA : EVIDENCE AS TO MEANING OF ILLEGIBLE CHARACTERS, ETC.

Corresponding provision

- Section 101 of the BSA corresponds to section 98 of the Evidence Act
- There are no changes

SECTION 102 OF BSA : WHO MAY GIVE EVIDENCE OF AGREEMENT VARYING TERMS OF DOCUMENT

Corresponding provision

- Section 102 of the BSA corresponds to section 99 of the Evidence Act
- There are no changes

SECTION 103 OF BSA : SAVING OF PROVISIONS OF INDIAN SUCCESSION ACT RELATING TO WILLS

Corresponding provision

- Section 103 of the BSA corresponds to section 100 of the Evidence Act
- There are no changes

SECTION 104 OF BSA : BURDEN OF PROOF

Corresponding provision

- Section 104 of the BSA corresponds to section 101 of the Evidence Act
- There are no changes

SECTION 105 OF BSA : ON WHOM BURDEN OF PROOF LIES

Corresponding provision

- Section 105 of the BSA corresponds to section 102 of the Evidence Act
- There are no changes

SECTION 106 OF BSA : BURDEN OF PROOF AS TO PARTICULAR FACT

Corresponding provision

- Section 106 of the BSA corresponds to section 103 of the Evidence Act
- There are no changes

SECTION 107 OF BSA : BURDEN OF PROVING FACT TO BE PROVED TO MAKE EVIDENCE ADMISSIBLE

Corresponding provision

- Section 107 of the BSA corresponds to section 104 of the Evidence Act
- There are no changes

SECTION 108 OF BSA : BURDEN OF PROVING THAT CASE OF ACCUSED COMES WITHIN EXCEPTIONS

Corresponding provision

- Section 108 of the BSA corresponds to section 105 of the Evidence Act
- There are no changes

SECTION 109 OF BSA : BURDEN OF PROVING FACT ESPECIALLY WITHIN KNOWLEDGE

Corresponding provision

- Section 109 of the BSA corresponds to section 106 of the Evidence Act
- There are no changes

SECTION 110 OF BSA : BURDEN OF PROVING DEATH OF PERSON KNOWN TO HAVE BEEN ALIVE WITHIN THIRTY YEARS

Corresponding provision

- Section 110 of the BSA corresponds to section 107 of the Evidence Act
- There are no changes

SECTION 111 OF BSA : BURDEN OF PROVING THAT PERSON IS ALIVE WHO HAS NOT BEEN HEARD OF FOR SEVEN YEARS

Corresponding provision

- Section 111 of the BSA corresponds to section 108 of the Evidence Act
- There are no changes

SECTION 112 OF BSA : BURDEN OF PROOF AS TO RELATIONSHIP IN THE CASES OF PARTNERS, LANDLORD AND TENANT, PRINCIPAL AND AGENT

Corresponding provision

- Section 112 of the BSA corresponds to section 109 of the Evidence Act
- There are no changes

SECTION 113 OF BSA : BURDEN OF PROOF AS TO OWNERSHIP

Corresponding provision

- Section 113 of the BSA corresponds to section 110 of the Evidence Act
- There are no changes

SECTION 114 OF BSA : PROOF OF GOOD FAITH IN TRANSACTIONS WHERE ONE PARTY IS IN RELATION OF ACTIVE CONFIDENCE

Corresponding provision

- Section 114 of the BSA corresponds to section 111 of the Evidence Act
- There are no changes

SECTION 115 OF BSA : PRESUMPTION AS TO CERTAIN OFFENCES

Corresponding provision

- Section 115 of the BSA corresponds to section 111A of the Evidence Act
- There are no changes

SECTION 116 OF BSA : BIRTH DURING MARRIAGE, CONCLUSIVE PROOF OF LEGITIMACY

Corresponding provision

- Section 116 of the BSA corresponds to section 112 of the Evidence Act
- There are no changes

SECTION 117 OF BSA : PRESUMPTION AS TO ABETMENT OF SUICIDE BY A MARRIED WOMAN

Corresponding provision

- Section 117 of the BSA corresponds to section 113A of the Evidence Act
- There are no changes

SECTION 118 OF BSA : PRESUMPTION AS TO DOWRY DEATH

Corresponding provision

- Section 118 of the BSA corresponds to section 113B of the Evidence Act
- There are no changes

SECTION 119 OF BSA : COURT MAY PRESUME EXISTENCE OF CERTAIN FACTS

Corresponding provision

- Section 119 of the BSA corresponds to section 114 of the Evidence Act
- There are no changes

SECTION 120 OF BSA : PRESUMPTION AS TO ABSENCE OF CONSENT IN CERTAIN PROSECUTION FOR RAPE

Corresponding provision

- Section 120 of the BSA corresponds to section 114A of the Evidence Act
- There are no changes

SECTION 121 OF BSA : ESTOPPEL

Corresponding provision

- Section 121 of the BSA corresponds to section 115 of the Evidence Act
- There are no changes

SECTION 122 OF BSA : ESTOPPEL OF TENANT AND OF LICENSEE OF PERSON IN POSSESSION

Corresponding provision

- Section 122 of the BSA corresponds to section 116 of the Evidence Act

During continuance of tenancy or anytime thereafter

- Section 116 of the Evidence Act provided that no tenant of immovable property, or person claiming through such tenant, shall, during the continuance of the tenancy, be permitted to deny that the landlord of such tenant had, at the beginning of the tenancy, a title to such immovable property
- Section 122 of BSA provides that no tenant of immovable property, or person claiming through such tenant, shall, during the continuance of the tenancy or *any time thereafter*, be permitted to deny

that the landlord of such tenant had, at the beginning of the tenancy, a title to such immovable property

SECTION 123 OF BSA : ESTOPPEL OF ACCEPTOR OF BILL OF EXCHANGE, BAILEE OR LICENSEE

Corresponding provision

- Section 123 of the BSA corresponds to section 117 of the Evidence Act
- There are no changes

SECTION 124 OF BSA : WHO MAY TESTIFY

Corresponding provision

- Section 124 of the BSA corresponds to section 118 of the Evidence Act

Person of unsound mind

- Reference to "lunatic" is replaced with reference to "person of unsound mind"

SECTION 125 OF BSA : WITNESS UNABLE TO COMMUNICATE VERBALLY

Corresponding provision

- Section 125 of the BSA corresponds to section 119 of the Evidence Act
- There are no changes

SECTION 126 OF BSA : COMPETENCY OF HUSBAND AND WIFE AS WITNESSES IN CERTAIN CASES

Corresponding provision

- Section 126 of the BSA corresponds to section 120 of the Evidence Act
- There are no changes

SECTION 127 OF BSA : JUDGES AND MAGISTRATES

Corresponding provision

- Section 127 of the BSA corresponds to section 121 of the Evidence Act
- There are no changes

SECTION 128 OF BSA : COMMUNICATIONS DURING MARRIAGE

Corresponding provision

- Section 128 of the BSA corresponds to section 122 of the Evidence Act
- There are no changes

SECTION 129 OF BSA : EVIDENCE AS TO AFFAIRS OF STATE

Corresponding provision

- Section 129 of the BSA corresponds to section 123 of the Evidence Act
- There are no changes

SECTION 130 OF BSA : OFFICIAL COMMUNICATIONS

Corresponding provision

- Section 130 of the BSA corresponds to section 124 of the Evidence Act
- There are no changes

SECTION 131 OF BSA : INFORMATION AS TO COMMISSION OF OFFENCES

Corresponding provision

- Section 131 of the BSA corresponds to section 125 of the Evidence Act
- There are no changes

SECTION 132 OF BSA : PROFESSIONAL COMMUNICATIONS

Corresponding provision

- Section 132(1) and (2) of the BSA corresponds to section 126 of the Evidence Act
- Section 132(3) of BSA corresponds to section 127 of Evidence Act

Advocate

- The words "barrister, attorney, pleader or vakil" are replaced by the word "advocate"

SECTION 133 OF BSA : PRIVILEGE NOT WAIVED BY VOLUNTEERING EVIDENCE

Corresponding provision

- Section 133 of the BSA corresponds to section 128 of the Evidence Act

Advocate

- The words "barrister, attorney, pleader or vakil" are replaced by the word "advocate"

SECTION 134 OF BSA : CONFIDENTIAL COMMUNICATION WITH LEGAL ADVISERS

Corresponding provision

- Section 134 of the BSA corresponds to section 129 of the Evidence Act

Legal Adviser

- The words "legal professional adviser" are replaced by words "legal adviser"

SECTION 135 OF BSA : PRODUCTION OF TITLE-DEEDS OF WITNESS NOT A PARTY

Corresponding provision

- Section 135 of the BSA corresponds to section 130 of the Evidence Act
- There are no changes

SECTION 136 OF BSA : PRODUCTION OF DOCUMENTS OR ELECTRONIC RECORDS WHICH ANOTHER PERSON, HAVING POSSESSION, COULD REFUSE TO PRODUCE

Corresponding provision

- Section 136 of the BSA corresponds to section 131 of the Evidence Act
- There are no changes

SECTION 137 OF BSA : WITNESS NOT EXCUSED FROM ANSWERING ON GROUND THAT ANSWER WILL CRIMINATE

Corresponding provision

- Section 137 of the BSA corresponds to section 132 of the Evidence Act
- There are no changes

SECTION 138 OF BSA : ACCOMPLICE

Corresponding provision

- Section 138 of the BSA corresponds to section 133 of the Evidence Act

Accomplice

- Words "if" is substituted in section 138 of BSA for words "merely because" in section 133 of Evidence Act
- Section 133 of Evidence Act provides that an accomplice shall be a competent witness against an accused person; and a conviction is not illegal *merely because* it proceeds upon the uncorroborated testimony of an accomplice.
- Section 138 of BSA provides that an accomplice shall be a competent witness against an accused person; and a conviction is not illegal if it proceeds upon the corroborated testimony of an accomplice.

SECTION 139 OF BSA : NUMBER OF WITNESSES

Corresponding provision

- Section 139 of the BSA corresponds to section 134 of the Evidence Act
- There are no changes

SECTION 140 OF BSA : ORDER OF PRODUCTION AND EXAMINATION OF WITNESSES

Corresponding provision

- Section 140 of the BSA corresponds to section 135 of the Evidence Act
- There are no changes

SECTION 141 OF BSA : JUDGE TO DECIDE AS TO ADMISSIBILITY OF EVIDENCE

Corresponding provision

- Section 141 of the BSA corresponds to section 136 of the Evidence Act
- There are no changes

SECTION 142 OF BSA : EXAMINATION OF WITNESSES

Corresponding provision

- Section 142 of the BSA corresponds to section 137 of the Evidence Act
- There are no changes

SECTION 143 OF BSA : ORDER OF EXAMINATIONS

Corresponding provision

- Section 143 of the BSA corresponds to section 138 of the Evidence Act
- There are no changes

SECTION 144 OF BSA : CROSS-EXAMINATION OF PERSON CALLED TO PRODUCE A DOCUMENT

Corresponding provision

- Section 144 of the BSA corresponds to section 139 of the Evidence Act
- There are no changes

SECTION 145 OF BSA : WITNESSES TO CHARACTER

Corresponding provision

- Section 145 of the BSA corresponds to section 140 of the Evidence Act
- There are no changes

SECTION 146 OF BSA : LEADING QUESTIONS

Corresponding provision

- Section 146(1) of the BSA corresponds to section 141 of the Evidence Act

- Section 146(2) and 146(3) of BSA corresponds to section 142, para 1 & para 2 of Evidence Act
- Section 146(4) of BSA corresponds to section 143 of Evidence Act
- There are no changes

SECTION 147 OF BSA : EVIDENCE AS TO MATTERS IN WRITING

Corresponding provision

- Section 147 of the BSA corresponds to section 144 of the Evidence Act
- There are no changes

SECTION 148 OF BSA : CROSS-EXAMINATION AS TO PREVIOUS STATEMENTS IN WRITING

Corresponding provision

- Section 148 of the BSA corresponds to section 145 of the Evidence Act
- There are no changes

SECTION 149 OF BSA : QUESTIONS LAWFUL IN CROSS-EXAMINATION

Corresponding provision

- Section 149 of the BSA corresponds to section 146 of the Evidence Act
- There are no changes

SECTION 150 OF BSA : WHEN WITNESS TO BE COMPELLED TO ANSWER

Corresponding provision

- Section 150 of the BSA corresponds to section 147 of the Evidence Act
- There are no changes

SECTION 151 OF BSA : COURT TO DECIDE WHEN QUESTION SHALL BE ASKED AND WHEN WITNESS COMPELLED TO ANSWER

Corresponding provision

- Section 151 of the BSA corresponds to section 148 of the Evidence Act
- There are no changes

SECTION 152 OF BSA : QUESTION NOT TO BE ASKED WITHOUT REASONABLE GROUNDS

Corresponding provision

- Section 152 of the BSA corresponds to section 149 of the Evidence Act

Advocate

- Words "advocate" is used for "barrister"

SECTION 153 OF BSA : PROCEDURE OF COURT IN CASE OF QUESTION BEING ASKED WITHOUT REASONABLE GROUNDS

Corresponding provision

- Section 153 of the BSA corresponds to section 150 of the Evidence Act

Advocate

- The words "barrister, attorney, pleader or vakil" are replaced by the word "advocate"

SECTION 154 OF BSA : INDECENT AND SCANDALOUS QUESTIONS

Corresponding provision

- Section 154 of the BSA corresponds to section 151 of the Evidence Act
- There are no changes

SECTION 155 OF BSA : QUESTIONS INTENDED TO INSULT OR ANNOY

Corresponding provision

- Section 155 of the BSA corresponds to section 152 of the Evidence Act
- There are no changes

SECTION 156 OF BSA : EXCLUSION OF EVIDENCE TO CONTRADICT ANSWERS TO QUESTIONS TESTING VERACITY

Corresponding provision

- Section 156 of the BSA corresponds to section 153 of the Evidence Act
- There are no changes

SECTION 157 OF BSA : QUESTION BY PARTY TO HIS OWN WITNESS

Corresponding provision

- Section 157 of the BSA corresponds to section 154 of the Evidence Act
- There are no changes

SECTION 158 OF BSA : IMPEACHING CREDIT OF WITNESS

Corresponding provision

- Section 158 of the BSA corresponds to section 155 of the Evidence Act
- There are no changes

SECTION 159 OF BSA : QUESTIONS TENDING TO CORROBORATE EVIDENCE OF RELEVANT FACT, ADMISSIBLE

Corresponding provision

- Section 159 of the BSA corresponds to section 156 of the Evidence Act
- There are no changes

SECTION 160 OF BSA : FORMER STATEMENTS OF WITNESS MAY BE PROVED TO CORROBORATE LATER TESTIMONY AS TO SAME FACT

Corresponding provision

- Section 160 of the BSA corresponds to section 157 of the Evidence Act
- There are no changes

SECTION 161 OF BSA : WHAT MATTERS MAY BE PROVED IN CONNECTION WITH PROVED STATEMENT RELEVANT UNDER SECTION 26 OR 27

Corresponding provision

- Section 161 of the BSA corresponds to section 158 of the Evidence Act
- There are no changes

SECTION 162 OF BSA : REFRESHING MEMORY

Corresponding provision

- Section 162 of the BSA corresponds to section 159 of the Evidence Act
- There are no changes

SECTION 163 OF BSA : TESTIMONY TO FACTS STATED IN DOCUMENT MENTIONED IN SECTION 162

Corresponding provision

- Section 163 of the BSA corresponds to section 160 of the Evidence Act
- There are no changes

SECTION 164 OF BSA : RIGHT OF ADVERSE PARTY AS TO WRITING USED TO REFRESH MEMORY

Corresponding provision

- Section 164 of the BSA corresponds to section 161 of the Evidence Act
- There are no changes

SECTION 165 OF BSA : PRODUCTION OF DOCUMENTS

Corresponding provision

- Section 165 of the BSA corresponds to section 162 of the Evidence Act

Communication between Ministers and President of India

- New proviso to section 165 of BSA provides that no Court shall require any communication between the Ministers and the President of India to be produced before it

SECTION 166 OF BSA : GIVING, AS EVIDENCE, OF DOCUMENT CALLED FOR AND PRODUCED ON NOTICE

Corresponding provision

- Section 166 of the BSA corresponds to section 163 of the Evidence Act
- There are no changes

SECTION 167 OF BSA : USING, AS EVIDENCE, OF DOCUMENT PRODUCTION OF WHICH WAS REFUSED ON NOTICE

Corresponding provision

- Section 167 of the BSA corresponds to section 164 of the Evidence Act
- There are no changes

SECTION 168 OF BSA : JUDGE'S POWER TO PUT QUESTIONS OR ORDER PRODUCTION

Corresponding provision

- Section 168 of the BSA corresponds to section 165 of the Evidence Act
- There are no changes

SECTION 169 OF BSA : NO NEW TRIAL FOR IM-PROPER ADMISSION OR REJECTION OF EVIDENCE

Corresponding provision

- Section 169 of the BSA corresponds to section 167 of the Evidence Act
- There are no changes

SECTION 170 OF BSA : REPEAL AND SAVINGS

Corresponding provision

- Section 170 of the BSA corresponds to section 2 of the Evidence Act

SCHEDULE OF BSA

Corresponding provision

- No corresponding Schedule in Evidence Act
- This is a new Schedule and prescribes certificate mentioned in section 63(4)(*c*) of BSA

BHARATIYA SAKSHYA ADHINIYAM, 2023

Arrangement of sections

PART I

CHAPTER I

PRELIMINARY

SECTION PAGE

How much of a statement is to be proved

Judgments of courts when relevant

Opinions of third persons when relevant

SECTION PAGE

CHAPTER V

OF DOCUMENTARY EVIDENCE

PART IV

PRODUCTION AND EFFECT OF EVIDENCE

CHAPTER VII

OF THE BURDEN OF PROOF

CHAPTER XI

OF IMPROPER ADMISSION AND REJECTION OF EVIDENCE

CHAPTER XII

REPEAL AND SAVINGS

BHARATIYA SAKSHYA ADHINIYAM, 2023
[47 OF 2023]

An Act to consolidate and to provide for general rules and principles of evidence for fair trial.

BE it enacted by Parliament in the Seventy-fourth Year of the Republic of India as follows:—

PART I

CHAPTER I

PRELIMINARY

Short title, application and commencement.

1. (1) This Act may be called the Bharatiya Sakshya Adhiniyam, 2023.

(2) It applies to all judicial proceedings in or before any Court, including Courts-martial, but not to affidavits presented to any Court or officer, nor to proceedings before an arbitrator.

(3) It shall come into force on such date as the Central Government may, by notification in the Official Gazette†, appoint.

Corresponding Provision **:** Section 1 of Indian Evidence Act, 1872

† **Notification No. S.O. 849(E), dated 23-2-2024** - In exercise of the powers conferred by sub-section (3) of section 1 of the Bharatiya Sakshya Adhiniyam, 2023 (47 of 2023), the Central Government hereby appoints the 1st day of July, 2024 as the date on which the provisions of the said Adhiniyam, shall come into force.

Definitions.

2. (*1*) In this Adhiniyam, unless the context otherwise requires,—

(*a*) "Court" includes all Judges and Magistrates, and all persons, except arbitrators, legally authorised to take evidence;

***Corresponding Provision*:** Section 3, para 1 of Indian Evidence Act, 1872

(*b*) "conclusive proof" means when one fact is declared by this Adhiniyam to be conclusive proof of another, the Court shall, on proof of the one fact, regard the other as proved, and shall not allow evidence to be given for the purpose of disproving it;

***Corresponding Provision*:** Section 4, para 3 of Indian Evidence Act, 1872

(*c*) "disproved" in relation to a fact, means when, after considering the matters before it, the Court either believes that it does not exist, or considers its non-existence so probable that a prudent man ought, under the circumstances of the particular case, to act upon the supposition that it does not exist;

***Corresponding Provision*:** Section 3, para 8 of Indian Evidence Act, 1872

(*d*) "document" means any matter expressed or described or otherwise recorded upon any substance by means of letters, figures or marks or any other means or by more than one of those means, intended to be used, or which may be used, for the purpose of recording that matter and includes electronic and digital records.

Illustrations

(*i*) A writing is a document.

(*ii*) Words printed, lithographed or photographed are documents.

(*iii*) A map or plan is a document.

(*iv*) An inscription on a metal plate or stone is a document.

(*v*) A caricature is a document.

(*vi*) An electronic record on emails, server logs, documents on computers, laptop or smartphone, messages, websites, locational evidence and voice mail messages stored on digital devices are documents;

***Corresponding Provision*:** Section 3, para 5 of Indian Evidence Act, 1872

(*e*) "evidence" means and includes—

(*i*) all statements including statements given electronically which the Court permits or requires to be made before it by witnesses in relation to matters of fact under inquiry and such statements are called oral evidence;

(*ii*) all documents including electronic or digital records produced for the inspection of the Court and such documents are called documentary evidence;

***Corresponding Provision* :** Section 3, para 6 of Indian Evidence Act, 1872

(*f*) "fact" means and includes—

(*i*) any thing, state of things, or relation of things, capable of being perceived by the senses;

(*ii*) any mental condition of which any person is conscious.

Illustrations

(*i*) That there are certain objects arranged in a certain order in a certain place, is a fact.

(*ii*) That a person heard or saw something, is a fact.

(*iii*) That a person said certain words, is a fact.

(*iv*) That a person holds a certain opinion, has a certain intention, acts in good faith, or fraudulently, or uses a particular word in a particular sense, or is or was at a specified time conscious of a particular sensation, is a fact;

Corresponding Provision **:** Section 3, para 2 of Indian Evidence Act, 1872

(*g*) "facts in issue" means and includes any fact from which, either by itself or in connection with other facts, the existence, non-existence, nature or extent of any right, liability or disability, asserted or denied in any suit or proceeding, necessarily follows.

Explanation.—Whenever, under the provisions of the law for the time being in force relating to Civil Procedure, any Court records an issue of fact, the fact to be asserted or denied in the answer to such issue is a fact in issue.

Illustrations

A is accused of the murder of B. At his trial, the following facts may be in issue:—

(*i*) That A caused B's death.

(*ii*) That A intended to cause B's death.

(*iii*) That A had received grave and sudden provocation from B.

(*iv*) That A, at the time of doing the act which caused B's death, was, by reason of unsoundness of mind, incapable of knowing its nature;

Corresponding Provision **:** Section 3, para 4 of Indian Evidence Act, 1872

(*h*) "may presume".—Whenever it is provided by this Adhiniyam that the Court may presume a fact, it may either regard such fact as proved, unless and until it is disproved or may call for proof of it;

Corresponding Provision **:** Section 4, para 1 of Indian Evidence Act, 1872

(*i*) "not proved".—A fact is said to be not proved when it is neither proved nor disproved;

Corresponding Provision: Section 3, para 9 of Indian Evidence Act, 1872

(*j*) "proved".—A fact is said to be proved when, after considering the matters before it, the Court either believes it to exist, or considers its existence so probable that a prudent man ought, under the circumstances of the particular case, to act upon the supposition that it exists;

Corresponding Provision: Section 3, para 7 of Indian Evidence Act, 1872

(*k*) "relevant".—A fact is said to be relevant to another when it is connected with the other in any of the ways referred to in the provisions of this Adhiniyam relating to the relevancy of facts;

Corresponding Provision: Section 3, para 3 of Indian Evidence Act, 1872

(*l*) "shall presume".—Whenever it is directed by this Adhiniyam that the Court shall presume a fact, it shall regard such fact as proved, unless and until it is disproved.

Corresponding Provision: Section 4, para 2 of Indian Evidence Act, 1872

(*2*) Words and expressions used herein and not defined but defined in the Information Technology Act, 2000 (21 of 2000), the Bharatiya Nagarik Suraksha Sanhita, 2023 and the Bharatiya Nyaya Sanhita, 2023 shall have the same meanings as assigned to them in the said Act and Sanhitas.

COMMENTS

Circumstantial evidence must prove guilt unerringly beyond reasonable doubt - It is trite law that to convict an accused on the basis of circumstantial evidence, the prosecution must prove beyond reasonable doubt each of the incriminating circumstances on which it proposes to rely; the circumstance(s) relied upon must be of a definite tendency unerringly pointing towards accused's guilt and must form a chain so far complete that there is no escape from the conclusion that within all human probability it is the accused and no one else who had committed the crime and they (it) must exclude all other hypothesis inconsistent with his guilt and consistent with his innocence. [Para 17] - *State of Punjab* v. *Kewal Krishan* AIR 2023 Supreme Court 3226.

Circumstantial evidence should not only be consistent with guilt of accused but should be inconsistent with his innocence - A basic principle of criminal jurisprudence is that in circumstantial evidence cases, the prosecution is obliged to prove each circumstance, beyond reasonable doubt, as well as the links between all circumstances; such circumstances, taken cumulatively, should form a chain so complete that there is no escape from the conclusion that within all human probability, the crime was committed by the accused and none else; further, the facts so proved should unerringly point towards the guilt of the accused. The circumstantial evidence, in order to sustain conviction, must be complete and incapable of explanation of any other hypothesis than that of the guilt of the accused, and such evidence should not only be consistent with the guilt of the accused but should be inconsistent with his innocence. [Para 21] - *Jabir* v. *State of Uttarakhand* AIR 2023 Supreme Court 488.

To establish guilt on accused, chain of evidence must point out to crime and none else - In a criminal trial, the prosecution has to prove its case beyond reasonable doubt. This heavy burden has to be discharged by the prosecution. It becomes even more difficult in a case of circumstantial evidence.

In order to establish a charge of guilt on the accused, the chain of evidence must be completed and the chain must point out to one and only one conclusion, which is that it is only the accused who have committed the crime and none else. [Para 14] - *Dinesh Kumar* v. *State of Haryana* AIR 2023 Supreme Court 2795.

In a case of circumstantial evidence, judgment remains essentially inferential and circumstances must be conclusive - In a case of circumstantial evidence, the judgment remains essentially inferential. The inference is drawn from the established facts as the circumstances lead to particular inferences. The Court has to draw an inference with respect to whether the chain of circumstances is complete, and when the circumstances therein are collectively considered, the same must lead only to the irresistible conclusion that the accused alone is the perpetrator of the crime in question. All the circumstances so established must be of a conclusive nature, and consistent only with the hypothesis of the guilt of the accused. [Para 49] - *Subramanya* v. *State of Karnataka* AIR 2022 Supreme Court 5110.

In case of circumstantial evidences which is "indirect evidence", a complete chain without a snap must point to hypothesis that except accused, no one had committed offence - All evidence let in before the court of law are classified either as direct or circumstantial evidence. "Direct evidence" means when the principal fact is attested directly by witnesses, things or documents. For all other forms, the term "circumstantial evidence" which is "indirect evidence" is referred, whether by witnesses, things or documents, which can be received as evidence. This is also of two kinds namely, conclusive and presumptive. Conclusive is when the connection between the principal and evidentiary facts - the factum probandum and factum probans - is a necessary consequence of the laws of nature; "presumptive" is when the inference of the principal fact from the evidence is only probable, whatever be the degree of the persuasion which it may generate. Thus, circumstantial evidence is evidence of circumstances as opposed to what is called direct evidence. The prosecution must take place and prove all necessary circumstances constituting a complete chain without a snap and pointing to the hypothesis that except the accused, no one had committed the offence.

The principal fact can be proved indirectly by means of certain inferences drawn from its existence or its connection with other circumstantial evidence. It is often said that witnesses may lie but not the circumstances. However, the court must adopt a cautious approach while basing its conviction purely on circumstantial evidence. Inference of guilt can be drawn only when all incriminating facts and circumstances are found to be incompatible with the innocence of an accused. In other words, circumstantial evidence is not direct to the point in issue but consists of evidence of various other facts which are so closely associated with the fact in issue that, taken together they form a chain of circumstances from which the existence of the principal fact can be legally inferred or presumed.

It is trite law that in cases dependent on circumstantial evidence, the inference of guilt can be made if all the incriminating facts and circumstances are incompatible with the innocence of the accused or any other reasonable hypotheses than that of his guilt, and provide a cogent and complete chain of events which leave no reasonable doubt in the judicial mind. When an incriminating circumstance is put to the accused and the said accused either offers no explanation or offers an explanation which is found to be untrue, then the same becomes an additional link in the chain of circumstances to make it complete. If the combined effect of all the proven facts taken together is conclusive in establishing the guilt of the accused, a conviction would be justified even though any one or more of those facts by itself is not decisive. [Paras 53, 54, 55] - *Neeraj Dutta* v. *State* (*Govt. of N.C.T. of Delhi*) AIR 2023 Supreme Court 330.

Circumstantial evidence means facts from which another fact is inferred; hence, it is also to be proved by direct evidence - Congruent to the principle of *res gestae*, a fact includes a state of things or events as well as the mental state *i.e.* intention or animus. A fact in law of evidence includes the factum probandum *i.e.*, the principal fact to be proved and the factum probans, *i.e.*, the evidentiary fact from which the principal fact follows immediately or by inference. On the other hand, the expression "fact in issue" means the matters which are in dispute or which form the subject of investigation (*vide* Section 3 of Evidence Act).

It is well settled that evidence is upon facts pleaded in a case and hence, the principal facts are sometimes the facts in issue. Facts relevant to the issue are evidentiary facts which render probable the existence or non-existence of a fact in issue or some relevant fact.

In criminal cases, the facts in issue are constituted in the charge, or acquisition, in cases of warrant or summon cases. The proof of facts in issue could be oral and documentary evidence. Evidence is the medium through which the court is convinced of the truth or otherwise of the matter under enquiry, *i.e.*, the actual words of witnesses, or documents produced and not the facts which have to be proved by oral and documentary evidence. Of course, the term evidence is not restricted to only oral and documentary evidence but also to other things like material objects, the demeanour of the witnesses, facts of which judicial notice could be taken, admissions of parties, local inspection made and answers given by the accused to questions put forth by the Magistrate or Judge under section 313 of the Criminal Procedure Code (Cr. PC).

Further, according to Sarkar on Law of Evidence, 20 Edition, Volume 1, "direct" or "original" evidence means that evidence which establishes the existence of a thing or fact either by actual production or by testimony or demonstrable declaration of someone who has himself perceived it, and believed that it established a fact in issue. Direct evidence proves the existence of a fact in issue without any inference of presumption.

On the other hand, "indirect evidence" or "substantial evidence" gives rise to the logical inference that such a fact exists, either conclusively or presumptively. The effect of substantial evidence under consideration must be such as not to admit more than one solution and must be inconsistent with any explanation that the fact is not proved. By direct or presumptive evidence (circumstantial evidence), one may say that other facts are proved from which, existence of a given fact may be logically inferred.

Again, oral evidence can be classified as original and hearsay evidence. Original evidence is that which a witness reports himself to have seen or heard through the medium of his own senses. Hearsay evidence is also called derivative, transmitted, or second-hand evidence in which a witness is merely reporting not what he himself saw or heard, and not what has come under the immediate observation of his own bodily senses, but what he has learnt in respect of the fact through the medium of a third person. Normally, a hearsay witness would be inadmissible, but when it is corroborated by substantive evidence of other witnesses, it would be admissible.

Evidence that does not establish the fact in issue directly but throws light on the circumstances in which the fact in issue did occur is circumstantial evidence (also called inferential or presumptive evidence). Circumstantial evidence means facts from which another fact is inferred. Although circumstantial evidence does not go to prove directly the fact in issue, it is equally direct. Circumstantial evidence has also to be proved by direct evidence of the circumstances. Further, letting in evidence should be in accordance with the provision of the Evidence Act by the examination of witnesses, *i.e.*, examination-in-chief, cross-examination, and re-examination. [Paras 30 to 35] - *Neeraj Dutta* v. *State (Govt. of N.C.T. of Delhi)* AIR 2023 Supreme Court 330.

Circumstantial evidence must be conclusive hypothesis of guilty discarding other hypothesis - The circumstances from which the conclusion of guilt is to be drawn should be fully established. It has been held that the circumstances concerned "must or should" and not "may be" established. It has been held that there is not only a grammatical but a legal distinction between "may be proved" and "must be or should be proved". It has been held that the facts so established should be consistent only with the hypothesis of the guilt of the accused, that is to say, they should not be explainable on any other hypothesis except that the accused is guilty. It has been held that the circumstances should be of a conclusive nature and tendency and they should exclude every possible hypothesis except the one sought to be proved, and that there must be a chain of evidence so complete so as not to leave any reasonable ground for the conclusion consistent with the innocence of the accused and must show that in all human probability the act must have been done by the accused. It is a settled principle of law that however strong a suspicion may be, it cannot take place of a proof beyond reasonable doubt. [Paras 10 and 11] - *Nikhil Chandra Mondal* v. *State of West Bengal* AIR 2023 Supreme Court 1323.

In case of circumstantial evidence, facts must exclude every hypothesis except guilt of accused - Suspicion, howsoever strong, cannot substitute proof beyond reasonable doubt. This Court has held that there is not only a grammatical but also a legal distinction between 'may' and 'must'. For proving a case based on circumstantial evidence, it is necessary for the prosecution to establish each and every circumstance beyond reasonable doubt, and further, that the circumstances so proved must form a complete chain of evidence so as not to leave any reasonable ground for the conclusion consistent with the innocence of the accused and must show, in all human probability, that the act has been done by the accused. Further, it has been held that the facts so established must exclude every hypothesis except the guilt of the accused. [Para 9] - *Ram Pratap* v. *State of Haryana* AIR 2023 Supreme Court 719.

Accused can be punished if he is found guilty even in cases of circumstantial evidence where prosecution is able to prove beyond reasonable doubt complete chain of events - Although there can be no straight jacket formula for appreciation of circumstantial evidence, yet to convict an accused on the basis of circumstantial evidence, the Court must follow certain tests which are broadly as follows:

1. Circumstances from which an inference of guilt is sought to be drawn must be cogently and firmly established;
2. Those circumstances must be of a definite tendency unerringly pointing towards guilt of the accused and must be conclusive in nature;
3. The circumstances, if taken cumulatively, should form a chain so complete that there is no escape from the conclusion that within all human probability the crime was committed by the accused and none else; and
4. The circumstantial evidence in order to sustain conviction must be complete and incapable of explanation of any other hypothesis than that of the guilt of the accused but should be inconsistent with his innocence. In other words, the circumstances should exclude every possible hypothesis except the one to be proved.

It is settled principle of law that an accused can be punished if he is found guilty even in cases of circumstantial evidence provided that the prosecution is able to prove beyond reasonable doubt the complete chain of events and circumstances which definitely points towards the involvement and guilty of the suspect or accused, as the case may be. The accused will not be entitled to acquittal merely because there is no eye witness in the case. It is also equally true that an accused can be convicted on the basis of circumstantial evidence subject to satisfaction of the expected principles in that regard. [Paras 46 and 47] - *Ramanand Alias Nandlal Bharti* v. *State of Uttar Pradesh* AIR 2022 Supreme Court 5273.

Before a court can convict, circumstances concerned "must or should be" established and not "may be" established - The law on the appreciation of circumstantial evidence is well settled. The circumstances concerned "must or should be" established and not "may be" established. The accused "must be" and not merely "may be" guilty before a court can convict him. The conclusions of guilt arrived at must be sure conclusions and must not be based on vague conjectures. The entire chain of circumstances on which the conclusion of guilt is to be drawn, should be fully established and should not leave any reasonable ground for the conclusion consistent with the innocence of the accused. [Para 7] - *Chandrapal* v. *State of Chhattisgarh (Earlier M.P.)* AIR 2022 Supreme Court 2542.

Circumstances should be of a conclusive nature and tendency - For resting a conviction in the case of circumstantial evidence, the circumstances from which the conclusion of guilt is to be drawn, should be fully established, and all the facts so established should be consistent only with the hypothesis of the guilt of the accused. The circumstances should be of a conclusive nature and tendency, and they should be such as to exclude every hypothesis, but the one proposed to be proved. There must be a chain of evidence so complete as not to leave any reasonable ground for a conclusion consistent with the innocence of the accused, and it must be such as to show that within all human probabilities, the act must have been done by the accused. [Para 14] - *Lochan Shrivas* v. *State of Chhattisgarh* AIR 2022 Supreme Court 252.

In a case of circumstantial evidence, facts should be consistent only with hypothesis of guilt of accused - In a case of circumstantial evidence, before the case can be said to be fully established against an accused, it is necessary that the circumstances from which the conclusion of guilt is to be drawn, should be fully established, and all the facts so established should be consistent only with the hypothesis of the guilt of the accused. They should not be explainable on any other hypothesis except that the accused is guilty. The circumstances should be of a conclusive nature and tendency. They should exclude every hypothesis except the one to be proved. There must be a chain of evidence so complete as not to leave any reasonable ground for the conclusion consistent with the innocence of the accused and must show that in all human probabilities, the act must have been done by the accused. [Para 16] - *Lochan Shrivas* v. *State of Chhattisgarh* AIR 2022 Supreme Court 252.

For circumstantial evidence, 5 Golden rules are laid down by Apex Court - The law with regard to the appreciation of evidence when the case of the prosecution hinges on the circumstantial evidence is very well settled. The five golden principles have been laid down by this Court. [Para 22] - *Mohd. Firoz* v. *State of Madhya Pradesh* AIR 2022 Supreme Court 1967.

In a case of circumstantial evidence, motive assumes significance - In a case of circumstantial evidence, motive assumes significance. Though, the motive may pale into insignificance in a case involving eyewitnesses, it may not be so when an accused is implicated based upon the circumstantial evidence. [Para 13] - *Ravi Sharma* v. *State (Government of NCT of Delhi)* AIR 2022 Supreme Court 4810.

Motive cannot be a substitute for proof of guilt - Even if it is believed that the accused appellant had a motive to commit the crime, the same may be an important circumstance in a case based on circumstantial evidence but cannot take the place as a conclusive proof that the person concerned was the author of the crime. One could even say that the presence of motive in the facts and circumstances of the case creates a strong suspicion against the accused appellant but suspicion, howsoever strong, cannot be a substitute for proof of the guilt of the accused beyond reasonable doubt. The trial court rightly disbelieved motive to commit the crime as the evidence in this regard is absolutely hearsay in nature. [Para 92] - *Subramanya* v. *State of Karnataka* AIR 2022 Supreme Court 5110.

Motive is an important link in chain of circumstances - In a case of circumstantial evidence, motive has an important role to play. Motive may also have a role to play even in a case of direct evidence but it carries much greater importance in a case of circumstantial evidence than a case of direct evidence. It is an important link in the chain of circumstances. [Para 15] - *Indrajit Das* v. *State of Tripura* AIR 2023 Supreme Court 1239.

Absence of motive cannot be a ground to reject prosecution case, but weighs in favour of accused - As regards the relevancy of motive in a case based on circumstantial evidence, the weight of authorities is on principles that if motive is proved, that would supply another link in the chain of circumstantial evidence but, absence of motive cannot be a ground to reject the prosecution case, though such an absence of motive is a factor that weighs in favour of the accused. [Para 15] - *Prem Singh* v. *State of NCT of Delhi* AIR 2023 Supreme Court 193.

Motive, when proved, supplies additional link in chain of circumstantial evidence - Motive, when proved, supplies additional link in the chain of circumstantial evidence but, absence thereof cannot, by itself, be a ground to reject the prosecution case; although absence of motive in a case based on circumstantial evidence is a factor that weighs in favour of the accused. [Para 17.1] - *Prem Singh* v. *State of NCT of Delhi* AIR 2023 Supreme Court 193.

Failure to prove motive in case of circumstantial evidence not fatal - It is a settled principle of criminal jurisprudence that in a case based on circumstantial evidence, motive for committing the crime on the part of the accused assumes greater importance. This Court in various decisions has laid down the principles holding that motive for commission of offence no doubt assumes greater importance in cases resting on circumstantial evidence than those in which direct evidence regarding commission of offence is available. It is equally true that failure to prove motive in cases resting on circumstantial evidence is not fatal by itself. However, it is also well settled and it is trite in law that absence of motive could be a missing link of incriminating circumstances, but once the prosecution has established the other incriminating circumstances to its entirety, absence of motive will not give any benefit to the accused. [Para 87] - *Ramanand Alias Nandlal Bharti* v. *State of Uttar Pradesh* AIR 2022 Supreme Court 5273.

Last seen theory requires corroboration from other circumstances and evidences - The evidence of last seen becomes an extremely important piece of evidence in a case of circumstantial evidence, particularly when there is a close proximity of time between when the accused was last seen with the deceased and the discovery of the body of the deceased, or in this case the time of the death of the deceased.

This does not mean that in cases where there is a long gap between the time of last seen and the death of the deceased the last seen evidence loses its value. It would not, but then a very heavy burden is placed upon the prosecution to prove that during this period of last seen and discovery of the body of the deceased or the time of the death of the deceased, no other person but the accused could have had an access to the deceased. The circumstances of last seen together in the present case by itself cannot form the basis of guilt.

The circumstances of last seen together does not by itself lead to an irrevocable conclusion that it is the accused who had committed the crime. The prosecution must come out with something more to establish this connectivity with the accused and the crime committed. Particularly, in the present case when there is no close proximity between circumstances of last seen together and the approximate time of death, the evidence of last seen becomes weak.

Where time gap between the last seen and time of death is long enough, as in the present case, then it would be dangerous to come to the conclusion that the accused is responsible for the murder. In such cases it is unsafe to base conviction on the "last seen theory" and it would be safer to look for corroboration from other circumstance and evidence which have been adduced by the prosecution. The other circumstances here is the so called discovery, and most of these, as we have already discussed, fail to meet the requirement of section 27 of the Evidence Act. [Para 12] - *Dinesh Kumar* v. *State of Haryana* AIR 2023 Supreme Court 2795.

Sole reliance on "last seen theory" not justified to convict accused - Where there is no other circumstance or evidence. Importantly, the time gap between when the deceased was seen in the company of the accused and the probable time of his death, based on the post mortem report, which was conducted two days later, was silent about the probable time of death, though it stated that death occurred approximately two days before the post mortem, is not narrow. Given this fact, and the serious inconsistencies in the depositions of the witnesses, as well as the fact that the FIR was lodged almost 6 weeks after the incident, the sole reliance on the "last seen" circumstance (even if it were to be assumed to have been proved) to convict the accused-appellants is not justified. [Para 25] - *Jabir* v. *State of Uttarakhand* AIR 2023 Supreme Court 488.

Last seen theory is applicable where time lag between time deceased was seen last with accused and time of murder is narrow - It has been repeatedly emphasized by this court, that the "last seen" doctrine has limited application, where the time lag between the time the deceased was seen last with the accused, and the time of murder, is narrow; furthermore, the court should not convict an accused only on the basis of the "last seen" circumstance. [Para 23] - *Jabir* v. *State of Uttarakhand* AIR 2023 Supreme Court 488.

PART II

CHAPTER II

RELEVANCY OF FACTS

Evidence may be given of facts in issue and relevant facts.

3. Evidence may be given in any suit or proceeding of the existence or non-existence of every fact in issue and of such other facts as are hereinafter declared to be relevant, and of no others.

Explanation.—This section shall not enable any person to give evidence of a fact which he is disentitled to prove by any provision of the law for the time being in force relating to Civil Procedure.

Illustrations

(*a*) A is tried for the murder of B by beating him with a club with the intention of causing his death.

At A's trial the following facts are in issue:—

A's beating B with the club;

A's causing B's death by such beating;

A's intention to cause B's death.

(*b*) A suitor does not bring with him, and have in readiness for production at the first hearing of the case, a bond on which he relies. This section does not enable him to produce the bond or prove its contents at a subsequent stage of the proceedings, otherwise than in accordance with the conditions prescribed by the Code of Civil Procedure, 1908 (5 of 1908).

Corresponding Provision : Section 5 of Indian Evidence Act, 1872

Closely connected facts

Relevancy of facts forming part of same transaction.

4. Facts which, though not in issue, are so connected with a fact in issue or a relevant fact as to form part of the same transaction, are relevant, whether they occurred at the same time and place or at different times and places.

Illustrations

(*a*) A is accused of the murder of B by beating him. Whatever was said or done by A or B or the bystanders at the beating, or so shortly before or after it as to form part of the transaction, is a relevant fact.

(*b*) A is accused of waging war against the Government of India by taking part in an armed insurrection in which property is destroyed, troops are attacked and jails are broken open. The occurrence of these facts is relevant, as forming part of the general transaction, though A may not have been present at all of them.

(*c*) A sues B for a libel contained in a letter forming part of a correspondence. Letters between the parties relating to the subject out of which the libel arose, and forming part of the correspondence in which it is contained, are relevant facts, though they do not contain the libel itself.

(*d*) The question is, whether certain goods ordered from B were delivered to A. The goods were delivered to several intermediate persons successively. Each delivery is a relevant fact.

Corresponding Provision : Section 6 of Indian Evidence Act, 1872

COMMENTS

Statement of accused to which section 6 is applicable cannot be treated as a confession of guilt - Section 5 of the Evidence Act provides that evidence may be given in a proceeding of the existence or non-existence of every fact in issue and of such other facts which are declared to be relevant under the provisions of Chapter II of the Evidence Act, 1872. Section 6 is applicable to facts which are not in issue. Such facts become relevant only when the same satisfy the tests laid down in section 6. Hence, the statement of an accused to which section 6 is applicable cannot be treated as a confession of guilt. The statement becomes relevant which can be read in evidence as it shows the conduct of the appellant immediately after the incident. [Para 18] - *Arvind Kumar* v. *State of NCT, Delhi* AIR 2023 Supreme Court 3653.

To form particular statement as part of same transaction utterances must be simultaneous with incident - The rule embodied in section 6 is usually known as the rule of *res gestae*. What it means is that a fact which, though not in issue, is so connected with the fact in issue "as to form part of the same transaction" becomes relevant by itself. To form particular statement as part of the same transaction utterances must be simultaneous with the incident or substantial contemporaneous that is made either during or immediately before or after its occurrence. [Para 49] - *Balu Sudam Khalde* v. *State of Maharashtra* AIR 2023 Supreme Court 1736.

A conduct of accused after incident may become admissible, though not in issue, but connected with fact in issue - The essence of the doctrine of *res gestae* is that a fact which, though not in issue, is so connected with the fact in issue "as to form part of the same transaction" that it becomes relevant by itself. A conduct of the accused after the incident may become admissible under section 6 of the Evidence Act, though not in issue, if it is so connected with the fact in issue. [Para 36] - *Veerendra* v. *State of Madhya Pradesh* AIR 2022 Supreme Court 2396.

Facts which are occasion, cause or effect of facts in issue or relevant facts.

5. Facts which are the occasion, cause or effect, immediate or otherwise, of relevant facts, or facts in issue, or which constitute the state of things under which they happened, or which afforded an opportunity for their occurrence or transaction, are relevant.

Illustrations

(*a*) The question is, whether A robbed B. The facts that, shortly before the robbery, B went to a fair with money in his possession, and that he showed it, or mentioned the fact that he had it, to third persons, are relevant.

(*b*) The question is, whether A murdered B. Marks on the ground, produced by a struggle at or near the place where the murder was committed, are relevant facts.

(*c*) The question is, whether A poisoned B. The state of B's health before the symptoms ascribed to poison, and habits of B, known to A, which afforded an opportunity for the administration of poison, are relevant facts.

Corresponding Provision **:** Section 7 of Indian Evidence Act, 1872

Motive, preparation and previous or subsequent conduct.

6. (1) Any fact is relevant which shows or constitutes a motive or preparation for any fact in issue or relevant fact.

(2) The conduct of any party, or of any agent to any party, to any suit or proceeding, in reference to such suit or proceeding, or in reference to any fact in issue therein or relevant thereto, and the conduct of any person, an offence against whom is the subject of any proceeding, is relevant, if such conduct influences or is influenced by any fact in issue or relevant fact, and whether it was previous or subsequent thereto.

Explanation 1.—The word "conduct" in this section does not include statements, unless those statements accompany and explain acts other than statements; but this explanation is not to affect the relevancy of statements under any other section of this Adhiniyam.

Explanation 2.—When the conduct of any person is relevant, any statement made to him or in his presence and hearing, which affects such conduct, is relevant.

Illustrations

(*a*) A is tried for the murder of B. The facts that A murdered C, that B knew that A had murdered C, and that B had tried to extort money from A by threatening to make his knowledge public, are relevant.

(*b*) A sues B upon a bond for the payment of money. B denies the making of the bond. The fact that, at the time when the bond was alleged to be made, B required money for a particular purpose, is relevant.

(*c*) A is tried for the murder of B by poison. The fact that, before the death of B, A procured poison similar to that which was administered to B, is relevant.

(*d*) The question is, whether a certain document is the will of A. The facts that, not long before, the date of the alleged will, A made inquiry into matters to which the provisions of the alleged will relate; that he consulted advocates in reference to making the will, and that he caused drafts of other wills to be prepared, of which he did not approve, are relevant.

(*e*) A is accused of a crime. The facts that, either before, or at the time of, or after the alleged crime, A provided evidence which would tend to give to the facts of the case an appearance favourable to himself, or that he destroyed or concealed evidence, or prevented the presence or procured the absence of persons who might have been witnesses, or suborned persons to give false evidence respecting it, are relevant.

(*f*) The question is, whether A robbed B. The facts that, after B was robbed, C said in A's presence—"the police are coming to look for the person who robbed B", and that immediately afterwards A ran away, are relevant.

(*g*) The question is, whether A owes B ten thousand rupees. The facts that A asked C to lend him money, and that D said to C in A's presence and hearing—"I advise you not to trust A, for he owes B ten thousand rupees", and that A went away without making any answer, are relevant facts.

(*h*) The question is, whether A committed a crime. The fact that A absconded, after receiving a letter, warning A that inquiry was being made for the criminal, and the contents of the letter, are relevant.

(*i*) A is accused of a crime. The facts that, after the commission of the alleged crime, A absconded, or was in possession of property or the proceeds of property acquired by the crime, or attempted to conceal things which were or might have been used in committing it, are relevant.

(*j*) The question is, whether A was raped. The fact that, shortly after the alleged rape, A made a complaint relating to the crime, the circumstances under which, and the terms in which, the complaint was made, are relevant. The fact that, without making a complaint, A said that A had been raped is not relevant as conduct under this section, though it may be relevant as a dying declaration under clause (*a*) of section 26, or as corroborative evidence under section 160.

(*k*) The question is, whether A was robbed. The fact that, soon after the alleged robbery, A made a complaint relating to the offence, the circumstances under which, and the terms in which, the complaint was made, are relevant. The fact that A said he had been robbed, without making any complaint, is not relevant, as conduct under this section, though it may be relevant as a dying declaration under clause *(a)* of section 26, or as corroborative evidence under section 160.

Corresponding Provision **:** Section 8 of Indian Evidence Act, 1872

COMMENTS

Conduct of accused, alone, though may be relevant under section 8, cannot form basis of conviction - Although the conduct of an accused may be a relevant fact under section 8 of the Evidence Act, yet the same, by itself, cannot be a ground to convict him or hold him guilty and that too, for a serious offence like murder. Like any other piece of evidence, the conduct of an accused is also one of the circumstances which the court may take into consideration along with the other evidence on record, direct or indirect. The conduct of the accused alone, though may be relevant under section 8 of the Evidence Act, cannot form the basis of conviction. [Para 74] - *Ramanand Alias Nandlal Bharti* v. *State of Uttar Pradesh* AIR 2022 Supreme Court 5273/*Subramanya* v. *State of Karnataka* AIR 2022 Supreme Court 5110.

Conduct of accused, when relevant - By virtue of section 8 of the Evidence Act, the conduct of an accused is relevant, if such conduct influences or influenced by any fact in issue or relevant fact. The evidence of the circumstance, simpliciter, that the accused pointed out to the police officer, the place where he had concealed the weapon of offence would be admissible as conduct under section 8 irrespective of the fact whether the statement made by the appellant convict contemporaneously with or antecedent to such conduct falls within the purview of section 27 of the Evidence Act or not. Even if the discovery statement made by the appellant convict is not admissible under section 27 of the Evidence Act, still it is relevant under section 8 of the Evidence Act. [Para 78] - *Mukesh Singh* v. *State (NCT of Delhi)* AIR 2023 Supreme Court 4097.

Where two accused talked on call, same only proves close relationship; same do not prove murder in furtherance of this proximity - When a conviction is based solely on circumstantial evidence, such evidence and the chain of circumstances must be conclusive enough to sustain a conviction. Where two accused talked on call, same only proves that they shared a close relationship. However, what these records do not prove, is that the murder was somehow in furtherance of this alleged proximity between them particularly when the prosecution has failed to establish by evidence the supposed objective of these murders and what was it that was sought to be achieved by such an act. [Para 13] - *Ravinder Singh Alias Kaku* v. *State of Punjab* AIR 2022 Supreme Court 2726.

Facts necessary to explain or introduce fact in issue or relevant facts.

7. Facts necessary to explain or introduce a fact in issue or relevant fact, or which support or rebut an inference suggested by a fact in issue or a relevant fact, or which establish the identity of anything, or person whose identity, is relevant, or fix the time or place at which any fact in issue or relevant fact happened, or which show the relation of parties by whom any such fact was transacted, are relevant in so far as they are necessary for that purpose.

Illustrations

(*a*) The question is, whether a given document is the will of A. The state of A's property and of his family at the date of the alleged will may be relevant facts.

(*b*) A sues B for a libel imputing disgraceful conduct to A; B affirms that the matter alleged to be libellous is true. The position and relations of the parties at the time when the libel was published may be relevant facts as introductory to the facts in issue. The particulars of a dispute between A and B about a matter unconnected with the alleged libel are irrelevant, though the fact that there was a dispute may be relevant if it affected the relations between A and B.

(*c*) A is accused of a crime. The fact that, soon after the commission of the crime, A absconded from his house, is relevant under section 6, as conduct subsequent to and affected by facts in issue. The fact that, at the time when he left home, A had sudden and urgent business at the place to which he went, is relevant, as tending to explain the fact that he left home suddenly. The details of the business on which he left are not relevant, except in so far as they are necessary to show that the business was sudden and urgent.

(*d*) A sues B for inducing C to break a contract of service made by him with A. C, on leaving A's service, says to A—"I am leaving you because B has made me a better offer". This statement is a relevant fact as explanatory of C's conduct, which is relevant as a fact in issue.

(*e*) A, accused of theft, is seen to give the stolen property to B, who is seen to give it to A's wife. B says as he delivers it—"A says you are to hide this". B's statement is relevant as explanatory of a fact which is part of the transaction.

(*f*) A is tried for a riot and is proved to have marched at the head of a mob. The cries of the mob are relevant as explanatory of the nature of the transaction.

Corresponding Provision : Section 9 of Indian Evidence Act, 1872

COMMENTS

Identification, meaning of - Facts which establish the identity of any person or thing whose identity is relevant are, by virtue of section 9 of the Evidence Act, always relevant. The term 'identification' means proving that a person, subject or article before the Court is the very same that he or it is alleged, charged or reputed to be. Identification is almost always a matter of opinion or belief. [Para 37] - *Mukesh Singh* v. *State (NCT of Delhi)* AIR 2023 Supreme Court 4097.

Identification in Court not preceded by test identification parade is a matter for courts of fact to examine - It is well settled that the substantive evidence is the evidence of identification in court and the test identification parade provides corroboration to the identification of the witness in court, if required. However, what weight must be attached to the evidence of identification in court, which is not preceded by a test identification parade, is a matter for the courts of fact to examine. [Para 48] - *Mukesh Singh* v. *State (NCT of Delhi)* AIR 2023 Supreme Court 4097.

It is always open for the accused to raise legitimacy of test identification parade or its evidentiary value but cannot decline or refuse to join it - The newly inserted section

54A Cr.PC provides for the identification of the arrested person where it is considered necessary for the purpose of investigation by the officer-in-charge of a police station. The said section empowers the court, on the request of the officer-in-charge of a police station, to direct for placing the accused at test identification parade for identification by any person or persons in such manner as the court may deem fit. This section is restricted to identification of persons only. So this section has no application where the question of identification of articles arises. TIP is part of investigation and the investigation of a case is to be conducted by the investigation agency and it is their statutory prerogatives. There was no statutory provision authorizing the accused to pray for placing him in the test parade. Some High Courts approved this right, while some other High Courts took a contrary view. In *State of Uttar Pradesh* v. *Rajju* AIR 1971 SC 708, this Court observed, "If the accused felt that the witnesses would not be able to identify them they should have requested for an identification parade." This observation indirectly approves the right to ask for test parade by the accused. In another case, the accused voluntarily accepted the risk of being identified in a parade but he was denied that opportunity. [Para 30] - *Mukesh Singh* v. *State (NCT of Delhi)* AIR 2023 Supreme Court 4097.

Things said or done by conspirator in reference to common design.

8. Where there is reasonable ground to believe that two or more persons have conspired together to commit an offence or an actionable wrong, anything said, done or written by any one of such persons in reference to their common intention, after the time when such intention was first entertained by any one of them, is a relevant fact as against each of the persons believed to be so conspiring, as well for the purpose of proving the existence of the conspiracy as for the purpose of showing that any such person was a party to it.

Illustration

Reasonable ground exists for believing that A has joined in a conspiracy to wage war against the State.

The facts that B procured arms in Europe for the purpose of the conspiracy, C collected money in Kolkata for a like object,

D persuaded persons to join the conspiracy in Mumbai, E published writings advocating the object in view at Agra, and F transmitted from Delhi to G at Singapore the money which C had collected at Kolkata, and the contents of a letter written by H giving an account of the conspiracy, are each relevant, both to prove the existence of the conspiracy, and to prove A's complicity in it, although he may have been ignorant of all of them, and although the persons by whom they were done were strangers to him, and although they may have taken place before he joined the conspiracy or after he left it.

Corresponding Provision : Section 10 of Indian Evidence Act, 1872

When facts not otherwise relevant become relevant.

9. Facts not otherwise relevant are relevant—

(1) if they are inconsistent with any fact in issue or relevant fact;

(2) if by themselves or in connection with other facts they make the existence or non-existence of any fact in issue or relevant fact highly probable or improbable.

Illustrations

(*a*) The question is, whether A committed a crime at Chennai on a certain day. The fact that, on that day, A was at Ladakh is relevant. The fact that, near the time when the crime was committed, A was at a distance from the place where it was committed, which would render it highly improbable, though not impossible, that he committed it, is relevant.

(*b*) The question is, whether A committed a crime. The circumstances are such that the crime must have been committed either by A, B, C or D. Every fact which shows that the crime could have been committed by no one else, and that it was not committed by either B, C or D, is relevant.

Corresponding Provision : Section 11 of Indian Evidence Act, 1872

Facts tending to enable Court to determine amount are relevant in suits for damages.

10. In suits in which damages are claimed, any fact which will enable the Court to determine the amount of damages which ought to be awarded, is relevant.

Corresponding Provision : Section 12 of Indian Evidence Act, 1872

Facts relevant when right or custom is in question.

11. Where the question is as to the existence of any right or custom, the following facts are relevant—

(*a*) any transaction by which the right or custom in question was created. claimed, modified, recognised, asserted or denied, or which was inconsistent with its existence;

(*b*) particular instances in which the right or custom was claimed, recognised or exercised, or in which its exercise was disputed, asserted or departed from.

Illustration

The question is, whether A has a right to a fishery. A deed conferring the fishery on A's ancestors, a mortgage of the fishery by A's father, a subsequent grant of the fishery by A's father, irreconcilable with the mortgage, particular instances in which A's father exercised the right, or in which the exercise of the right was stopped by A's neighbours, are relevant facts.

Corresponding Provision : Section 13 of Indian Evidence Act, 1872

Facts showing existence of state of mind, or of body or bodily feeling.

12. Facts showing the existence of any state of mind, such as intention, knowledge, good faith, negligence, rashness, ill-will or goodwill towards any particular person, or showing the existence of any state of body or bodily feeling, are relevant, when the existence of any such state of mind or body or bodily feeling is in issue or relevant.

Explanation 1.—A fact relevant as showing the existence of a relevant state of mind must show that the state of mind exists, not generally, but in reference to the particular matter in question.

Explanation 2.—But where, upon the trial of a person accused of an offence, the previous commission by the accused of an offence is relevant within the meaning of this section, the previous conviction of such person shall also be a relevant fact.

Illustrations

(*a*) A is accused of receiving stolen goods knowing them to be stolen. It is proved that he was in possession of a particular stolen article. The fact that, at the same time, he was in possession of many other stolen articles is relevant, as tending to show that he knew each and all of the articles of which he was in possession to be stolen.

(*b*) A is accused of fraudulently delivering to another person a counterfeit currency which, at the time when he delivered it, he knew to be counterfeit. The fact that, at the time of its delivery, A was possessed of a number of other pieces of counterfeit currency is relevant. The fact that A had been previously convicted of delivering to another person as genuine a counterfeit currency knowing it to be counterfeit is relevant.

(*c*) A sues B for damage done by a dog of B's, which B knew to be ferocious. The fact that the dog had previously bitten X, Y and Z, and that they had made complaints to B, are relevant.

(*d*) The question is, whether A, the acceptor of a bill of exchange, knew that the name of the payee was fictitious. The fact that A had accepted other bills drawn in the same manner before they could have been transmitted to him by the payee if the payee had been a real person, is relevant, as showing that A knew that the payee was a fictitious person.

(*e*) A is accused of defaming B by publishing an imputation intended to harm the reputation of B. The fact of previous publications by A respecting B, showing ill-will on the part of A towards B is relevant, as proving A's intention to harm B's reputation by the particular publication in question. The facts that there was no previous quarrel between A and B, and that A repeated the matter complained of as he heard it, are relevant, as showing that A did not intend to harm the reputation of B.

(*f*) A is sued by B for fraudulently representing to B that C was solvent, whereby B, being induced to trust C, who was insolvent, suffered loss. The fact that, at the time when A represented C to be solvent, C was supposed to be solvent by his neighbours and by persons dealing with him, is relevant, as showing that A made the representation in good faith.

(*g*) A is sued by B for the price of work done by B, upon a house of which A is owner, by the order of C, a contractor. A's defence is that B's contract was with C. The fact that A paid C for the work in question is relevant, as proving that A did, in good faith, make over to C the management of the work in question, so that C was in a position to contract with B on C's own account, and not as agent for A.

(*h*) A is accused of the dishonest misappropriation of property which he had found, and the question is whether, when he appropriated it, he believed in good faith that the real owner could not be found. The fact that public notice of the loss of the property had been given in the place where A was, is relevant, as showing that A did not in good faith believe that the real owner of the property could not be found. The fact that A knew, or had reason to believe, that the notice was given fraudulently by C, who had heard of the loss of the property and wished to set up a false claim to it, is relevant, as showing that the fact that A knew of the notice did not disprove A's good faith.

(*i*) A is charged with shooting at B with intent to kill him. In order to show A's intent, the fact of A's having previously shot at B may be proved.

(*j*) A is charged with sending threatening letters to B. Threatening letters previously sent by A to B may be proved, as showing the intention of the letters.

(*k*) The question is, whether A has been guilty of cruelty towards B, his wife. Expressions of their feeling towards each other shortly before or after the alleged cruelty are relevant facts.

(*l*) The question is, whether A's death was caused by poison. Statements made by A during his illness as to his symptoms are relevant facts.

(*m*) The question is, what was the state of A's health at the time when an assurance on his life was effected.

Statements made by A as to the state of his health at or near the time in question are relevant facts.

(*n*) A sues B for negligence in providing him with a car for hire not reasonably fit for use, whereby A was injured. The fact that B's attention was drawn on other occasions to the defect of that particular car is relevant. The fact that B was habitually negligent about the cars which he let to hire is irrelevant.

(*o*) A is tried for the murder of B by intentionally shooting him dead. The fact that A on other occasions shot at B is relevant as showing his intention to shoot B. The fact that A was in the habit of shooting at people with intent to murder them is irrelevant.

(*p*) A is tried for a crime. The fact that he said something indicating an intention to commit that particular crime is relevant. The fact that he said something indicating a general disposition to commit crimes of that class is irrelevant.

Corresponding Provision **:** Section 14 of Indian Evidence Act, 1872

COMMENTS

Motive cannot be a substitute for proof of guilt - Even if it is believed that the accused appellant had a motive to commit the crime, the same may be an important circumstance in a case based on circumstantial evidence but cannot take the place as a conclusive proof that the person concerned was the author of the crime. One could even say that the presence of motive in the facts and circumstances of the case creates a strong suspicion against the accused appellant but suspicion, howsoever strong, cannot be a substitute for proof of the guilt of the accused beyond reasonable doubt. The trial court rightly disbelieved motive to commit the crime as the evidence in this regard is absolutely hearsay in nature. [Para 92] - *Subramanya* v. *State of Karnataka* AIR 2022 Supreme Court 5110.

Motive is an important link in chain of circumstances - In a case of circumstantial evidence, motive has an important role to play. Motive may also have a role to play even in a case of direct evidence but it carries much greater importance in a case of circumstantial evidence than a case of direct evidence. It is an important link in the chain of circumstances. [Para 15] - *Indrajit Das* v. *State of Tripura* AIR 2023 Supreme Court 1239.

Absence of motive cannot be a ground to reject prosecution case, but weighs in favour of accused - As regards the relevancy of motive in a case based on circumstantial evidence, the weight of authorities is on principles that if motive is proved, that would supply another link in the chain of circumstantial evidence but, absence of motive cannot be a ground to reject the prosecution case, though such an absence of motive is a factor that weighs in favour of the accused. [Para 15] - *Prem Singh* v. *State of NCT of Delhi* AIR 2023 Supreme Court 193.

Motive, when proved, supplies additional link in chain of circumstantial evidence - Motive, when proved, supplies additional link in the chain of circumstantial evidence but, absence thereof cannot, by itself, be a ground to reject the prosecution case; although absence of motive in a case based on circumstantial evidence is a factor that weighs in favour of the accused. [Para 17.1] - *Prem Singh* v. *State of NCT of Delhi* AIR 2023 Supreme Court 193.

Failure to prove motive in case of circumstantial evidence not fatal - It is a settled principle of criminal jurisprudence that in a case based on circumstantial evidence, motive for committing the crime on the part of the accused assumes greater importance. This Court in various decisions has laid down the principles holding that motive for commission of offence no doubt assumes greater importance in cases resting on circumstantial evidence than those in which direct evidence regarding commission of offence is available. It is equally true that failure to prove motive in cases resting on circumstantial evidence is not fatal by itself. However, it is also well settled and it is trite in law that absence of motive could be a missing link of incriminating circumstances, but once the prosecution has established the other incriminating circumstances to its entirety, absence of motive will not give any benefit to the accused. [Para 87] - *Ramanand Alias Nandlal Bharti* v. *State of Uttar Pradesh* AIR 2022 Supreme Court 5273.

Facts bearing on question whether act was accidental or intentional.

13. When there is a question whether an act was accidental or intentional, or done with a particular knowledge or intention, the fact that such act formed part of a series of similar occurrences, in each of which the person doing the act was concerned, is relevant.

Illustrations

(*a*) A is accused of burning down his house in order to obtain money for which it is insured. The facts that A lived in several houses successively each of which he insured, in each of which a fire occurred, and after each of which fires A received payment from a different insurance company, are relevant, as tending to show that the fires were not accidental.

(*b*) A is employed to receive money from the debtors of B. It is A's duty to make entries in a book showing the amounts received by him. He makes an entry showing that on a particular occasion he received less than he really did receive. The question is, whether this false entry was accidental or intentional. The facts that other entries made by A in the same book are false, and that the false entry is in each case in favour of A, are relevant.

(*c*) A is accused of fraudulently delivering to B a counterfeit currency. The question is, whether the delivery of the currency was accidental. The facts that, soon before or soon after the delivery to B, A delivered counterfeit currency to C, D and E are relevant, as showing that the delivery to B was not accidental.

Corresponding Provision : Section 15 of Indian Evidence Act, 1872

Existence of course of business when relevant.

14. When there is a question whether a particular act was done, the existence of any course of business, according to which it naturally would have been done, is a relevant fact.

Illustrations

(*a*) The question is, whether a particular letter was dispatched. The facts that it was the ordinary course of business for all letters put in a certain place to be carried to the post, and that particular letter was put in that place are relevant.

(*b*) The question is, whether a particular letter reached A. The facts that it was posted in due course, and was not returned through the Return Letter Office, are relevant.

Corresponding Provision : Section 16 of Indian Evidence Act, 1872

Admissions

Admission defined.

15. An admission is a statement, oral or documentary or contained in electronic form, which suggests any inference as to any fact in issue or relevant fact, and which is made by any of the persons, and under the circumstances, hereinafter mentioned.

Corresponding Provision : Section 17 of Indian Evidence Act, 1872

Admission by party to proceeding or his agent.

16. (1) Statements made by a party to the proceeding, or by an agent to any such party, whom the Court regards, under the circumstances of the case, as expressly or impliedly authorised by him to make them, are admissions.

(2) Statements made by—

(*i*) parties to suits suing or sued in a representative character, are not admissions, unless they were made while the party making them held that character; or

(*ii*) (*a*) persons who have any proprietary or pecuniary interest in the subject matter of the proceeding, and who make the statement in their character of persons so interested; or

(*b*) persons from whom the parties to the suit have derived their interest in the subject matter of the suit,

are admissions, if they are made during the continuance of the interest of the persons making the statements.

Corresponding Provision : Section 18 of Indian Evidence Act, 1872

Admissions by persons whose position must be proved as against party to suit.

17. Statements made by persons whose position or liability, it is necessary to prove as against any party to the suit, are admissions, if such statements would be relevant as against such persons in relation to such position or liability in a suit brought by or against them, and if they are made whilst the person making them occupies such position or is subject to such liability.

Illustration

A undertakes to collect rents for B. B sues A for not collecting rent due from C to B. A denies that rent was due from C to B. A statement by C that he owed B rent is an admission, and is a relevant fact as against A, if A denies that C did owe rent to B.

Corresponding Provision : Section 19 of Indian Evidence Act, 1872

Admissions by persons expressly referred to by party to suit.

18. Statements made by persons to whom a party to the suit has expressly referred for information in reference to a matter in dispute are admissions.

Illustration

The question is, whether a horse sold by A to B is sound. A says to B—"Go and ask C, C knows all about it". C's statement is an admission.

Corresponding Provision : Section 20 of Indian Evidence Act, 1872

Proof of admissions against persons making them, and by or on their behalf.

19. Admissions are relevant and may be proved as against the person who makes them, or his representative in interest; but they cannot be proved by or on behalf of the person who makes them or by his representative in interest, except in the following cases, namely:—

(1) an admission may be proved by or on behalf of the person making it, when it is of such a nature that, if the person making it were dead, it would be relevant as between third persons under section 26;

(2) an admission may be proved by or on behalf of the person making it, when it consists of a statement of the existence of any state of mind or body, relevant or in issue, made at or about the time when such state of mind or body existed, and is accompanied by conduct rendering its falsehood improbable;

(3) an admission may be proved by or on behalf of the person making it, if it is relevant otherwise than as an admission.

Illustrations

(*a*) The question between A and B is, whether a certain deed is or is not forged. A affirms that it is genuine, B that it is forged. A may prove a statement by B that the deed is genuine, and B may prove a statement by A that deed is forged; but A cannot prove a statement by himself that the deed is genuine, nor can B prove a statement by himself that the deed is forged.

(*b*) A, the captain of a ship, is tried for casting her away. Evidence is given to show that the ship was taken out of her proper course. A produces a book kept by him in the ordinary course of his business showing observations alleged to have been taken by him from day to day, and indicating that the ship was not taken out of her proper course. A may prove these statements, because they would be admissible between third parties, if he were dead, under clause *(b)* of section 26.

(*c*) A is accused of a crime committed by him at Kolkata. He produces a letter written by himself and dated at Chennai on that day, and bearing the Chennai post-mark of that day. The statement in the date of the letter is admissible, because, if A were dead, it would be admissible under clause *(b)* of section 26.

(*d*) A is accused of receiving stolen goods knowing them to be stolen. He offers to prove that he refused to sell them below their value. A may prove these statements, though they are admissions, because they are explanatory of conduct influenced by facts in issue.

(*e*) A is accused of fraudulently having in his possession counterfeit currency which he knew to be counterfeit. He offers to prove that he asked a skilful person to examine the currency as he doubted whether it was counterfeit or not, and that person did examine it and told him it was genuine. A may prove these facts.

Corresponding Provision : Section 21 of Indian Evidence Act, 1872

When oral admissions as to contents of documents are relevant.

20. Oral admissions as to the contents of a document are not relevant, unless and until the party proposing to prove them shows that he is entitled to give secondary evidence of the contents of such document under the rules hereinafter contained, or unless the genuineness of a document produced is in question.

Corresponding Provision : Section 22 of Indian Evidence Act, 1872

Admissions in civil cases when relevant.

21. In civil cases no admission is relevant, if it is made either upon an express condition that evidence of it is not to be given, or under circumstances from which the Court can infer that the parties agreed together that evidence of it should not be given.

Explanation.—Nothing in this section shall be taken to exempt any advocate from giving evidence of any matter of which he may be compelled to give evidence under sub-sections (1) and (2) of section 132.

Corresponding Provision : Section 23 of Indian Evidence Act, 1872

Confession caused by inducement, threat, coercion or promise, when irrelevant in criminal proceeding.

22. A confession made by an accused person is irrelevant in a criminal proceeding, if the making of the confession appears to the Court to have been caused by any inducement, threat, coercion or promise having reference to the charge against the accused person, proceeding from a person in authority and sufficient, in the opinion of the Court, to give the accused person grounds which would appear to him reasonable for supposing that by making it he would gain any advantage or avoid any evil of a temporal nature in reference to the proceedings against him:

Provided that if the confession is made after the impression caused by any such inducement, threat, coercion or promise has, in the opinion of the Court, been fully removed, it is relevant:

Provided further that if such a confession is otherwise relevant, it does not become irrelevant merely because it was made under a promise of secrecy, or in consequence of a deception practised on the accused person for the purpose of obtaining it, or when he was drunk, or because it was made in answer to questions which he need not have answered, whatever may have been the form of those questions, or because he was not warned that he was not bound to make such confession, and that evidence of it might be given against him.

Corresponding Provision **:** Sections 24, 28 and 29 of Indian Evidence Act, 1872

COMMENTS

Extra judicial confession must be voluntary not caused by any inducement, threat or promise - Confessions may be divided into two classes, *i.e.* judicial and extra judicial. Judicial confessions are those which are made before Magistrate or Court in the course of judicial proceedings. Extra judicial confessions are those which are made by the party elsewhere than before a Magistrate or Court. Extra judicial confessions are generally those made by a party to or before a private individual which includes even a judicial officer in his private capacity. It also includes a Magistrate who is not especially empowered to record confessions under section 164 of the Cr.P.C. or a Magistrate so empowered but receiving the confession at a stage when section 164 does not apply. As to extra judicial confessions, two questions arise: (*i*) were they made voluntarily? And (*ii*) are they true? As the Section enacts, a confession made by an accused person is irrelevant in a criminal proceedings, if the making of the confession appears to the Court to have been caused by any inducement, threat or promise, (1) having reference to the charge against the accused person, (2) proceeding from a person in authority, and (3) sufficient, in the opinion of the Court to give the accused person grounds which would appear to him reasonable for supposing that by making it he would gain any advantage or avoid any evil of a temporal nature in reference to the proceedings against him. It follows that a confession would be voluntary if it is made by the accused in a fit state of mind, and if it is not caused by any inducement, threat or promise which has reference to the charge against him, proceeding from a person in authority. It would not be involuntary, if the inducement, (*a*) does not have reference to the charge against the accused person, or (*b*) it does not proceed from a person in authority; or (*c*) it is not sufficient, in the opinion of the Court to give the accused person grounds which would appear to him reasonable for supposing that, by making it, he would gain any advantage or avoid any evil of a temporal nature in reference to the proceedings against him. Whether or not the confession was voluntary would depend upon the facts and circumstances of each case, judged in the light of section 24 of the Evidence Act. The law is clear that a confession cannot be used against an accused person unless the Court is satisfied that it was voluntary and at that stage the question whether it is true or false does not arise. If the facts and circumstances surrounding the making of a confession appear to cast a doubt on the veracity or voluntariness of the confession, the Court may refuse to act upon the confession, even if it is admissible in evidence. One important question, in regard to which the Court has to be satisfied with is, whether when the accused made confession, he was a free man or his movements were controlled by the police either by themselves or through some other agency employed by them for the purpose of securing such a confession. The question whether a confession is voluntary or not is always a question of fact. All the factors and all the circumstances of the case, including the important factors at the time given for reflection, scope of the accused getting a feeling of threat, inducement or promise, must be considered before deciding whether the Court is satisfied that its opinion, the impression caused by the inducement, threat or promise, if any, has been fully removed. A free and voluntary confession is deserving of highest credit, because it is presumed to flow from the highest sense of guilt. [*See R.V. Warwickshall* (1783) Lesch 263].

It is not to be conceived that a man would be induced to make a free and voluntary confession of guilt, so contrary to the feelings and principles of human nature, if the facts confessed were not true. Deliberate and voluntary confessions of guilt, if clearly proved, are among the most effectual proofs in law. An involuntary confession is one which is not the result of the free will of the maker of it. So, where the statement is made as a result of the harassment and continuous interrogation for several hours after the person is treated as an offender and accused, such statement must be regarded as involuntary. The inducement may take the form of a promise or of threat, and often the inducement involves both promise and threat, a promise of forgiveness if disclosure is made and threat of prosecution if it is not. (*See Woodroffe Evidence*, 9th Edn. Page 284).

A promise is always attached to the confession, alternative while a threat is always attached to the silence alternative; thus, in the one case the prisoner is measuring the net advantage of the promise, minus the general undesirability of a false confession, as against the present unsatisfactory situation; while in the other case he is measuring the net advantages of the present satisfactory situation, minus the general undesirability of the confession against the threatened harm. It must be borne in mind that every inducement, threat or promise does not vitiate a confession. Since the object of the rule is to exclude only those confessions which are testimonially untrustworthy, the inducement, threat or promise must be such as is calculated to lead to an untrue confession. On the aforesaid analysis the Court is to determine the absence or presence of inducement, promise etc. or its sufficiency and how or in what measure it worked on the mind of the accused. If the inducement, promise or threat is sufficient in the opinion of the Court, to give the accused person grounds which would appear to him reasonable for supposing that by making it he would gain any advantage or avoid any evil, it is enough to exclude the confession. The words 'appear to him' in the last part of the section refer to the mentality of the accused. [*See State of Rajasthan* v. *Raja Ram* (2003) 8 SCC 180/AIR 2003 SC 3601].

An extra judicial confession, if voluntary and true and made in a fit state of mind, can be relied upon by the Court. The confession will have to be proved like any other fact. The value of the evidence as to confession, like any other evidence, depends upon the veracity of the witness to whom it has been made. The value of the evidence as to the confession depends on the reliability of the witness who gives the evidence. It is not open to any Court to start with a presumption that extra judicial confession is a weak type of evidence. It would depend on the nature of the circumstances, the time when the confession was made and the credibility of the witnesses who speak to such a confession. Such a confession can be relied upon and conviction can be founded thereon if the evidence about the confession comes from the mouth of witnesses who appear to be unbiased, not even remotely inimical to the accused, and in respect of whom nothing is brought out which may tend to indicate that he may have a motive for attributing an untruthful statement to the accused, the words spoken to by the witness are clear, unambiguous and unmistakably convey that the accused is the perpetrator of the crime and nothing is omitted by the witness which may militate against it. After subjecting the evidence of the witness to a rigorous test on the touchstone of credibility, the extra judicial confession can be accepted and can be the basis of a conviction if it passes the test of credibility.

Extra judicial confession is a weak piece of evidence and the court must ensure that the same inspires confidence and is corroborated by other prosecution evidence. It is considered to be a weak piece of evidence as it can be easily procured whenever direct evidence is not available. In order to accept extra judicial confession, it must be voluntary and must inspire confidence. If the court is satisfied that the extra judicial confession is voluntary, it can be acted upon to base the conviction. [Paras 80, 81 and 82] - *Ramanand Alias Nandlal Bharti* v. *State of Uttar Pradesh* AIR 2022 Supreme Court 5273.

Extra judicial confession, if voluntary and true and made in a fit state of mind, can be relied but it being a weak piece

of evidence, it is to be corroborated by other prosecution evidence - An extra judicial confession, if voluntary and true and made in a fit state of mind, can be relied upon by the Court. The confession will have to be proved like any other fact. The value of the evidence as to confession, like any other evidence, depends upon the veracity of the witness to whom it has been made. The value of the evidence as to the confession depends on the reliability of the witness who gives the evidence. It is not open to any court to start with a presumption that extra judicial confession is a weak type of evidence. It would depend on the nature of the circumstances, the time when the confession was made and the credibility of the witnesses who speak to such a confession. Such a confession can be relied upon and conviction can be founded thereon if the evidence about the confession comes from the mouth of witnesses who appear to be unbiased, not even remotely inimical to the accused, and in respect of whom nothing is brought out which may tend to indicate that he may have a motive for attributing an untruthful statement to the accused, the words spoken to by the witness are clear, unambiguous and unmistakably convey that the accused is the perpetrator of the crime and nothing is omitted by the witness which may militate against it. After subjecting the evidence of the witness to a rigorous test on the touchstone of credibility, the extra judicial confession can be accepted and can be the basis of a conviction if it passes the test of credibility.

Extra judicial confession is a weak piece of evidence and the court must ensure that the same inspires confidence and is corroborated by other prosecution evidence. It is considered to be a weak piece of evidence as it can be easily procured whenever direct evidence is not available. In order to accept extra judicial confession, it must be voluntary and must inspire confidence. If the court is satisfied that the extra judicial confession is voluntary, it can be acted upon to base the conviction. [Para 53] - *Subramanya* v. *State of Karnataka* AIR 2022 Supreme Court 5110.

If voluntary statement is recorded in language not known to accused, assistance of interpreter is to be taken - Illustration - The statement of the accused having been recorded being voluntary and when the statement is being recorded in the language not known to the accused, the assistance of interpreter if taken by the police cannot be found fault with.

The ultimate test of the said statement made by the accused having been noted down as told by the accused or not would be of paramount consideration. If the answer is in the affirmative then necessarily said statement will have to be held as passing the test of law as otherwise not. Merely because the translation was made from Malayalam to Tamil and written down in Kannada would not suggest that such statement be held to be either not being voluntary or the said statement having been recorded improperly. The interpreter having entered the witness box and tendered himself for cross-examination which resulted in nothing worthwhile having been elicited for discarding his evidence, it cannot be gainsaid by the accused that said statement is to be ignored or rejected or discarded. Merely because the accused did not know how to read and write Malayalam does not *ipso facto* make the contents of statement to be disbelieved. [Para 19] - *Siju Kurian* v. *State of Karnataka* AIR 2023 Supreme Court 2239.

Confession to police officer.

23. (1) No confession made to a police officer shall be proved as against a person accused of any offence.

Corresponding Provision **:** Section 25 of Indian Evidence Act, 1872

(2) No confession made by any person while he is in the custody of a police officer, unless it is made in the immediate presence of a Magistrate shall be proved against him:

Provided that when any fact is deposed to as discovered in consequence of information received from a person accused of any offence, in the custody of a police officer, so much of such information, whether it amounts to a confession or not, as relates distinctly to the fact discovered, may be proved.

Corresponding Provision **:** Sections 26 and 27 of Indian Evidence Act, 1872

COMMENTS

Statement is inadmissible if given while in police custody - Section 25 of the Evidence Act in no uncertain terms makes it clear that no confession made to a police officer shall be proved as against a person accused of any offence. Likewise, section 26 states that any such statement is inadmissible if given while in police custody. When the confessional statement of the accused relied upon by the prosecution was admittedly recorded after the arrest of those accused persons when other accused were in police custody, said statement would become inadmissible having regard to the provisions of sections 25 and 26 of the Evidence Act, 1872. Section 25 of the Act in no uncertain terms makes it clear that no confession made to a police officer shall be proved as against a person accused of any offence. Likewise, section 26 states that any such statement is inadmissible if given while in police custody. [Para 9] - *Naresh Alias Nehru* v. *State of Haryana* AIR 2023 Supreme Court 5054.

Appreciation of evidence by Supreme Court - Though in cases of concurrent findings of fact the Apex Court will not ordinarily interfere with the said findings, in exceptional circumstances, the Apex Court is empowered to do so. If this Court finds that the appreciation of evidence and findings is vitiated by any error of law or procedure or found contrary to the principles of natural justice, errors of record and misreading of the evidence, or where the conclusions of the High Court are manifestly perverse, the Apex Court would not be powerless to reappreciate the evidence. [Para 26] - *Khema Alias Khem Chandra* v. *State of Uttar Pradesh* AIR 2022 Supreme Court 3765.

Testimonies of family members cannot be rejected - Merely because the witnesses are family members apart from being chance witnesses, their testimonies cannot be rejected. [Para 34] - *Jafarudheen* v. *State of Kerala* AIR 2022 Supreme Court 3627.

Section 27 of Evidence Act incorporates theory of "confirmation by subsequent facts" facilitating a link to chain of events - Section 27 of the Evidence Act is an exception to sections 24 to 26. Admissibility under section 27 is relatable to the information pertaining to a fact discovered. This provision merely facilitates proof of a fact discovered in consequence of information received from a person in custody, accused of an offence. Thus, it incorporates the theory of "confirmation by subsequent facts" facilitating a link to the chain of events. It is for the prosecution to prove that the information received from the accused is relatable to the fact discovered. The object is to utilize it for the purpose of recovery as it ultimately touches upon the issue pertaining to the discovery of a new fact through the information furnished by the accused. Therefore, Section 27 is an exception to sections 24 to 26 meant for a specific purpose and thus be construed as a proviso. The onus is on the prosecution to prove the fact discovered from the information obtained from the accused. This is also for the reason that the information has been obtained while the accused is still in the custody of the police. Having understood the aforesaid object behind the provision, any recovery under section 27 will have to satisfy the Court's conscience. One cannot lose sight of the fact that the prosecution may at times take advantage of the custody of the accused, by other means. The Court will have to be conscious of the witness's credibility and the other evidence produced when dealing with a recovery under section 27 of the Evidence Act. [Paras 30 and 31] - *Jafarudheen* v. *State of Kerala* AIR 2022 Supreme Court 3627.

Only if contents of discovery panchnama is proved, such evidence can be relied upon - The requirement of law that needs to be fulfilled before accepting the evidence of discovery is that by proving the contents of the panchnama. The investigating officer in his deposition is obliged in law to prove the contents of the panchnama and it is only if the investigating officer has successfully proved the contents of the discovery panchnama in accordance with law, then in that case the prosecution may be justified in relying upon such evidence and the trial court may also accept the evidence. [Para 56] - *Ramanand Alias Nandlal Bharti* v. *State of Uttar Pradesh* AIR 2022 Supreme Court 5273.

Voluntary custodial statement is admissibility as legal evidence when facts stated is not in knowledge of others - Section 27 of Evidence Act permits the derivative use of custodial statement in the ordinary course of events. There is no automatic presumption that the custodial statements have been extracted through compulsion. A fact discovered is an information supplied by the accused in his disclosure statement is a relevant fact and that is only admissible in evidence if something new is discovered or recovered at the instance of the accused which was not within the knowledge of the police before recording the disclosure statement of the accused. The statement of an accused recorded while being in police custody can be split into its components and can be separated from the admissible portions. Such of those components or portions which were the immediate cause of the discovery would be the legal evidence and the rest can be rejected. It is a trite law that in pursuance to a voluntary statement made by the accused, a fact must be discovered which was in the exclusive knowledge of the accused alone. In such circumstances, that part of the voluntary statement which leads to the discovery of a new fact which was only in the knowledge of the accused would become admissible under section 27. Such statement should have been voluntarily made and the facts stated therein should not have been in the knowledge of others. [Paras 18 and 19] - *Siju Kurian* v. *State of Karnataka* AIR 2023 Supreme Court 2239.

Being in 'custody of a police officer' and being 'accused of an offence', are pre-requisites to render a confession made to police admissible to a limited extent - Section 26 of the Indian Evidence Act, 1872 provides that no confession made by any person whilst he is in the custody of a police officer shall be proved against such person, unless it is made in the immediate presence of a Magistrate. Section 27 of Evidence Act, thereafter, is in the nature of an exception to section 26 of the Evidence Act. It states that, when any fact is deposed to as discovered in consequence of information received from a person accused of any offence, in the custody of a police officer, so much of such information, whether it amounts to a confession or not, as relates distinctly to the fact thereby discovered, may be proved. Therefore, it is essential under section 27 of the Evidence Act that the person concerned must be 'accused of an offence' and being in the 'custody of a police officer', he or she must give information leading to the discovery of a fact and so much of that information, whether it amounts to a confession or not, that relates distinctly to the fact discovered, may be proved against him. In effect, both aspects, *viz.*, being in 'the custody of a police officer' and being 'accused of an offence', are indispensable pre-requisites to render a confession made to the police admissible to a limited extent, by bringing into play the exception postulated under section 27 of the Evidence Act. [Para 22] - *Rajesh* v. *State of Madhya Pradesh* AIR 2023 Supreme Court 4759.

After recording statement (Panchnama) in presence of two independent witnesses, would proceed to particular place as may be led by accused - If, it is say of the investigating officer that the accused appellant while in custody on his own free will and volition made a statement that he would lead to the place where he had hidden the weapon of offence along with his blood stained clothes then the first thing that the investigating officer should have done was to call for two independent witnesses at the police station itself. Once the two independent witnesses arrive at the police station thereafter in their presence the accused should be asked to make an appropriate statement as he may desire in regard to pointing out the place where he is said to have hidden the weapon of offence. When the accused while in custody makes such statement before the two independent witnesses (panch witnesses) the exact statement or rather the exact words uttered by the accused should be incorporated in the first part of the panchnama that the investigating officer may draw in accordance with law. This first part of the panchnama for the purpose of section 27 of the Evidence Act is always drawn at the police station in the presence of the independent witnesses so as to lend credence that a particular statement was made by the accused expressing his willingness on his own free will and volition to point out the place where the weapon of offence or any other article used in the commission of the offence had been hidden. Once the first part of the panchnama is completed thereafter the police party along with the accused and the two independent witnesses (panch witnesses) would proceed to the particular place as may be led by the accused. If from that particular place anything like the weapon of offence or blood stained clothes or any other article is discovered then that part of the entire process would form the second part of the panchnama. This is how the law expects the investigating officer to draw the discovery panchnama as contemplated under section 27 of the Evidence Act. [Para 53] - *Ramanand Alias Nandlal Bharti* v. *State of Uttar Pradesh* AIR 2022 Supreme Court 5273.

Disclosure statement of co-accused cannot be solely relied - The law on the evidentiary value of disclosure statements of co-accused too is settled; the courts have hesitated to place reliance solely on disclosure statements of co-accused and used them merely to support the conviction or, as Sir Lawrence Jenkins observed in *Emperor* v. *Lalit Mohan Chucker burty* to "lend assurance to other evidence against a co-accused". [Para 23] - *Manoj Kumar Soni* v. *State of Madhya Pradesh* AIR 2023 Supreme Court 3857.

Consideration of proved confession affecting person making it and others jointly under trial for same offence.

24. When more persons than one are being tried jointly for the same offence, and a confession made by one of such persons affecting himself and some other of such persons is proved, the Court may take into consideration such confession as against such other person as well as against the person who makes such confession.

Explanation I.—"Offence", as used in this section, includes the abetment of, or attempt to commit, the offence.

Explanation II.—A trial of more persons than one held in the absence of the accused who has absconded or who fails to comply with a proclamation issued under section 84 of the Bharatiya Nagarik Suraksha Sanhita, 2023 shall be deemed to be a joint trial for the purpose of this section.

Illustrations

(*a*) A and B are jointly tried for the murder of C. It is proved that A said—"B and I murdered C". The Court may consider the effect of this confession as against B.

(*b*) A is on his trial for the murder of C. There is evidence to show that C was murdered by A and B, and that B said—"A and I murdered C". This statement may not be taken into consideration by the Court against A, as B is not being jointly tried.

Corresponding Provision : Section 30 of Indian Evidence Act, 1872

COMMENTS

Extra judicial confession of co-accused could be admitted only as a corroborative piece of evidence - As per section 30 of the Evidence Act, when more persons than one are being tried jointly for the same offence, and a confession made by one of such persons affecting himself and some other of such persons is proved, the court may take into consideration such confession as against such other person as well as against the person who makes such confession. However, Apex Court has consistently held that an extra judicial confession is a weak kind of evidence and unless it inspires confidence or is fully corroborated by some other evidence of clinching nature, ordinarily conviction for the offence of murder should not be made only on the evidence of extra judicial confession.

The extra judicial confession made by the co-accused could be admitted in evidence only as a corroborative piece of evidence. In absence of any substantive evidence against the accused, the extra judicial confession allegedly made by the co-accused loses its significance and there cannot be any conviction based on such extra judicial confession of the co-accused. [Para 11] - *Chandrapal* v. *State of Chhattisgarh (Earlier M.P.)* AIR 2022 Supreme Court 2542.

Admissions not conclusive proof, but may estop.

25. Admissions are not conclusive proof of the matters admitted but they may operate as estoppels under the provisions hereinafter contained.

Corresponding Provision : Section 31 of Indian Evidence Act, 1872

Statements by persons who cannot be called as witnesses

Cases in which statement of relevant fact by person who is dead or cannot be found, etc., is relevant.

26. Statements, written or verbal, of relevant facts made by a person who is dead, or who cannot be found, or who has become incapable of giving evidence, or whose attendance cannot be procured without an amount of delay or expense which under the circumstances of the case appears to the Court unreasonable, are themselves relevant facts in the following cases, namely:—

(*a*) when the statement is made by a person as to the cause of his death, or as to any of the circumstances of the transaction which resulted in his death, in cases in which the cause of that person's death comes into question. Such statements are relevant whether the person who made them was or was not, at the time when they were made, under expectation of death, and whatever may be the nature of the proceeding in which the cause of his death comes into question;

(*b*) when the statement was made by such person in the ordinary course of business, and in particular when it consists of any entry or memorandum made by him in books kept in the ordinary course of business, or in the discharge of professional duty; or of an acknowledgement written or signed by him of the receipt of money, goods, securities or property of any kind; or of a document used in commerce written or signed by him; or of the date of a letter or other document usually dated, written or signed by him;

(*c*) when the statement is against the pecuniary or proprietary interest of the person making it, or when, if true, it would expose him or would have exposed him to a criminal prosecution or to a suit for damages;

(*d*) when the statement gives the opinion of any such person, as to the existence of any public right or custom or matter of public or general interest, of the existence of which, if it existed, he would have been likely to be aware, and when such statement was made before any controversy as to such right, custom or matter had arisen;

(*e*) when the statement relates to the existence of any relationship by blood, marriage or adoption between persons as to whose relationship by blood, marriage or adoption the person making the statement had special means of knowledge, and when the statement was made before the question in dispute was raised;

(*f*) when the statement relates to the existence of any relationship by blood, marriage or adoption between persons deceased, and is made in any will or deed relating to the affairs of the family to which any such deceased person belonged, or in any family pedigree, or upon any tombstone, family portrait or other thing on which such statements are usually made, and when such statement was made before the question in dispute was raised;

(*g*) when the statement is contained in any deed, will or other document which relates to any such transaction as is specified in clause *(a)* of section 11;

(*h*) when the statement was made by a number of persons, and expressed feelings or impressions on their part relevant to the matter in question.

Illustrations

(*a*) The question is, whether A was murdered by B; or A dies of injuries received in a transaction in the course of which she was raped. The question is whether she was raped by B; or the question is, whether A was killed by B under such circumstances that a suit would lie against B by A's widow. Statements made by A as to the cause of his or her death, referring respectively to the murder, the rape and the actionable wrong under consideration, are relevant facts.

(*b*) The question is as to the date of A's birth. An entry in the diary of a deceased surgeon regularly kept in the course of business, stating that, on a given day he attended A's mother and delivered her of a son, is a relevant fact.

(*c*) The question is, whether A was in Nagpur on a given day. A statement in the diary of a deceased solicitor, regularly kept in the course of business, that on a given day the solicitor attended A at a place mentioned, in Nagpur, for the purpose of conferring with him upon specified business, is a relevant fact.

(*d*) The question is, whether a ship sailed from Mumbai harbour on a given day. A letter written by a deceased member of a merchant's firm by which she was chartered to their correspondents in Chennai, to whom the cargo was consigned, stating that the ship sailed on a given day from Mumbai port, is a relevant fact.

(*e*) The question is, whether rent was paid to A for certain land. A letter from A's deceased agent to A, saying that he had received the rent on A's account and held it at A's orders is a relevant fact.

(*f*) The question is, whether A and B were legally married. The statement of a deceased clergyman that he married them under such circumstances that the celebration would be a crime is relevant.

(*g*) The question is, whether A, a person who cannot be found, wrote a letter on a certain day. The fact that a letter written by him is dated on that day is relevant.

(*h*) The question is, what was the cause of the wreck of a ship. A protest made by the captain, whose attendance cannot be procured, is a relevant fact.

(*i*) The question is, whether a given road is a public way. A statement by A, a deceased headman of the village, that the road was public, is a relevant fact.

(*j*) The question is, what was the price of grain on a certain day in a particular market. A statement of the price, made by a deceased business person in the ordinary course of his business, is a relevant fact.

(*k*) The question is, whether A, who is dead, was the father of B. A statement by A that B was his son, is a relevant fact.

(*l*) The question is, what was the date of the birth of A. A letter from A's deceased father to a friend, announcing the birth of A on a given day, is a relevant fact.

(*m*) The question is, whether, and when, A and B were married. An entry in a memorandum book by C, the deceased father of B, of his daughter's marriage with A on a given date, is a relevant fact.

(*n*) A sues B for a libel expressed in a painted caricature exposed in a shop window. The question is as to the similarity of the caricature and its libellous character. The remarks of a crowd of spectators on these points may be proved.

Corresponding Provision **:** Section 32 of Indian Evidence Act, 1872

COMMENTS

Dying declaration cannot be unreliable if weapon is not recovered - Merely because the weapon used is not recovered cannot be a ground not to rely upon the dying declaration, which was recorded before the Executive Magistrate, which has been proved by the prosecution. [Para 9] - *State of Uttar Pradesh* v. *Subhash Alias Pappu* AIR 2022 Supreme Court 1651.

Credibility of dying declaration depends upon surrounding circumstances - The weight and utility of a dying declaration depend upon the surrounding circumstances and the credibility which the court attaches to it, having regard to the evidence led before it. Therefore, whether it is essential to have medical certification before the statement is recorded, who records it, etc. are all fact dependent, and no stereotypical approach can be adopted by courts. [Para 14] - *Rajaram* v. *State of Madhya Pradesh* AIR 2023 Supreme Court 94.

There is no rule that a dying declaration is inadmissible if recorded by a police officer instead of a Magistrate - There is no rule to the effect that a dying declaration is inadmissible when it is recorded by a police officer instead of a Magistrate. Although a dying declaration ought to ideally be recorded by a Magistrate if possible, it cannot be said that dying declarations recorded by police personnel are inadmissible for that reason alone. The issue of whether a dying declaration recorded by the police is admissible must be decided after considering the facts and circumstances of each case. [Para 41] - *State of Jharkhand* v. *Shailendra Kumar Rai Alias Pandav Rai* AIR 2022 Supreme Court 5393.

Dying declaration is relevant, if relates to cause of death or circumstances of resulting in death - In terms of section 32, statements (either written or verbal) of relevant facts are themselves relevant facts when they are made by the following classes of people:

(*a*) a person who is dead;

(*b*) a person who cannot be found;

(*c*) a person who is incapable of giving evidence; or

(*d*) a person whose attendance cannot be procured without an amount of delay or expense.

Clause (1) indicates that in cases where the cause of a person's death comes into question, a statement made by that person is relevant when it relates to:

(*a*) the cause of death; or

(*b*) any of the circumstances of the transaction which resulted in death. [Para 38] - *State of Jharkhand* v. *Shailendra Kumar Rai Alias Pandav Rai* AIR 2022 Supreme Court 5393.

Statement by an injured person recorded as FIR can be treated as dying declaration leading to conviction - About the treatment of the FIR/Bayan Tahriri as dying declaration and in this respect various earlier pronouncements of this Court have clarified the position of law that the statement by an injured person recorded as FIR can be treated as a dying declaration and such a statement is admissible under section 32 of the Indian Evidence Act. It was also held that the dying declaration must not cover the whole incident or narrate the case history. Corroboration is not necessary for this situation; a dying declaration can be the sole basis for conviction. [Para 91] - *Harendra Rai* v. *State of Bihar* AIR 2023 Supreme Court 4331.

Relevancy of certain evidence for proving, in subsequent proceeding, truth of facts therein stated.

27. Evidence given by a witness in a judicial proceeding, or before any person authorised by law to take it, is relevant for the purpose of proving, in a subsequent judicial proceeding, or in a later stage of the same judicial proceeding, the truth of the facts which it states, when the witness is dead or cannot be found, or is incapable of giving evidence, or is kept out of the way by the adverse party, or if his presence cannot be obtained without an amount of delay or expense which, under the circumstances of the case, the Court considers unreasonable:

Provided that the proceeding was between the same parties or their representatives in interest; that the adverse party in the first proceeding had the right and opportunity to cross-examine and the questions in issue were substantially the same in the first as in the second proceeding.

Explanation.—A criminal trial or inquiry shall be deemed to be a proceeding between the prosecutor and the accused within the meaning of this section.

Corresponding Provision : Section 33 of Indian Evidence Act, 1872

Statements made under special circumstances

Entries in books of account when relevant.

28. Entries in the books of account, including those maintained in an electronic form, regularly kept in the course of business are relevant whenever they refer to a matter into which the Court has to inquire, but such statements shall not alone be sufficient evidence to charge any person with liability.

Illustration

A sues B for one thousand rupees, and shows entries in his account books showing B to be indebted to him to this amount. The entries are relevant, but are not sufficient, without other evidence, to prove the debt.

Corresponding Provision : Section 34 of Indian Evidence Act, 1872

Relevancy of entry in public record or an electronic record made in performance of duty.

29. An entry in any public or other official book, register or record or an electronic record, stating a fact in issue or relevant fact, and made by a public servant in the discharge of his official duty, or by any other person in performance of a duty specially enjoined by the law of the country in which such book, register or record or an electronic record, is kept, is itself a relevant fact.

Corresponding Provision : Section 35 of Indian Evidence Act, 1872

Relevancy of statements in maps, charts and plans.

30. Statements of facts in issue or relevant facts, made in published maps or charts generally offered for public sale, or in maps or plans made under the authority of the Central Government or any State Government, as to matters usually represented or stated in such maps, charts or plans, are themselves relevant facts.

Corresponding Provision : Section 36 of Indian Evidence Act, 1872

Relevancy of statement as to fact of public nature contained in certain Acts or notifications.

31. When the Court has to form an opinion as to the existence of any fact of a public nature, any statement of it, made in a recital contained in any Central Act or State Act or in a Central Government or State Government notification appearing in the respective Official Gazette or in any printed paper or in electronic or digital form purporting to be such Gazette, is a relevant fact.

Corresponding Provision : Section 37 of Indian Evidence Act, 1872

Relevancy of statements as to any law contained in law books including electronic or digital form.

32. When the Court has to form an opinion as to a law of any country, any statement of such law contained in a book purporting to be printed or published including in electronic or digital form under the authority of the Government of such country and to contain any such law, and any report of a ruling of the Courts of such country contained in a book including in electronic or digital form purporting to be a report of such rulings, is relevant.

Corresponding Provision : Section 38 of Indian Evidence Act, 1872

How much of a statement is to be proved

What evidence to be given when statement forms part of a conversation, document, electronic record, book or series of letters or papers.

33. When any statement of which evidence is given forms part of a longer statement, or of a conversation or part of an isolated document, or is contained in a document which forms part of a book, or is contained in part of electronic record or of a connected series of letters or papers, evidence shall be given of so much and no more of the statement, conversation, document, electronic record, book or series of letters or papers as the Court considers necessary in that particular case to the full understanding of the nature and effect of the statement, and of the circumstances under which it was made.

Corresponding Provision : Section 39 of Indian Evidence Act, 1872

Judgments of Courts when relevant

Previous judgments relevant to bar a second suit or trial.

34. The existence of any judgment, order or decree which by law prevents any Court from taking cognizance of a suit or holding a trial, is a relevant fact when the question is whether such Court ought to take cognizance of such suit or to hold such trial.

Corresponding Provision : Section 40 of Indian Evidence Act, 1872

Relevancy of certain judgments in probate, etc., jurisdiction.

35. (1) A final judgment, order or decree of a competent Court or Tribunal, in the exercise of probate, matrimonial, admiralty or insolvency jurisdiction, which confers upon or takes away from any person any legal character, or which declares any person to be entitled to any such character, or to be entitled to any specific thing, not as against any specified person but absolutely, is relevant when the existence of any such legal character, or the title of any such person to any such thing, is relevant.

(2) Such judgment, order or decree is conclusive proof that—

(*i*) any legal character, which it confers accrued at the time when such judgment, order or decree came into operation;

(*ii*) any legal character, to which it declares any such person to be entitled, accrued to that person at the time when such judgment, order or decree declares it to have accrued to that person;

(*iii*) any legal character which it takes away from any such person ceased at the time from which such judgment, order or decree declared that it had ceased or should cease; and

(*iv*) anything to which it declares any person to be so entitled was the property of that person at the time from which such judgment, order or decree declares that it had been or should be his property.

Corresponding Provision : Section 41 of Indian Evidence Act, 1872

Relevancy and effect of judgments, orders or decrees, other than those mentioned in section 35.

36. Judgments, orders or decrees other than those mentioned in section 35 are relevant if they relate to matters of a public nature relevant to the enquiry; but such judgments, orders or decrees are not conclusive proof of that which they state.

Illustration

A sues B for trespass on his land. B alleges the existence of a public right of way over the land, which A denies. The existence of a decree in favour of the defendant, in a suit by A against C for a trespass on the same land, in which C alleged the existence of the same right of way, is relevant, but it is not conclusive proof that the right of way exists.

Corresponding Provision : Section 42 of Indian Evidence Act, 1872

Judgments, etc., other than those mentioned in sections 34, 35 and 36 when relevant.

37. Judgments or orders or decrees, other than those mentioned in sections 34, 35 and 36, are irrelevant, unless the existence of such judgment, order or decree is a fact in issue, or is relevant under some other provision of this Adhiniyam.

Illustrations

(*a*) A and B separately sue C for a libel which reflects upon each of them. C in each case says that the matter alleged to be libellous is true, and the circumstances are such that it is probably true in each case, or in neither. A obtains a decree against C for damages on the ground that C failed to make out his justification. The fact is irrelevant as between B and C.

(*b*) A prosecutes B for stealing a cow from him. B is convicted. A afterwards sues C for the cow, which B had sold to him before his conviction. As between A and C, the judgment against B is irrelevant.

(*c*) A has obtained a decree for the possession of land against B. C, B's son, murders A in consequence. The existence of the judgment is relevant, as showing motive for a crime.

(*d*) A is charged with theft and with having been previously convicted of theft. The previous conviction is relevant as a fact in issue.

(*e*) A is tried for the murder of B. The fact that B prosecuted A for libel and that A was convicted and sentenced is relevant under section 6 as showing the motive for the fact in issue.

Corresponding Provision : Section 43 of Indian Evidence Act, 1872

Fraud or collusion in obtaining judgment, or incompetency of Court, may be proved.

38. Any party to a suit or other proceeding may show that any judgment, order or decree which is relevant under section 34, 35 or 36, and which has been proved by the adverse party, was delivered by a Court not competent to deliver it, or was obtained by fraud or collusion.

Corresponding Provision : Section 44 of Indian Evidence Act, 1872

Opinions of third persons when relevant

Opinions of experts.

39. (1) When the Court has to form an opinion upon a point of foreign law or of science or art, or any other field, or as to identity of handwriting or finger impressions, the opinions upon that point of persons specially skilled in such foreign law, science or art or any other field, or in questions as to identity of handwriting or finger impressions are relevant facts and such persons are called experts.

Illustrations

(*a*) The question is, whether the death of A was caused by poison. The opinions of experts as to the symptoms produced by the poison by which A is supposed to have died, are relevant.

(*b*) The question is, whether A, at the time of doing a certain act, was, by reason of unsoundness of mind, incapable of knowing the nature of the act, or that he was doing what was either wrong or contrary to law. The opinions of experts upon the question whether the symptoms exhibited by A commonly show unsoundness of mind, and whether such unsoundness of mind usually renders persons incapable of knowing the nature of the acts which they do, or of knowing that what they do is either wrong or contrary to law, are relevant.

(*c*) The question is, whether a certain document was written by A. Another document is produced which is proved or admitted to have been written by A. The opinions of experts on the question whether the two documents were written by the same person or by different persons, are relevant.

Corresponding Provision : Section 45 of Indian Evidence Act, 1872

(2) When in a proceeding, the court has to form an opinion on any matter relating to any information transmitted or stored in any computer resource or any other electronic or digital form, the opinion of the Examiner of Electronic Evidence referred to in section 79A* of the Information Technology Act, 2000 (21 of 2000), is a relevant fact.

Explanation.—For the purposes of this sub-section, an Examiner of Electronic Evidence shall be an expert.

* For text of section 79A of Information Technology Act, 2000, *see* **Appendix**.

Corresponding Provision : Section 45A of Indian Evidence Act, 1872

COMMENTS

Medical witness is very crucial independent testimony, and it is not merely a check upon testimony of eyewitnesses - The evidentiary value of a medical witness is very crucial to corroborate the case of prosecution and it is not merely a check upon testimony of eyewitnesses, it is also independent testimony, because it may establish certain facts, quite apart from the other oral evidence. It has been reiterated by this court that the medical evidence adduced by the prosecution has great corroborative value as it proves that the injuries could have been caused in the manner alleged. [Para 18] - *Anuj Singh Alias Ramanuj Singh Alias Seth Singh* v. *State of Bihar* AIR 2022 Supreme Court 2817.

Report of Ballistic Expert being a scientific evidence is required to use along with other substantive available evidence - The report of the Ballistic Expert is obviously a scientific evidence in the nature of an opinion. It is required to use this evidence along with the other substantive piece of evidence available. [Para 18] - *Ravi Sharma* v. *State (Government of NCT of Delhi)* AIR 2022 Supreme Court 4810.

Facts bearing upon opinions of experts.

40. Facts, not otherwise relevant, are relevant if they support or are inconsistent with the opinions of experts, when such opinions are relevant.

Illustrations

(*a*) The question is, whether A was poisoned by a certain poison. The fact that other persons, who were poisoned by that poison, exhibited certain symptoms which experts affirm or deny to be the symptoms of that poison, is relevant.

(*b*) The question is, whether an obstruction to a harbour is caused by a certain sea-wall. The fact that other harbours similarly situated in other respects, but where there were no such sea-walls, began to be obstructed at about the same time, is relevant.

Corresponding Provision : Section 46 of Indian Evidence Act, 1872

Opinion as to handwriting and signature, when relevant.

41. (1) When the Court has to form an opinion as to the person by whom any document was written or signed, the opinion of any person acquainted with the handwriting of the person by whom it is supposed to be written or signed that it was or was not written or signed by that person, is a relevant fact.

Explanation.—A person is said to be acquainted with the handwriting of another person when he has seen that person write, or when he has received documents purporting to be written by that person in answer to documents written by himself or under his authority and addressed to that person, or when, in the ordinary course of business, documents purporting to be written by that person have been habitually submitted to him.

Illustration

The question is, whether a given letter is in the handwriting of A, a merchant in Itanagar. B is a merchant in Bengaluru, who has written letters addressed to A and received letters purporting to be written by him. C, is B's clerk whose duty it was to examine and file B's correspondence. D is B's broker, to whom B habitually submitted the letters purporting to be written by A for the purpose of advising him thereon. The opinions of B, C and D on the question whether the letter is in the handwriting of A are relevant, though neither B, C nor D ever saw A write.

Corresponding Provision : Section 47 of Indian Evidence Act, 1872

(2) When the Court has to form an opinion as to the electronic signature of any person, the opinion of the Certifying Authority which has issued the Electronic Signature Certificate is a relevant fact.

Corresponding Provision : Section 47A of Indian Evidence Act, 1872

Opinion as to existence of general custom or right, when relevant.

42. When the Court has to form an opinion as to the existence of any general custom or right, the opinions, as to the existence of such custom or right, of persons who would be likely to know of its existence if it existed, are relevant.

Explanation.—The expression "general custom or right" includes customs or rights common to any considerable class of persons.

Illustration

The right of the villagers of a particular village to use the water of a particular well is a general right within the meaning of this section.

Corresponding Provision : Section 48 of Indian Evidence Act, 1872

Opinion as to usages, tenets, etc., when relevant.

43. When the Court has to form an opinion as to—

(*i*) the usages and tenets of any body of men or family;

(*ii*) the constitution and governance of any religious or charitable foundation; or

(*iii*) the meaning of words or terms used in particular districts or by particular classes of people,

the opinions of persons having special means of knowledge thereon, are relevant facts.

Corresponding Provision : Section 49 of Indian Evidence Act, 1872

Opinion on relationship, when relevant.

44. When the Court has to form an opinion as to the relationship of one person to another, the opinion, expressed by conduct, as to the existence of such relationship, of any person who, as a member of the family or otherwise, has special means of knowledge on the subject, is a relevant fact:

Provided that such opinion shall not be sufficient to prove a marriage in proceedings under the Divorce Act, 1869 (4 of 1869), or in prosecution under sections 82 and 84 of the Bharatiya Nyaya Sanhita, 2023.

Illustrations

(*a*) The question is, whether A and B were married. The fact that they were usually received and treated by their friends as husband and wife, is relevant.

(*b*) The question is, whether A was the legitimate son of B. The fact that A was always treated as such by members of the family, is relevant.

Corresponding Provision **:** Section 50 of Indian Evidence Act, 1872

Grounds of opinion, when relevant.

45. Whenever the opinion of any living person is relevant, the grounds on which such opinion is based are also relevant.

Illustration

An expert may give an account of experiments performed by him for the purpose of forming his opinion.

Corresponding Provision **:** Section 51 of Indian Evidence Act, 1872

Character when relevant

In civil cases character to prove conduct imputed, irrelevant.

46. In civil cases the fact that the character of any person concerned is such as to render probable or improbable any conduct imputed to him, is irrelevant, except in so far as such character appears from facts otherwise relevant.

Corresponding Provision **:** Section 52 of Indian Evidence Act, 1872

In criminal cases previous good character relevant.

47. In criminal proceedings the fact that the person accused is of a good character, is relevant.

Corresponding Provision **:** Section 53 of Indian Evidence Act, 1872

COMMENT

Previous bad character is not relevant except unless good character is pleaded - Section 53 of the Indian Evidence Act,

1872 stipulates that the previous bad character is not relevant except in reply, *i.e.*, unless evidence has been given of a good character in which case it becomes relevant. [Para 37] - *Pappu Tiwary* v. *State of Jharkhand* AIR 2022 Supreme Court 758.

Evidence of character or previous sexual experience not relevant in certain cases.

48. In a prosecution for an offence under section 64, section 65, section 66, section 67, section 68, section 69, section 70, section 71, section 74, section 75, section 76, section 77 or section 78 of the Bharatiya Nyaya Sanhita, 2023 or for attempt to commit any such offence, where the question of consent is in issue, evidence of the character of the victim or of such person's previous sexual experience with any person shall not be relevant on the issue of such consent or the quality of consent.

Corresponding Provision **:** Section 53A of Indian Evidence Act, 1872

COMMENTS

Whether a woman is 'habitual to sexual intercourse' is irrelevant; "two-finger test" or per vaginum examination cannot be adopted - Whether a woman is "habituated to sexual intercourse" or "habitual to sexual intercourse" is irrelevant for the purposes of determining whether the ingredients of section 375 of the IPC are present in a particular case. The so-called test is based on the incorrect assumption that a sexually active woman cannot be raped. Nothing could be further from the truth - a woman's sexual history is wholly immaterial while adjudicating whether the accused raped her. Further, the probative value of a woman's testimony does not depend upon her sexual history. It is patriarchal and sexist to suggest that a woman cannot be believed when she states that she was raped, merely for the reason that she is sexually active.

The legislature explicitly recognized this fact when it enacted the Criminal Law (Amendment) Act, 2013 which *inter alia* amended the Evidence Act to insert section 53A. In terms of section 53A of the Evidence Act, evidence of a victim's character or of her previous sexual experience with any person shall not be relevant to the issue of consent or the quality of consent, in prosecutions of sexual offences.

The Ministry of Health and Family Welfare issued guidelines for health providers in cases of sexual violence. These guidelines prescribe the application of the "two-finger test":

"Per-Vaginum examination commonly referred to by lay persons as 'two-finger test', must not be conducted for establishing rape/sexual violence and the size of the vaginal introitus has no bearing on a case of sexual violence. Per vaginum examination can be done only in adult women when medically indicated.

The status of hymen is irrelevant because the hymen can be torn due to several reasons such as cycling, riding or masturbation among other things. An intact hymen does not rule out sexual violence, and a torn hymen does not prove previous sexual intercourse. Hymen should therefore be treated like any other part of the genitals while documenting examination findings in cases of sexual violence. Only those that are relevant to the episode of assault (findings such as fresh tears, bleeding, edema etc.) are to be documented."

Although the "two-finger test" in this case was conducted over a decade ago, it is a regrettable fact that it continues to be conducted even today.

We direct the Union Government as well as the State Governments to:

(*a*) Ensure that the guidelines formulated by the Ministry of Health and Family Welfare are circulated to all government and private hospitals;

(*b*) Conduct workshops for health providers to communicate the appropriate procedure to be adopted while examining survivors of sexual assault and rape; and

(*c*) Review the curriculum in medical schools with a view to ensuring that the "two-finger test" or per vaginum examination is not prescribed as one of the procedures to be adopted while examining survivors of sexual assault and rape.

A copy of this judgment shall be shared with the Secretary, Ministry of Health and Family Welfare, Government of India. The Secretary, Ministry of Health and Family Welfare, Government of India shall transmit copies of this judgment to the Principal Secretary (Department of Public Health) of each state. The Principal Secretaries in the Departments of Health of each state shall also be responsible for ensuring the implementation of the directions issued in Part E of this judgment. The Secretaries in the Departments of Home of each state shall in addition issue directions to the Directors General of Police in this regard. The Directors General of Police shall, in turn, communicate these directions to the Superintendents of Police. [Paras 62, 63, 64, 65, 66 and 67] - *State of Jharkhand* v. *Shailendra Kumar Rai Alias Pandav Rai* AIR 2022 Supreme Court 5393.

Person conducting "two-finger test" to be held guilty of misconduct - Any person who conducts the "two-finger test" or per vaginum examination (while examining a person alleged to have been subjected to a sexual assault) in contravention of the directions of this Court shall be guilty of misconduct. [Para 68] - *State of Jharkhand* v. *Shailendra Kumar Rai Alias Pandav Rai* AIR 2022 Supreme Court 5393.

Previous bad character not relevant, except in reply.

49. In criminal proceedings, the fact that the accused has a bad character, is irrelevant, unless evidence has been given that he has a good character, in which case it becomes relevant.

Explanation 1.—This section does not apply to cases in which the bad character of any person is itself a fact in issue.

Explanation 2.—A previous conviction is relevant as evidence of bad character.

Corresponding Provision : Section 54 of Indian Evidence Act, 1872

Character as affecting damages.

50. In civil cases, the fact that the character of any person is such as to affect the amount of damages which he ought to receive, is relevant.

Explanation.—In this section and sections 46, 47 and 49, the word "character" includes both reputation and disposition; but, except as provided in section 49, evidence may be given only of general reputation and general disposition, and not of particular acts by which reputation or disposition has been shown.

Corresponding Provision : Section 55 of Indian Evidence Act, 1872

PART III

ON PROOF

CHAPTER III

FACTS WHICH NEED NOT BE PROVED

Fact judicially noticeable need not be proved.

51. No fact of which the Court will take judicial notice need be proved.

Corresponding Provision **:** Section 56 of Indian Evidence Act, 1872

COMMENTS

Doctrine of judicial notice - Scope and application of - The law, in respect of taking judicial notice of any fact, may be summarised in the following manner:

(*i*) The doctrine of judicial notice, as provided under section 56 of the Evidence Act, 1872, is an exception to general rules of evidence applicable for proving any fact by adducing evidence in the Court of law.

(*ii*) According to section 56 of the Evidence Act, judicial notice of any such fact can be taken by the Court, which is well-known to everyone, which is in the common knowledge of everyone, which is authoritatively attested, which is so apparent on the face of the record, etc.

(*iii*) Except in the rarest of rare cases, judicial notice of any fact is generally not taken in criminal matters in the normal course of proceeding, and the case is decided on the basis of oral, material and documentary evidence adduced by the parties to find out the guilt or innocence.

As discussed above, the judicial notice of any fact is generally not taken in criminal matters, but the present matter stands on an altogether different footing in view of what has been noted hereinbefore. It falls in the category of rarest of rare cases and hence, it requires a different approach. [Paras 66 and 67] - *Harendra Rai* v. *State of Bihar* AIR 2023 Supreme Court 4331.

Court can accept certain facts without establishing such facts - According to the general procedure, facts need to be proved by adducing evidence in the Court of law, and the evidence must be produced in accordance with the procedure mentioned in the Indian Evidence Act, 1872. The doctrine of judicial notice, as provided under section 56, is an exception to this rule.

Section 56 of the Evidence Act says that "No fact of which the Court will take judicial notice need to be proved." Section 57 of the Evidence Act goes one step further by providing that the Court has no other option but to take judicial notice of the facts mentioned in the list given in the section as it uses the word "shall" and not "may". Section 58 of the Evidence Act says that if the parties or their agents have agreed to admit a fact during the court proceeding or in writing before the hearing, then such fact need not be proved unless the Court believes that it needs to be proved.

Section 56 of the Evidence Act, deals with the authority of a Court to accept certain facts, which are either of common knowledge or from sources which guarantee the accuracy or are a matter of authoritative official record or court record, without the need to establish such fact. The judicial notice of any fact is taken when the facts cannot reasonably be doubted. [Paras 62, 63 and 64] - *Harendra Rai* v. *State of Bihar* AIR 2023 Supreme Court 4331.

Facts of which Court shall take judicial notice.

52. (1) The Court shall take judicial notice of the following facts, namely:—

(*a*) all laws in force in the territory of India including laws having extra-territorial operation;

(*b*) international treaty, agreement or convention with country or countries by India, or decisions made by India at international associations or other bodies;

(*c*) the course of proceeding of the Constituent Assembly of India, of Parliament of India and of the State Legislatures;

(*d*) the seals of all Courts and Tribunals;

(*e*) the seals of Courts of Admiralty and Maritime Jurisdiction, Notaries Public, and all seals which any person is authorised to use by the Constitution, or by an Act of Parliament or State Legislatures, or Regulations having the force of law in India;

(*f*) the accession to office, names, titles, functions, and signatures of the persons filling for the time being any public office in any State, if the fact of their appointment to such office is notified in any Official Gazette;

(*g*) the existence, title and national flag of every country or sovereign recognised by the Government of India;

(*h*) the divisions of time, the geographical divisions of the world, and public festivals, fasts and holidays notified in the Official Gazette;

(*i*) the territory of India;

(*j*) the commencement, continuance and termination of hostilities between the Government of India and any other country or body of persons;

(*k*) the names of the members and officers of the Court and of their deputies and subordinate officers and assistants, and also of all officers acting in execution of its process, and of advocates and other persons authorised by law to appear or act before it;

(*l*) the rule of the road on land or at sea.

(2) In the cases referred to in sub-section (1) and also on all matters of public history, literature, science or art, the Court may resort for its aid to appropriate books or documents of reference and if the Court is called upon by any person to take judicial notice of any fact, it may refuse to do so unless and until such person produces any such book or document as it may consider necessary to enable it to do so.

Corresponding Provision : Section 57 of Indian Evidence Act, 1872

Facts admitted need not be proved.

53. No fact needs to be proved in any proceeding which the parties thereto or their agents agree to admit at the hearing, or which, before the hearing, they agree to admit by any writing under their hands, or which by any rule of pleading in force at the time they are deemed to have admitted by their pleadings:

Provided that the Court may, in its discretion, require the facts admitted to be proved otherwise than by such admissions.

Corresponding Provision **:** Section 58 of Indian Evidence Act, 1872

CHAPTER IV

OF ORAL EVIDENCE

Proof of facts by oral evidence.

54. All facts, except the contents of documents may be proved by oral evidence.

Corresponding Provision **:** Section 59 of Indian Evidence Act, 1872

COMMENT

Oral evidence means testimony of living persons including deaf and dumb - Section 59 of the Evidence Act states that all facts, except the contents of documents or electronic records, may be proved by oral evidence. Oral evidence means the testimony of living persons examined in the presence of the court or commissioners appointed by the court. Deaf and dumb persons may also adduce evidence by signs or through interpretation or by writing, if they are literate. [Para 36] - *Neeraj Dutta* v. *State (Govt. of N.C.T. of Delhi)* AIR 2023 Supreme Court 330.

Oral evidence to be direct.

55. Oral evidence shall, in all cases whatever, be direct; if it refers to,—

(*i*) a fact which could be seen, it must be the evidence of a witness who says he saw it;

(*ii*) a fact which could be heard, it must be the evidence of a witness who says he heard it;

(*iii*) a fact which could be perceived by any other sense or in any other manner, it must be the evidence of a witness who says he perceived it by that sense or in that manner;

(*iv*) an opinion or to the grounds on which that opinion is held, it must be the evidence of the person who holds that opinion on those grounds:

Provided that the opinions of experts expressed in any treatise commonly offered for sale, and the grounds on which such opinions are held, may be proved by the production of such treatises if the author is dead or cannot be found, or has become incapable of giving evidence, or cannot be called as a witness without an amount of delay or expense which the Court regards as unreasonable:

Provided further that, if oral evidence refers to the existence or condition of any material thing other than a document, the Court may, if it thinks fit, require the production of such material thing for its inspection.

Corresponding Provision **:** Section 60 of Indian Evidence Act, 1872

COMMENT

In section 60 of Evidence Act, 1872 word "direct" is used in juxtaposition to derivative or hearsay evidence - Section 60 of the Evidence Act requires that oral evidence must be direct or positive. Direct evidence is when it goes straight to establish the main fact in issue. The word "direct" is used in juxtaposition to derivative or hearsay evidence where a witness gives evidence that he received information from some other person. If that person does not, himself, state such information, such evidence would be inadmissible being hearsay evidence. On the other hand, forensic procedure as circumstantial or inferential evidence or presumptive evidence (Section 3) is indirect evidence. It means proof of other facts from which the existence of the fact in issue may be logically inferred. In this context, the expression 'circumstantial evidence' is used in a loose sense as, sometimes, circumstantial evidence may also be direct.

Although the expression "hearsay evidence" is not defined under the Evidence Act, it is, nevertheless, in constant use in the courts. However, hearsay evidence is inadmissible to prove a fact which is deposed to on hearsay, but it does not necessarily preclude evidence as to a statement having been made upon which certain action was taken or certain results followed such as evidence of an informant of the crime.

At this stage, it must be distinguished that even with regard to oral evidence, there are sub-categories - primary evidence and secondary evidence. Primary evidence is an oral account of the original evidence *i.e.* of a person who saw what happened and gives an account of it recorded by the Court, or the original document itself, or the original thing when produced in Court. Secondary evidence is a report or an oral account of the original evidence or a copy of a document or a model of the original thing. [Paras 39 to 41] - *Neeraj Dutta* v. *State (Govt. of N.C.T. of Delhi)* AIR 2023 Supreme Court 330.

Oral testimony - Scope and application of - Generally speaking, oral testimony may be classified into three categories, *viz.*:

(*i*) Wholly reliable;

(*ii*) Wholly unreliable;

(*iii*) Neither wholly reliable nor wholly unreliable.

The first two category of cases may not pose serious difficulty for the court in arriving at its conclusion(s). However, in the third category of cases, the court has to be circumspect and look for corroboration of any material particulars by reliable testimony, direct or circumstantial, as a requirement of the rule of prudence. [Para 28] - *Munna Lal* v. *State of Uttar Pradesh* AIR 2023 Supreme Court 634.

Oral testimony requires further corroboration from reliable testimony, direct or circumstantial - Generally speaking, oral testimony in this context may be classified into three categories, namely:

(1) Wholly reliable.

(2) Wholly unreliable.

(3) Neither wholly reliable nor wholly unreliable.

It could thus be seen that in the category of "wholly reliable" witness, there is no difficulty for the prosecution to press for conviction on the basis of the testimony of such a witness. In case of "wholly unreliable" witness, again, there is no difficulty, inasmuch as no conviction could be made on the basis of oral testimony provided by a "wholly unreliable" witness. The real difficulty comes in case of the third category of evidence which is partly reliable and partly unreliable. In such cases, the court is required to be circumspect and separate the chaff from the grain, and seek further corroboration from reliable testimony, direct or circumstantial. [Paras 32 and 33] - *Nand Lal* v. *State of Chhattisgarh* AIR 2023 Supreme Court 1599.

CHAPTER V

OF DOCUMENTARY EVIDENCE

Proof of contents of documents.

56. The contents of documents may be proved either by primary or by secondary evidence.

Corresponding Provision : Section 61 of Indian Evidence Act, 1872

COMMENT

Primary evidence is best evidence, only when it is lost, secondary evidence is allowed - Section 61 deals with proof of contents of documents which is by either primary or by secondary evidence. When a document is produced as primary evidence, it will have to be proved in the manner laid down in sections 67 to 73 of the Evidence Act. Mere production and marking of a document as an exhibit by the court cannot be held to be due proof of its contents. Its execution has to be proved by admissible evidence. On the other hand, when a document is produced and admitted by the opposite party and is marked as an exhibit by the court, the contents of the document must be proved either by the production of the original document *i.e.*, primary evidence or by copies of the same as per section 65 as secondary evidence. So long as an original document is in existence and is available, its contents must be proved by primary evidence. It is only when the primary evidence is lost, in the interest of justice, the secondary evidence must be allowed. Primary evidence is the best evidence and it affords the greatest certainty of the fact in question. Thus, when a particular fact is to be established by production of documentary evidence, there is no scope for leading oral evidence. What is to be produced is the primary evidence *i.e.*, document itself. It is only when the absence of the primary source has been satisfactorily explained that secondary evidence is permissible to prove the contents of documents. Secondary evidence, therefore, should not be accepted without a sufficient reason being given for non-production of the original. [Para 42] - *Neeraj Dutta* v. *State (Govt. of N.C.T. of Delhi)* AIR 2023 Supreme Court 330.

Primary evidence.

57. Primary evidence means the document itself produced for the inspection of the Court.

Explanation 1.—Where a document is executed in several parts, each part is primary evidence of the document.

Explanation 2.—Where a document is executed in counterpart, each counterpart being executed by one or some of the parties only, each counterpart is primary evidence as against the parties executing it.

Explanation 3.—Where a number of documents are all made by one uniform process, as in the case of printing, lithography or photography, each is primary evidence of the contents of the rest; but, where they are all copies of a common original, they are not primary evidence of the contents of the original.

Explanation 4.—Where an electronic or digital record is created or stored, and such storage occurs simultaneously or sequentially in multiple files, each such file is primary evidence.

Explanation 5.—Where an electronic or digital record is produced from proper custody, such electronic and digital record is primary evidence unless it is disputed.

Explanation 6.—Where a video recording is simultaneously stored in electronic form and transmitted or broadcast or transferred to another, each of the stored recordings is primary evidence.

Explanation 7.—Where an electronic or digital record is stored in multiple storage spaces in a computer resource, each such automated storage, including temporary files, is primary evidence.

Illustration

A person is shown to have been in possession of a number of placards, all printed at one time from one original. Any one of the placards is primary evidence of the contents of any other, but no one of them is primary evidence of the contents of the original.

Corresponding Provision **:** Section 62 of Indian Evidence Act, 1872

COMMENTS

Primary evidence v. Secondary evidence - Section 62 of the Evidence Act defines primary evidence to mean the documents itself produced for the inspection of the court. If primary evidence is available, it would exclude secondary evidence. Section 63 of the Evidence Act deals with secondary evidence and defines what it means and includes. Section 63 mentions five kinds of secondary evidence, namely,—

(*i*) Certified copies given under the provisions hereinafter contained;

(*ii*) Copies made from the original by mechanical processes which in themselves ensure the accuracy of the copy, and copies compared with such copies;

(*iii*) Copies made from or compared with the original;

(*iv*) Counterparts of documents as against the parties who did not execute them;

(*v*) Oral accounts of the contents of a document given by some person who has himself seen it.

Section 64 of the Evidence Act states that documents must be proved by primary evidence except in certain cases mentioned above.

Once a document is admitted, the contents of that document are also admitted in evidence, though those contents may not be conclusive evidence. Moreover, once certain evidence is conclusive it shuts out any other evidence which would detract from the conclusiveness of that evidence. There is a prohibition for any other evidence to be led which may detract from the conclusiveness of that evidence and the court has no option to hold the existence of the fact otherwise when such evidence is made conclusive. Thus, once a document has been properly admitted, the contents of the documents would stand admitted in evidence, and if no objection has been raised with regard to its mode of proof at the stage of tendering in evidence of such a document, no such objection could be allowed to be raised at any later stage of the case or in appeal. [Paras 43 to 44] - *Neeraj Dutta* v. *State (Govt. of N.C.T. of Delhi)* AIR 2023 Supreme Court 330.

Secondary evidence.

58. Secondary evidence includes—

(*i*) certified copies given under the provisions hereinafter contained;

(*ii*) copies made from the original by mechanical processes which in themselves ensure the accuracy of the copy, and copies compared with such copies;

(*iii*) copies made from or compared with the original;

(*iv*) counterparts of documents as against the parties who did not execute them;

(*v*) oral accounts of the contents of a document given by some person who has himself seen it;

(*vi*) oral admissions;

(*vii*) written admissions;

(*viii*) evidence of a person who has examined a document, the original of which consists of numerous accounts or other documents which cannot conveniently be examined in Court, and who is skilled in the examination of such documents.

Illustrations

(*a*) A photograph of an original is secondary evidence of its contents, though the two have not been compared, if it is proved that the thing photographed was the original.

(*b*) A copy compared with a copy of a letter made by a copying machine is secondary evidence of the contents of the letter, if it is shown that the copy made by the copying machine was made from the original.

(*c*) A copy transcribed from a copy, but afterwards compared with the original, is secondary evidence; but the copy not so compared is not secondary evidence of the original, although the copy from which it was transcribed was compared with the original.

(*d*) Neither an oral account of a copy compared with the original, nor an oral account of a photograph or machine-copy of the original, is secondary evidence of the original.

Corresponding Provision **:** Section 63 of Indian Evidence Act, 1872

Proof of documents by primary evidence.

59. Documents shall be proved by primary evidence except in the cases hereinafter mentioned.

Corresponding Provision **:** Section 64 of Indian Evidence Act, 1872

Cases in which secondary evidence relating to documents may be given.

60. Secondary evidence may be given of the existence, condition, or contents of a document in the following cases, namely: —

(*a*) when the original is shown or appears to be in the possession or power—

(*i*) of the person against whom the document is sought to be proved; or

(*ii*) of any person out of reach of, or not subject to, the process of the Court; or

(*iii*) of any person legally bound to produce it,

and when, after the notice mentioned in section 64 such person does not produce it;

(*b*) when the existence, condition or contents of the original have been proved to be admitted in writing by the person against whom it is proved or by his representative in interest;

(*c*) when the original has been destroyed or lost, or when the party offering evidence of its contents cannot, for any other reason not arising from his own default or neglect, produce it in reasonable time;

(*d*) when the original is of such a nature as not to be easily movable;

(*e*) when the original is a public document within the meaning of section 74;

(*f*) when the original is a document of which a certified copy is permitted by this Adhiniyam, or by any other law in force in India to be given in evidence;

(*g*) when the originals consist of numerous accounts or other documents which cannot conveniently be examined in Court, and the fact to be proved is the general result of the whole collection.

Explanation.—For the purposes of—

(*i*) clauses (*a*), (*c*) and (*d*), any secondary evidence of the contents of the document is admissible;

(*ii*) clause (*b*), the written admission is admissible;

(*iii*) clause (*e*) or (*f*), a certified copy of the document, but no other kind of secondary evidence, is admissible;

(*iv*) clause (*g*), evidence may be given as to the general result of the documents by any person who has examined them, and who is skilled in the examination of such document.

Corresponding Provision : Section 65 of Indian Evidence Act, 1872

COMMENT

Oral evidence v. documentary evidence - Section 59 of the Evidence Act states that all facts, except the contents of documents or electronic records, may be proved by oral evidence. Oral evidence means the testimony of living persons examined in the presence of the court or commissioners appointed by the court. Deaf and dumb persons may also adduce evidence by signs or through interpretation or by writing, if they are literate. Documentary evidences, on the other hand, are to be proved by the production of the documents themselves or, in their absence, by secondary evidence under section 65 of the Act. Further, facts showing the existence of any state of mind, such as intention, knowledge, good faith, negligence, or ill will need not be proved by direct testimony. It may be proved inferentially from conduct, surrounding circumstances, etc.). [Paras 36, 37] - *Neeraj Dutta* v. *State (Govt. of N.C.T. of Delhi)* AIR 2023 Supreme Court 330.

Electronic or digital record.

61. Nothing in this Adhiniyam shall apply to deny the admissibility of an electronic or digital record in the evidence on the ground that it is an electronic or digital record and such record shall, subject to section 63, have the same legal effect, validity and enforceability as other document.

Special provisions as to evidence relating to electronic record.

62. The contents of electronic records may be proved in accordance with the provisions of section 63.

Corresponding Provision : Section 65A of Indian Evidence Act, 1872

Admissibility of electronic records.

63. (1) Notwithstanding anything contained in this Adhiniyam, any information contained in an electronic record which is printed on paper, stored, recorded or copied in optical or magnetic media or semiconductor memory which is produced by a computer or any communication device or otherwise stored, recorded or copied in any electronic form (hereinafter referred to as the computer output) shall be deemed to be also a document, if the conditions mentioned in this section are satisfied in relation to the information and computer in question and shall be admissible in any proceedings, without further proof or production of the original, as evidence or any contents of the original or of any fact stated therein of which direct evidence would be admissible.

(2) The conditions referred to in sub-section (1) in respect of a computer output shall be the following, namely:—

(*a*) the computer output containing the information was produced by the computer or communication device during the period over which the computer or communication device was used regularly to create, store or process information for the purposes of any activity regularly carried on over that period by the person having lawful control over the use of the computer or communication device;

(*b*) during the said period, information of the kind contained in the electronic record or of the kind from which the information so contained is derived was regularly fed into the computer or communication device in the ordinary course of the said activities;

(*c*) throughout the material part of the said period, the computer or communication device was operating properly or, if not, then in respect of any period in which it was not operating properly or was out of operation during that part of the period, was not such as to affect the electronic record or the accuracy of its contents; and

(*d*) the information contained in the electronic record reproduces or is derived from such information fed into the computer or communication device in the ordinary course of the said activities.

(3) Where over any period, the function of creating, storing or processing information for the purposes of any activity regularly carried on over that period as mentioned in clause (*a*) of sub-section (2) was regularly performed by means of one or more computers or communication device, whether—

(*a*) in standalone mode; or

(*b*) on a computer system; or

(*c*) on a computer network; or

(*d*) on a computer resource enabling information creation or providing information processing and storage; or

(*e*) through an intermediary,

all the computers or communication devices used for that purpose during that period shall be treated for the purposes of this section as constituting a single computer or communication device; and references in this section to a computer or communication device shall be construed accordingly.

(4) In any proceeding where it is desired to give a statement in evidence by virtue of this section, a certificate doing any of the following things shall be submitted along with the electronic record at each instance where it is being submitted for admission, namely:—

(*a*) identifying the electronic record containing the statement and describing the manner in which it was produced;

(*b*) giving such particulars of any device involved in the production of that electronic record as may be appropriate for the purpose of showing that the electronic record was produced by a computer or a communication device referred to in clauses (*a*) to (*e*) of sub-section (3);

(*c*) dealing with any of the matters to which the conditions mentioned in sub-section (2) relate,

and purporting to be signed by a person in charge of the computer or communication device or the management of the relevant activities (whichever is appropriate) and an expert shall be evidence of any matter stated in the certificate; and for the purposes of this sub-section it shall be sufficient for a matter to be stated to the best of the knowledge and belief of the person stating it in the certificate specified in the Schedule.

(5) For the purposes of this section,—

(*a*) information shall be taken to be supplied to a computer or communication device if it is supplied thereto in any appropriate form and whether it is so supplied directly or (with or without human intervention) by means of any appropriate equipment;

(*b*) a computer output shall be taken to have been produced by a computer or communication device whether it was produced by it directly or (with or without human intervention) by means of any appropriate equipment or by other electronic means as referred to in clauses (*a*) to (*e*) of sub-section (3).

Corresponding Provision **:** Section 65B of Indian Evidence Act, 1872

COMMENT

Electronic evidence should have complied with certification requirement - The electronic evidence produced before the Court should have been in accordance with the statute and should have complied with the certification requirement, for it to be admissible in the court of law. Oral evidence in the place of such certificate, cannot possibly suffice as section 65B(4) of the Evidence Act, 1872 is a mandatory requirement of the law. [Para 21] - *Ravinder Singh Alias Kaku* v. *State of Punjab* AIR 2022 Supreme Court 2726.

Rules as to notice to produce.

64. Secondary evidence of the contents of the documents referred to in clause (*a*) of section 60, shall not be given unless the party proposing to give such secondary evidence has previously given to the party in whose possession or power the document is, or to his advocate or representative, such notice to produce it as is prescribed by law; and if no notice is prescribed by law, then such notice as the Court considers reasonable under the circumstances of the case:

Provided that such notice shall not be required in order to render secondary evidence admissible in any of the following cases, or in any other case in which the Court thinks fit to dispense with it: —

(*a*) when the document to be proved is itself a notice;

(*b*) when, from the nature of the case, the adverse party must know that he will be required to produce it;

(*c*) when it appears or is proved that the adverse party has obtained possession of the original by fraud or force;

(*d*) when the adverse party or his agent has the original in Court;

(*e*) when the adverse party or his agent has admitted the loss of the document;

(*f*) when the person in possession of the document is out of reach of, or not subject to, the process of the Court.

Corresponding Provision : Section 66 of Indian Evidence Act, 1872

Proof of signature and handwriting of person alleged to have signed or written document produced.

65. If a document is alleged to be signed or to have been written wholly or in part by any person, the signature or the handwriting of so much of the document as is alleged to be in that person's handwriting must be proved to be in his handwriting.

Corresponding Provision : Section 67 of Indian Evidence Act, 1872

Proof as to electronic signature.

66. Except in the case of a secure electronic signature, if the electronic signature of any subscriber is alleged to have been affixed to an electronic record, the fact that such electronic signature is the electronic signature of the subscriber must be proved.

Corresponding Provision : Section 67A of Indian Evidence Act, 1872

Proof of execution of document required by law to be attested.

67. If a document is required by law to be attested, it shall not be used as evidence until one attesting witness at least has been called for the purpose of proving its execution, if there be an attesting witness alive, and subject to the process of the Court and capable of giving evidence:

Provided that it shall not be necessary to call an attesting witness in proof of the execution of any document, not being a will, which has been registered in accordance with the provisions of the Indian Registration Act, 1908 (16 of 1908), unless its execution by the person by whom it purports to have been executed is specifically denied.

Corresponding Provision : Section 68 of Indian Evidence Act, 1872

Proof where no attesting witness found.

68. If no such attesting witness can be found, it must be proved that the attestation of one attesting witness at least is in his handwriting, and that the signature of the person executing the document is in the handwriting of that person.

Corresponding Provision : Section 69 of Indian Evidence Act, 1872

Admission of execution by party to attested document.

69. The admission of a party to an attested document of its execution by himself shall be sufficient proof of its execution as against him, though it be a document required by law to be attested.

Corresponding Provision : Section 70 of Indian Evidence Act, 1872

Proof when attesting witness denies execution.

70. If the attesting witness denies or does not recollect the execution of the document, its execution may be proved by other evidence.

Corresponding Provision : Section 71 of Indian Evidence Act, 1872

Proof of document not required by law to be attested.

71. An attested document not required by law to be attested may be proved as if it was unattested.

Corresponding Provision : Section 72 of Indian Evidence Act, 1872

Comparison of signature, writing or seal with others admitted or proved.

72. (1) In order to ascertain whether a signature, writing or seal is that of the person by whom it purports to have been written or made, any signature, writing, or seal admitted or proved to the satisfaction of the Court to have been written or made by that person may be compared with the one which is to be proved, although that signature, writing or seal has not been produced or proved for any other purpose.

(2) The Court may direct any person present in Court to write any words or figures for the purpose of enabling the Court to compare the words or figures so written with any words or figures alleged to have been written by such person.

(3) This section applies also, with any necessary modifications, to finger impressions.

Corresponding Provision : Section 73 of Indian Evidence Act, 1872

Proof as to verification of digital signature.

73. In order to ascertain whether a digital signature is that of the person by whom it purports to have been affixed, the Court may direct—

(*a*) that person or the Controller or the Certifying Authority to produce the Digital Signature Certificate;

(*b*) any other person to apply the public key listed in the Digital Signature Certificate and verify the digital signature purported to have been affixed by that person.

Corresponding Provision : Section 73A of Indian Evidence Act, 1872

Public documents

Public and private documents.

74. (1) The following documents are public documents:—

(*a*) documents forming the acts, or records of the acts—

(*i*) of the sovereign authority;

(*ii*) of official bodies and tribunals; and

(*iii*) of public officers, legislative, judicial and executive of India or of a foreign country;

(*b*) public records kept in any State or Union territory of private documents.

Corresponding Provision : Section 74 of Indian Evidence Act, 1872

(2) All other documents except the documents referred to in sub-section (1) are private.

Corresponding Provision : Section 75 of Indian Evidence Act, 1872

Certified copies of public documents.

75. Every public officer having the custody of a public document, which any person has a right to inspect, shall give that person on demand a copy of it on payment of the legal fees therefor, together with a certificate written at the foot of such copy that it is a true copy of such document or part thereof, as the case may be, and such certificate shall be dated and subscribed by such officer with his name and his official title, and shall be sealed, whenever such officer is authorised by law to make use of a seal; and such copies so certified shall be called certified copies.

Explanation.—Any officer who, by the ordinary course of official duty, is authorised to deliver such copies, shall be deemed to have the custody of such documents within the meaning of this section.

Corresponding Provision **:** Section 76 of Indian Evidence Act, 1872

COMMENTS

Certified copy of public documents is permissible as secondary evidence - Section 74 of Evidence Act, 1872 deals with documents which are public documents. Sub-section (2) thereof makes public records kept [in any State] of private documents within the purview of "public document" under section 74 of the Evidence Act, 1872. Going by section 76 of the Evidence Act, 1872, certified copies of public documents shall be given, on demand, by the public officer having the custody of public document, together with a certificate written at the foot of such copy that it is a true copy of such document or part thereof, as the case may be, and such certificate shall be dated and subscribed by such officer with his name and his official title. Such copies so certified shall be called certified copies in terms of section 76.

A certified copy of sale deed produced being registered with the Sub-Registrar's Office, in the light of the aforementioned provisions under the Evidence Act there can be no doubt with respect to the permissibility for the production of such a certified copy as secondary evidence in law, in regard to the existence, condition or contents of a document. As per section 77 of the Evidence Act such certified copies may be produced in proof of the contents of the public document concerned. Section 79 deals with presumption as to genuineness of certified copies. [Para 21] - *Appaiya* v. *Andimuthu Alias Thangapandi* AIR 2023 Supreme Court 4810.

Proof of documents by production of certified copies.

76. Such certified copies may be produced in proof of the contents of the public documents or parts of the public documents of which they purport to be copies.

Corresponding Provision **:** Section 77 of Indian Evidence Act, 1872

COMMENTS

Certified copy is admissible to prove content of original document - Section 77 of the Evidence Act, provides for the production of certified copy of a public document as secondary evidence in proof of contents of its original. Section 79 of the Evidence Act, 1872 is the provision for presumption as to the genuineness of certified copies provided the existence of a law declaring certified copy of a document of such nature to be admissible as evidence. When that be the position under the aforesaid provisions, taking note of the fact that the document in question is a registered sale deed, falling within the definition of a public document, the question is whether there exists any law declaring such certified copy of a document as admissible in evidence for the purpose of proving the contents of its original document. Sub-section (5) of section 57 of the Registration Act is the relevant provision that provides that certified copy given under section 57 of the Registration Act shall be admissible for the purpose of proving the contents of its original document. In this context it is to be noted that certified copy issued thereunder is not a copy of the original document, but is a copy of the registration entry which is itself a copy of the original and is a public document under section 74(2) of the Evidence Act and sub-section (5) thereof, makes it admissible in evidence for proving the contents of its original. There is no ease that foundation for letting in secondary evidence was not laid and as noted earlier, both the trial Court and the First Appellate Court found it admissible in evidence. Thus, the cumulative effect of the aforementioned sections of the Evidence Act and section 57(5) of the Registration Act would make the certified copy of the sale deed of SRO admissible in evidence for the purpose of proving the contents of the said original document. When this be the position in the light of the specific provisions referred hereinbefore under the Evidence Act and the Registration Act, the finding of the High Court that the certified copy of sale deed owing to the failure in production of the original and proving through an independent witness is inadmissible in evidence, is legally unsustainable. [Para 29] - *Appaiya* v. *Andimuthu Alias Thangapandi* AIR 2023 Supreme Court 4810.

Proof of other official documents.

77. The following public documents may be proved as follows:—

(*a*) Acts, orders or notifications of the Central Government in any of its Ministries and Departments or of any State Government or any Department of any State Government or Union territory Administration—

(*i*) by the records of the Departments, certified by the head of those Departments respectively; or

(*ii*) by any document purporting to be printed by order of any such Government;

(*b*) the proceedings of Parliament or a State Legislature, by the journals of those bodies respectively, or by published Acts or abstracts, or by copies purporting to be printed by order of the Government concerned;

(*c*) proclamations, orders or Regulations issued by the President of India or the Governor of a State or the Administrator or Lieutenant Governor of a Union territory, by copies or extracts contained in the Official Gazette;

(*d*) the Acts of the Executive or the proceedings of the Legislature of a foreign country, by journals published by their authority, or commonly received in that country as such, or by a copy certified under the seal of the country or sovereign, or by a recognition thereof in any Central Act;

(*e*) the proceedings of a municipal or local body in a State, by a copy of such proceedings, certified by the legal keeper thereof, or by a printed book purporting to be published by the authority of such body;

(*f*) public documents of any other class in a foreign country, by the original or by a copy certified by the legal keeper thereof, with a certificate under the seal of a Notary Public, or of an Indian Consul or diplomatic agent, that the copy is duly certified by the officer having the legal custody of the original, and upon proof of the character of the document according to the law of the foreign country.

Corresponding Provision **:** Section 78 of Indian Evidence Act, 1872

Presumptions as to documents

Presumption as to genuineness of certified copies.

78. (1) The Court shall presume to be genuine every document purporting to be a certificate, certified copy or other document, which is by law declared to be admissible as evidence of any particular fact and which purports to be duly certified by any officer of the Central Government or of a State Government:

Provided that such document is substantially in the form and purports to be executed in the manner directed by law in that behalf.

(2) The Court shall also presume that any officer by whom any such document purports to be signed or certified, held, when he signed it, the official character which he claims in such paper.

Corresponding Provision **:** Section 79 of Indian Evidence Act, 1872

Presumption as to documents produced as record of evidence, etc.

79. Whenever any document is produced before any Court, purporting to be a record or memorandum of the evidence, or of any part of the evidence, given by a witness in a judicial proceeding or before any officer authorised by law to take such evidence or to be a statement or confession by any prisoner or accused person, taken in accordance with law, and purporting to be signed by any Judge or Magistrate, or by any such officer as aforesaid, the Court shall presume that—

(*i*) the document is genuine;

(*ii*) any statements as to the circumstances under which it was taken, purporting to be made by the person signing it, are true; and

(*iii*) such evidence, statement or confession was duly taken.

Corresponding Provision : Section 80 of Indian Evidence Act, 1872

Presumption as to Gazettes, newspapers, and other documents.

80. The Court shall presume the genuineness of every document purporting to be the Official Gazette, or to be a newspaper or journal, and of every document purporting to be a document directed by any law to be kept by any person, if such document is kept substantially in the form required by law and is produced from proper custody.

Explanation.—For the purposes of this section and section 92, document is said to be in proper custody if it is in the place in which, and looked after by the person with whom such document is required to be kept; but no custody is improper if it is proved to have had a legitimate origin, or if the circumstances of the particular case are such as to render that origin probable.

Corresponding Provision : Section 81 of Indian Evidence Act, 1872

Presumption as to Gazettes in electronic or digital record.

81. The Court shall presume the genuineness of every electronic or digital record purporting to be the Official Gazette, or purporting to be electronic or digital record directed by any law to be kept by any person, if such electronic or digital record is kept substantially in the form required by law and is produced from proper custody.

Explanation.—For the purposes of this section and section 93 electronic records are said to be in proper custody if they are in the place in which, and looked after by the person with whom such document is required to be kept; but no custody is improper if it is proved to have had a legitimate origin, or the circumstances of the particular case are such as to render that origin probable.

Corresponding Provision : Section 81A of Indian Evidence Act, 1872

Presumption as to maps or plans made by authority of Government.

82. The Court shall presume that maps or plans purporting to be made by the authority of the Central Government or any State Government were so made, and are accurate; but maps or plans made for the purposes of any cause must be proved to be accurate.

Corresponding Provision : Section 83 of Indian Evidence Act, 1872

Presumption as to collections of laws and reports of decisions.

83. The Court shall presume the genuineness of, every book purporting to be printed or published under the authority of the Government of any country, and to contain any of the laws of that country, and of every book purporting to contain reports of decisions of the Courts of such country.

Corresponding Provision : Section 84 of Indian Evidence Act, 1872

Presumption as to powers-of-attorney.

84. The Court shall presume that every document purporting to be a power-of-attorney, and to have been executed before, and authenticated by, a Notary Public, or any Court, Judge, Magistrate, Indian Consul or Vice-Consul, or representative of the Central Government, was so executed and authenticated.

Corresponding Provision : Section 85 of Indian Evidence Act, 1872

Presumption as to electronic agreements.

85. The Court shall presume that every electronic record purporting to be an agreement containing the electronic or digital signature of the parties was so concluded by affixing the electronic or digital signature of the parties.

Corresponding Provision : Section 85A of Indian Evidence Act, 1872

Presumption as to electronic records and electronic signatures.

86. (1) In any proceeding involving a secure electronic record, the Court shall presume unless contrary is proved, that the secure electronic record has not been altered since the specific point of time to which the secure status relates.

(2) In any proceeding, involving secure electronic signature, the Court shall presume unless the contrary is proved that—

(*a*) the secure electronic signature is affixed by subscriber with the intention of signing or approving the electronic record;

(*b*) except in the case of a secure electronic record or a secure electronic signature, nothing in this section shall create any presumption, relating to authenticity and integrity of the electronic record or any electronic signature.

Corresponding Provision : Section 85B of Indian Evidence Act, 1872

Presumption as to Electronic Signature Certificates.

87. The Court shall presume, unless contrary is proved, that the information listed in an

Electronic Signature Certificate is correct, except for information specified as subscriber information which has not been verified, if the certificate was accepted by the subscriber.

Corresponding Provision **:** Section 85C of Indian Evidence Act, 1872

Presumption as to certified copies of foreign judicial records.

88. (1) The Court may presume that any document purporting to be a certified copy of any judicial record of any country beyond India is genuine and accurate, if the document purports to be certified in any manner which is certified by any representative of the Central Government in or for such country to be the manner commonly in use in that country for the certification of copies of judicial records.

(2) An officer who, with respect to any territory or place outside India is a Political Agent therefor, as defined in clause *(43)* of section 3* of the General Clauses Act, 1897 (10 of 1897), shall, for the purposes of this section, be deemed to be a representative of the Central Government in and for the country comprising that territory or place.

Corresponding Provision **:** Section 86 of Indian Evidence Act, 1872

Presumption as to books, maps and charts.

89. The Court may presume that any book to which it may refer for information on matters of public or general interest, and that any published map or chart, the statements of which are relevant facts, and which is produced for its inspection, was written and published by the person, and at the time and place, by whom or at which it purports to have been written or published.

Corresponding Provision **:** Section 87 of Indian Evidence Act, 1872

---

* For text of section 3(43) of General Clauses Act, 1897, *see* **Appendix**.

Presumption as to electronic messages.

90. The Court may presume that an electronic message, forwarded by the originator through an electronic mail server to the addressee to whom the message purports to be addressed corresponds with the message as fed into his computer for transmission; but the Court shall not make any presumption as to the person by whom such message was sent.

***Corresponding Provision* :** Section 88A of Indian Evidence Act, 1872

Presumption as to due execution, etc., of documents not produced.

91. The Court shall presume that every document, called for and not produced after notice to produce, was attested, stamped and executed in the manner required by law.

***Corresponding Provision* :** Section 89 of Indian Evidence Act, 1872

Presumption as to documents thirty years old.

92. Where any document, purporting or proved to be thirty years old, is produced from any custody which the Court in the particular case considers proper, the Court may presume that the signature and every other part of such document, which purports to be in the handwriting of any particular person, is in that person's handwriting, and, in the case of a document executed or attested, that it was duly executed and attested by the persons by whom it purports to be executed and attested.

Explanation.—The *Explanation* to section 80 shall also apply to this section.

Illustrations

(*a*) A has been in possession of landed property for a long time. He produces from his custody deeds relating to the land showing his titles to it. The custody shall be proper.

(*b*) A produces deeds relating to landed property of which he is the mortgagee. The mortgagor is in possession. The custody shall be proper.

(*c*) A, a connection of B, produces deeds relating to lands in B's possession, which were deposited with him by B for safe custody. The custody shall be proper.

Corresponding Provision : Section 90 of Indian Evidence Act, 1872

Presumption as to electronic records five years old.

93. Where any electronic record, purporting or proved to be five years old, is produced from any custody which the Court in the particular case considers proper, the Court may presume that the electronic signature which purports to be the electronic signature of any particular person was so affixed by him or any person authorised by him in this behalf.

Explanation.—The *Explanation* to section 81 shall also apply to this section.

Corresponding Provision : Section 90A of Indian Evidence Act, 1872

CHAPTER VI

OF THE EXCLUSION OF ORAL EVIDENCE BY DOCUMENTARY EVIDENCE

Evidence of terms of contracts, grants and other dispositions of property reduced to form of document.

94. When the terms of a contract, or of a grant, or of any other disposition of property, have been reduced to the form of a document, and in all cases in which any matter is required by law to be reduced to the form of a document, no evidence shall be given in proof of the terms of such contract, grant or other disposition of property, or of such matter, except the document itself, or secondary evidence of its contents in cases in which secondary evidence is admissible under the provisions hereinbefore contained.

Exception 1.—When a public officer is required by law to be appointed in writing, and when it is shown that any particular person has acted as such officer, the writing by which he is appointed need not be proved.

Exception 2.—Wills admitted to probate in India may be proved by the probate.

Explanation 1.—This section applies equally to cases in which the contracts, grants or dispositions of property referred to are contained in one document, and to cases in which they are contained in more documents than one.

Explanation 2.—Where there are more originals than one, one original only need be proved.

Explanation 3.—The statement, in any document whatever, of a fact other than the facts referred to in this section, shall not preclude the admission of oral evidence as to the same fact.

Illustrations

(*a*) If a contract be contained in several letters, all the letters in which it is contained must be proved.

(*b*) If a contract is contained in a bill of exchange, the bill of exchange must be proved.

(*c*) If a bill of exchange is drawn in a set of three, one only need be proved.

(*d*) A contracts, in writing, with B, for the delivery of indigo upon certain terms. The contract mentions the fact that B had paid A the price of other indigo contracted for verbally on another occasion. Oral evidence is offered that no payment was made for the other indigo. The evidence is admissible.

(*e*) A gives B a receipt for money paid by B. Oral evidence is offered of the payment. The evidence is admissible.

Corresponding Provision **:** Section 91 of Indian Evidence Act, 1872

Exclusion of evidence of oral agreement.

95. When the terms of any such contract, grant or other disposition of property, or any matter required by law to be reduced to the form of a document, have been proved according to section 94, no evidence of any oral agreement or statement shall be admitted, as between the parties to any such instrument or their representatives in interest, for the purpose of contradicting, varying, adding to, or subtracting from, its terms:

Provided that any fact may be proved which would invalidate any document, or which would entitle any person to any decree or order relating thereto; such as fraud, intimidation, illegality, want of due execution, want of capacity in any contracting party, want or failure of consideration, or mistake in fact or law:

Provided further that the existence of any separate oral agreement as to any matter on which a document is silent, and which is not inconsistent with its terms, may be proved. In considering whether or not this proviso applies, the Court shall have regard to the degree of formality of the document:

Provided also that the existence of any separate oral agreement, constituting a condition precedent to the attaching of any obligation under any such contract, grant or disposition of property, may be proved:

Provided also that the existence of any distinct subsequent oral agreement to rescind or modify any such contract, grant or disposition of property, may be proved, except in cases in which such contract, grant or disposition of property is by law required to be in writing, or has been registered according to the law in force for the time being as to the registration of documents:

Provided also that any usage or custom by which incidents not expressly mentioned in any contract are usually annexed to contracts of that description, may be proved:

Provided also that the annexing of such incident would not be repugnant to, or inconsistent with, the express terms of the contract:

Provided also that any fact may be proved which shows in what manner the language of a document is related to existing facts.

Illustrations

(*a*) A policy of insurance is effected on goods "in ships from Kolkata to Visakhapatnam". The goods are shipped in a particular ship which is lost. The fact that particular ship was orally excepted from the policy, cannot be proved.

(*b*) A agrees absolutely in writing to pay B one thousand rupees on the 1st March, 2023. The fact that, at the same time, an oral agreement was made that the money should not be paid till the 31st March, 2023, cannot be proved.

(*c*) An estate called "the Rampur tea estate" is sold by a deed which contains a map of the property sold. The fact that land not included in the map had always been regarded as part of the estate and was meant to pass by the deed cannot be proved.

(*d*) A enters into a written contract with B to work certain mines, the property of B, upon certain terms. A was induced to do so by a misrepresentation of B's as to their value. This fact may be proved.

(*e*) A institutes a suit against B for the specific performance of a contract, and also prays that the contract may be reformed as to one of its provisions, as that provision was inserted in it by mistake. A may prove that such a mistake was made as would by law entitle him to have the contract reformed.

(*f*) A orders goods of B by a letter in which nothing is said as to the time of payment, and accepts the goods on delivery. B sues A for the price. A may show that the goods were supplied on credit for a term still unexpired.

(*g*) A sells B a horse and verbally warrants him sound. A gives B a paper in these words—"Bought of A a horse for thirty thousand rupees". B may prove the verbal warranty.

(*h*) A hires lodgings of B and gives B a card on which is written—"Rooms, ten thousand rupees a month". A may prove a verbal agreement that these terms were to include partial board. A hires lodging of B for a year, and a regularly stamped agreement, drawn up by an advocate, is made between them. It is silent on the subject of board. A may not prove that board was included in the term verbally.

(*i*) A applies to B for a debt due to A by sending a receipt for the money. B keeps the receipt and does not send the money. In a suit for the amount, A may prove this.

(*j*) A and B make a contract in writing to take effect upon the happening of a certain contingency. The writing is left with B who sues A upon it. A may show the circumstances under which it was delivered.

Corresponding Provision : Section 92 of Indian Evidence Act, 1872

Exclusion of evidence to explain or amend ambiguous document.

96. When the language used in a document is, on its face, ambiguous or defective, evidence may not be given of facts which would show its meaning or supply its defects.

Illustrations

(*a*) A agrees, in writing, to sell a horse to B for "one lakh rupees or one lakh fifty thousand rupees". Evidence cannot be given to show which price was to be given.

(*b*) A deed contains blanks. Evidence cannot be given of facts which would show how they were meant to be filled.

Corresponding Provision : Section 93 of Indian Evidence Act, 1872

Exclusion of evidence against application of document to existing facts.

97. When language used in a document is plain in itself, and when it applies accurately to existing facts, evidence may not be given to show that it was not meant to apply to such facts.

Illustration

A sells to B, by deed, "my estate at Rampur containing one hundred *bighas*". A has an estate at Rampur containing one hundred *bighas*. Evidence may not be given of the fact that the estate meant to be sold was one situated at a different place and of a different size.

Corresponding Provision : Section 94 of Indian Evidence Act, 1872

Evidence as to document unmeaning in reference to existing facts.

98. When language used in a document is plain in itself, but is unmeaning in reference to existing facts, evidence may be given to show that it was used in a peculiar sense.

Illustration

A sells to B, by deed, "my house in Kolkata". A had no house in Kolkata, but it appears that he had a house at Howrah, of which B had been in possession since the execution of the deed. These facts may be proved to show that the deed related to the house at Howrah.

Corresponding Provision **:** Section 95 of Indian Evidence Act, 1872

Evidence as to application of language which can apply to one only of several persons.

99. When the facts are such that the language used might have been meant to apply to any one, and could not have been meant to apply to more than one, of several persons or things, evidence may be given of facts which show which of those persons or things it was intended to apply to.

Illustrations

(*a*) A agrees to sell to B, for one thousand rupees, "my white horse". A has two white horses. Evidence may be given of facts which show which of them was meant.

(*b*) A agrees to accompany B to Ramgarh. Evidence may be given of facts showing whether Ramgarh in Rajasthan or Ramgarh in Uttarakhand was meant.

Corresponding Provision **:** Section 96 of Indian Evidence Act, 1872

Evidence as to application of language to one of two sets of facts, to neither of which the whole correctly applies.

100. When the language used applies partly to one set of existing facts, and partly to another set of existing facts, but the whole of it does not apply correctly to either, evidence may be given to show to which of the two it was meant to apply.

Illustration

A agrees to sell to B "my land at X in the occupation of Y". A has land at X, but not in the occupation of Y, and he has land in the occupation of Y but it is not at X. Evidence may be given of facts showing which he meant to sell.

Corresponding Provision : Section 97 of Indian Evidence Act, 1872

Evidence as to meaning of illegible characters, etc.

101. Evidence may be given to show the meaning of illegible or not commonly intelligible characters, of foreign, obsolete, technical, local and regional expressions, of abbreviations and of words used in a peculiar sense.

Illustration

A, sculptor, agrees to sell to B, "all my mods". A has both models and modelling tools. Evidence may be given to show which he meant to sell.

Corresponding Provision : Section 98 of Indian Evidence Act, 1872

Who may give evidence of agreement varying terms of document.

102. Persons who are not parties to a document, or their representatives in interest, may give evidence of any facts tending to show a contemporaneous agreement varying the terms of the document.

Illustration

A and B make a contract in writing that B shall sell A certain cotton, to be paid for on delivery. At the same time, they make an oral agreement that three months' credit shall be given to A. This could not be shown as between A and B, but it might be shown by C, if it affected his interests.

Corresponding Provision : Section 99 of Indian Evidence Act, 1872

Saving of provisions of Indian Succession Act relating to wills.

103. Nothing in this Chapter shall be taken to affect any of the provisions of the Indian Succession Act, 1925 (39 of 1925) as to the construction of wills.

Corresponding Provision : Section 100 of Indian Evidence Act, 1872

PART IV

PRODUCTION AND EFFECT OF EVIDENCE

CHAPTER VII

OF THE BURDEN OF PROOF

Burden of proof.

104. Whoever desires any Court to give judgment as to any legal right or liability dependent on the existence of facts which he asserts must prove that those facts exist, and when a person is bound to prove the existence of any fact, it is said that the burden of proof lies on that person.

Illustrations

(*a*) A desires a Court to give judgment that B shall be punished for a crime which A says B has committed. A must prove that B has committed the crime.

(*b*) A desires a Court to give judgment that he is entitled to certain land in the possession of B, by reason of facts which he asserts, and which B denies, to be true. A must prove the existence of those facts.

Corresponding Provision : Section 101 of Indian Evidence Act, 1872

On whom burden of proof lies.

105. The burden of proof in a suit or proceeding lies on that person who would fail if no evidence at all were given on either side.

Illustrations

(*a*) A sues B for land of which B is in possession, and which, as A asserts, was left to A by the will of

C, B's father. If no evidence were given on either side, B would be entitled to retain his possession. Therefore, the burden of proof is on A.

(*b*) A sues B for money due on a bond. The execution of the bond is admitted, but B says that it was obtained by fraud, which A denies. If no evidence were given on either side, A would succeed, as the bond is not disputed and the fraud is not proved. Therefore, the burden of proof is on B.

***Corresponding Provision* :** Section 102 of Indian Evidence Act, 1872

Burden of proof as to particular fact.

106. The burden of proof as to any particular fact lies on that person who wishes the Court to believe in its existence, unless it is provided by any law that the proof of that fact shall lie on any particular person.

Illustration

A prosecutes B for theft, and wishes the Court to believe that B admitted the theft to C. A must prove the admission. B wishes the Court to believe that, at the time in question, he was elsewhere. He must prove it.

***Corresponding Provision* :** Section 103 of Indian Evidence Act, 1872

Burden of proving fact to be proved to make evidence admissible.

107. The burden of proving any fact necessary to be proved in order to enable any person to give evidence of any other fact is on the person who wishes to give such evidence.

Illustrations

(*a*) A wishes to prove a dying declaration by B. A must prove B's death.

(*b*) A wishes to prove, by secondary evidence, the contents of a lost document. A must prove that the document has been lost.

***Corresponding Provision* :** Section 104 of Indian Evidence Act, 1872

Burden of proving that case of accused comes within exceptions.

108. When a person is accused of any offence, the burden of proving the existence of circumstances bringing the case within any of the General Exceptions in the Bharatiya Nyaya Sanhita, 2023 or within any special exception or proviso contained in any other part of the said Sanhita, or in any law defining the offence, is upon him, and the Court shall presume the absence of such circumstances.

Illustrations

(*a*) A, accused of murder, alleges that, by reason of unsoundness of mind, he did not know the nature of the act. The burden of proof is on A.

(*b*) A, accused of murder, alleges that, by grave and sudden provocation, he was deprived of the power of self-control. The burden of proof is on A.

(*c*) Section 117 of the Bharatiya Nyaya Sanhita, 2023 provides that whoever, except in the case provided for by sub-section (2) of section 122, voluntarily causes grievous hurt, shall be subject to certain punishments. A is charged with voluntarily causing grievous hurt under section 117. The burden of proving the circumstances bringing the case under sub-section (2) of section 122 lies on A.

Corresponding Provision : Section 105 of Indian Evidence Act, 1872

Burden of proving fact especially within knowledge.

109. When any fact is especially within the knowledge of any person, the burden of proving that fact is upon him.

Illustrations

(*a*) When a person does an act with some intention other than that which the character and circumstances of the act suggest, the burden of proving that intention is upon him.

(*b*) A is charged with travelling on a railway without a ticket. The burden of proving that he had a ticket is on him.

Corresponding Provision **:** Section 106 of Indian Evidence Act, 1872

COMMENTS

Burden of proof is on accused - Section 106 of the Evidence Act clearly lays down that when any fact is specially within the knowledge of a person, the burden approving that fact is upon him namely, on such person. [Para 16.5] - *Siju Kurian* v. *State of Karnataka* AIR 2023 Supreme Court 2239.

Burden of proving guilt of accused rests on prosecution; section 106 of Evidence Act does not shift burden of prosecution on accused - In criminal jurisprudence, entire burden of proving guilt of accused rests on prosecution, nonetheless if accused does not throw any light upon facts which are proved to be within his special knowledge in view of section 106 of Evidence Act, such failure on part of accused may also provide an additional link in chain of circumstances required to be proved against him. Of course, section 106 of Evidence Act does not shift burden of prosecution on accused, nor requires accused to furnish an explanation with regard to facts which are especially within his knowledge, nonetheless furnishing or non-furnishing of explanation by accused would be a very crucial fact, when theory of "last seen together" as propounded by prosecution is proved against him, to know as to how and when accused parted company of victim. [Para 26] - *Mohd. Firoz* v. *State of Madhya Pradesh* AIR 2022 Supreme Court 1967.

When prosecution lead evidence, corresponding burden is on accused to explain situation of death - It is, of course, the duty of prosecution to lead the primary evidence of proving its case beyond reasonable doubt but, when necessary evidence had indeed been led, the corresponding burden was heavy on the appellant in terms of section 106 of the Evidence Act to explain as to what had happened at the time of incident and as to how the death of the deceased occurred. [Para 16.4.1] - *Prem Singh* v. *State of NCT of Delhi* AIR 2023 Supreme Court 193.

Onus of proving specific intention falls onto individual and not on prosecution - Section 106 of the Evidence Act postulates that the burden of proving things which are within the special knowledge of an individual is on that individual. Although the section in no way exonerates the prosecution from discharging its burden of proof beyond reasonable doubt, it merely prescribes that when an individual has done an act, with an intention other than that which the circumstances indicate, the onus of proving that specific intention falls onto the individual and not on the prosecution. If the accused had a different intention than the facts are specially within his knowledge which he must prove. Thus, although section 106 is in no way aimed at relieving the prosecution from its burden to establish the guilt of an accused, it applies to cases where chain of events has been successfully established by the prosecution, from which a reasonable inference is made out against the accused. Moreover, in a case based on circumstantial evidence, whenever an incriminating question is posed to the accused and he or she either evades response, or offers a response which is not true, then such a response in itself becomes an additional link in the chain of events. [Para 18] - *Sabitri Samantaray* v. *State of Odisha* AIR 2022 Supreme Court 2591.

Burden of proof to dislodge prosecution case is on accused - Where the prosecution had succeeded in establishing intention of the appellants for the commission of the offence and such an intention, when analyzed in the light of the statements made by all the sets of witnesses, and fatal injuries sustained by the deceased at the relevant place and time, certainly makes out a strong case that death of the deceased was indeed caused by the appellants, once the prosecution has successfully established the chain of events, the burden is on the appellants to prove it otherwise. [Para 24] - *Sabitri Samantaray* v. *State of Odisha* AIR 2022 Supreme Court 2591.

Once prosecution makes out a *prima facie* case, burden of proof would lie upon accused - Section 106 of the Evidence Act does not absolve the prosecution of discharging its primary burden of proving the prosecution case beyond reasonable doubt. It is only when the prosecution has led evidence which, if believed, will sustain a conviction, or which makes out a *prima facie* case, the question arises of considering facts of which the burden of proof would lie upon the accused. [Para 22] - *State of Punjab* v. *Kewal Krishan* AIR 2023 Supreme Court 3226.

Burden of proof is always with prosecution; section 106 only places burden for disclosure of a fact on establishment of certain circumstances by prosecution - Section 106 of the Act is an exception to the rule which is section 101 of the Evidence Act, and it comes into play only in a limited sense where the evidence is of a nature which is especially within the knowledge of that person and then the burden of proving that fact shifts upon him that person.

The burden of proof is always with the prosecution. It is the prosecution which has to prove its case beyond a reasonable doubt. Section 106 of the Evidence Act does not alter that position. It only places burden for disclosure of a fact on the establishment of certain circumstances.

What has to be kept in mind is that section 106 of the Evidence Act, only comes into play when the other facts have been established by the prosecution. When the evidence of last seen itself is on a weak footing, considering the long gap of time between last seen and the time of death of the deceased, section 106 of the Act would not be applicable. [Paras 12 and 13] - *Dinesh Kumar* v. *State of Haryana* AIR 2023 Supreme Court 2795.

Burden to prove unsoundness of mind is on accused - It remains trite that the burden of proving the existence of circumstances so as to bring the case within the purview of section 84 IPC lies on the accused in terms of section 105 of the Evidence Act; and where the accused is charged of murder, the burden to prove that as a result of unsoundness of mind, the accused was incapable of knowing the consequences of his acts is on the defence, as duly exemplified by illustration (*a*) to the said section 105 of the Evidence Act. As noticed, the mandate of law is that the Court shall presume absence of the circumstances so as to take the case within any of the General Exceptions in the Indian Penal Code, 1860. [Para 21] - *Prem Singh* v. *State of NCT of Delhi* AIR 2023 Supreme Court 193.

"Last seen theory", application of - The fact of last seen should not be weighed in isolation or be segregated from the other evidence led by the prosecution. The last seen theory should rather be applied taking into account the case of the prosecution in its entirety. Hence, the Courts have to not only consider the factum of last seen, but also have to keep in mind the circumstances that preceded and followed from the point of the deceased being so last seen in the presence of the Accused. [Para 30] - *Mohd. Firoz* v. *State of Madhya Pradesh* AIR 2022 Supreme Court 1967.

"Last seen together" theory, rebuttal of - Once the theory of "last seen together" was established, the accused was expected to offer some explanation as to under which circumstances, he had parted the company of the victim. In the criminal jurisprudence, the entire burden of proving the guilt of the accused rests on the prosecution, nonetheless if the accused does not throw any light upon the facts which are proved to be within his special knowledge in view of section 106 of the Evidence Act, such failure on the part of the accused may also provide an additional link in the chain of circumstances required to be proved against him. Of course, section 106 of the Evidence Act does not shift the burden of the prosecution on the accused, nor requires the accused to furnish an explanation with regard to the facts which are especially within his knowledge, nonetheless furnishing or non-furnishing of the explanation by the accused would be a very crucial fact, when the theory of "last seen together" as propounded by the prosecution is proved against him, to know as to how and when the accused parted the company of the victim. [Para 26] - *Mohd. Firoz v. State of Madhya Pradesh* AIR 2022 Supreme Court 1967.

Last seen together theory - Accused owe an explanation regarding circumstances of death - Once theory of 'last seen together' was established by prosecution, accused was expected to offer some explanation as to when and under what circumstances he had parted company of deceased. It is true that burden to prove guilt of accused is always on prosecution, however in view of section 106 of Evidence Act, when any fact is within knowledge of any person, burden of proving that fact is upon him. Of course, section 106 is certainly not intended to relieve prosecution of its duty to prove guilt of accused, nonetheless it is also equally settled legal position that if accused does not throw any light upon facts which are proved to be within his special knowledge, in view of section 106 of Evidence Act, such failure on part of accused may be used against accused as it may provide an additional link in chain of circumstances required to be proved against him. In case based on circumstantial evidence, furnishing or non-furnishing of explanation by accused would be a very crucial fact, when theory of 'last seen together' as propounded by prosecution was proved against him. Though last seen theory as propounded by prosecution in a case based on circumstantial evidence may be a weak kind of evidence by itself to base conviction solely on such theory, when said theory is proved coupled with other circumstances such as time when deceased was last seen with accused, and recovery of corpse being in very close proximity of time, accused does owe an Explanation under section 106 of Evidence Act with regard to circumstances under which death might have taken place. If accused offers no explanation or furnishes a wrong explanation, absconds, motive is established and some other corroborative evidence in form of recovery of weapon etc. forming a chain of circumstances is established, conviction could be based on such evidence. [Paras 6 and 9] - *Ram Gopal* v. *State of Madhya Pradesh* AIR 2023 Supreme Court 1145.

Burden of proving death of person known to have been alive within thirty years.

110. When the question is whether a man is alive or dead, and it is shown that he was alive within thirty years, the burden of proving that he is dead is on the person who affirms it.

Corresponding Provision **:** Section 107 of Indian Evidence Act, 1872

Burden of proving that person is alive who has not been heard of for seven years.

111. When the question is whether a man is alive or dead, and it is proved that he has not been heard of for seven years by those who would naturally have heard of him if he had been alive, the burden of proving that he is alive is shifted to the person who affirms it.

Corresponding Provision **:** Section 108 of Indian Evidence Act, 1872

Burden of proof as to relationship in the cases of partners, landlord and tenant, principal and agent.

112. When the question is whether persons are partners, landlord and tenant, or principal and agent, and it has been shown that they have been acting as such, the burden of proving that they do not stand, or have ceased to stand, to each other in those relationships respectively, is on the person who affirms it.

Corresponding Provision **:** Section 109 of Indian Evidence Act, 1872

Burden of proof as to ownership.

113. When the question is whether any person is owner of anything of which he is shown to be in possession, the burden of proving that he is not the owner is on the person who affirms that he is not the owner.

Corresponding Provision **:** Section 110 of Indian Evidence Act, 1872

Proof of good faith in transactions where one party is in relation of active confidence.

114. Where there is a question as to the good faith of a transaction between parties, one of whom stands to the other in a position of active confidence, the burden of proving the good faith of the transaction is on the party who is in a position of active confidence.

Illustrations

(*a*) The good faith of a sale by a client to an advocate is in question in a suit brought by the client. The burden of proving the good faith of the transaction is on the advocate.

(*b*) The good faith of a sale by a son just come of age to a father is in question in a suit brought by the son. The burden of proving the good faith of the transaction is on the father.

Corresponding Provision **:** Section 111 of Indian Evidence Act, 1872

Presumption as to certain offences.

115. (1) Where a person is accused of having committed any offence specified in sub-section (2), in—

(*a*) any area declared to be a disturbed area under any enactment for the time being in force, making provision for the suppression of disorder and restoration and maintenance of public order; or

(*b*) any area in which there has been, over a period of more than one month, extensive disturbance of the public peace,

and it is shown that such person had been at a place in such area at a time when firearms or explosives were used at or from that place to attack or resist the members of any armed forces or the forces charged with the maintenance of public order acting in the discharge of their duties, it shall be presumed, unless the contrary is shown, that such person had committed such offence.

(2) The offences referred to in sub-section (1) are the following, namely:—

(*a*) an offence under section 147, section 148, section 149 or section 150 of the Bharatiya Nyaya Sanhita, 2023;

(*b*) criminal conspiracy or attempt to commit, or abetment of, an offence under section 149 or section 150 of the Bharatiya Nyaya Sanhita, 2023.

Corresponding Provision : Section 111A of Indian Evidence Act, 1872

Birth during marriage, conclusive proof of legitimacy.

116. The fact that any person was born during the continuance of a valid marriage between his mother and any man, or within two hundred and eighty days after its dissolution, the mother remaining unmarried, shall be conclusive proof that he is the legitimate child of that man, unless it can be shown that the parties to the marriage had no access to each other at any time when he could have been begotten.

Corresponding Provision : Section 112 of Indian Evidence Act, 1872

Presumption as to abetment of suicide by a married woman.

117. When the question is whether the commission of suicide by a woman had been abetted by her husband or any relative of her husband and it is shown that she had committed suicide within a period of seven years from the date of her marriage and that her husband or such relative of her husband had subjected her to cruelty, the Court may presume, having regard to all the other circumstances of the case, that such suicide had been abetted by her husband or by such relative of her husband.

Explanation.—For the purposes of this section, "cruelty" shall have the same meaning as in section 86 of the Bharatiya Nyaya Sanhita, 2023.

Corresponding Provision **:** Section 113A of Indian Evidence Act, 1872

Presumption as to dowry death.

118. When the question is whether a person has committed the dowry death of a woman and it is shown that soon before her death, such woman had been subjected by such person to cruelty or harassment for, or in connection with, any demand for dowry, the Court shall presume that such person had caused the dowry death.

Explanation.—For the purposes of this section, "dowry death" shall have the same meaning as in section 80 of the Bharatiya Nyaya Sanhita, 2023.

Corresponding Provision **:** Section 113B of Indian Evidence Act, 1872

COMMENTS

Presumption of cruelty and harassment causing dowry death is rebuttable through cogent evidence - Section 304B, IPC read in conjunction with section 113B of the Evidence Act leaves no manner of doubt that once the prosecution has been able to demonstrate that a woman has been subjected to cruelty or harassment for or in connection with any demand for dowry, soon before her death, the Court shall proceed on a presumption that the persons who have subjected her to cruelty or harassment in connection with the demand for dowry, have caused a dowry death within the meaning of section 304B, IPC. The said presumption is, however, rebuttable and can be dispelled on the accused being able to demonstrate through cogent evidence that all the ingredients of section 304B, IPC have not been satisfied. [Para 17] - *Parvati Devi* v. *State of Bihar Now State of Jharkhand* AIR 2022 Supreme Court 1268.

Court may presume existence of certain facts.

119. (1) The Court may presume the existence of any fact which it thinks likely to have happened, regard being had to the common course of natural events, human conduct and public and private business, in their relation to the facts of the particular case.

Illustrations

The Court may presume that—

(*a*) a man who is in possession of stolen goods soon, after the theft is either the thief or has received the goods knowing them to be stolen, unless he can account for his possession;

(*b*) an accomplice is unworthy of credit, unless he is corroborated in material particulars;

(*c*) a bill of exchange, accepted or endorsed, was accepted or endorsed for good consideration;

(*d*) a thing or state of things which has been shown to be in existence within a period shorter than that within which such things or state of things usually cease to exist, is still in existence;

(*e*) judicial and official acts have been regularly performed;

(*f*) the common course of business has been followed in particular cases;

(*g*) evidence which could be and is not produced would, if produced, be unfavourable to the person who withholds it;

(*h*) if a man refuses to answer a question which he is not compelled to answer by law, the answer, if given, would be unfavourable to him;

(*i*) when a document creating an obligation is in the hands of the obligor, the obligation has been discharged.

(2) The Court shall also have regard to such facts as the following, in considering whether such maxims do or do not apply to the particular case before it:—

(*i*) as to *Illustration* (*a*)—a shop-keeper has in his bill a marked rupee soon after it was stolen, and cannot account for its possession specifically, but is continually receiving rupees in the course of his business;

(*ii*) as to *Illustration* (*b*)—A, a person of the highest character, is tried for causing a man's death by an act of negligence in arranging certain machinery. B, a person of equally good character, who also took part in the arrangement, describes precisely what was done, and admits and explains the common carelessness of A and himself;

(*iii*) as to *Illustration* (*b*)—A crime is committed by several persons. A, B and C, three of the criminals, are captured on the spot and kept apart from each other. Each gives an account of the crime implicating D, and the accounts corroborate each other in such a manner as to render previous concert highly improbable;

(*iv*) as to *Illustration* (*c*)—A, the drawer of a bill of exchange, was a man of business. B, the acceptor, was a young and ignorant person, completely under A's influence;

(*v*) as to *Illustration* (*d*)—it is proved that a river ran in a certain course five years ago, but it is known that there have been floods since that time which might change its course;

(*vi*) as to *Illustration* (*e*)—a judicial act, the regularity of which is in question, was performed under exceptional circumstances;

(*vii*) as to *Illustration* (*f*)—the question is, whether a letter was received. It is shown to have been posted, but the usual course of the post was interrupted by disturbances;

(*viii*) as to *Illustration* (*g*)—a man refuses to produce a document which would bear on a contract of small importance on which he is sued, but which might also injure the feelings and reputation of his family;

(*ix*) as to *Illustration* (*h*)—a man refuses to answer a question which he is not compelled by law to answer, but the answer to it might cause loss to him in matters unconnected with the matter in relation to which it is asked;

(*x*) as to *Illustration* (*i*)—a bond is in possession of the obligor, but the circumstances of the case are such that he may have stolen it.

***Corresponding Provision* :** Section 114 of Indian Evidence Act, 1872

COMMENTS

Presumption of marriage is to be drawn if a man and a woman live together for many years as husband and wife - It is well settled that if a man and a woman live together for long years as husband and wife, there would be a presumption in favour of wedlock. Such a presumption could be drawn under section 114 of the Evidence Act. Although, the presumption is rebuttable, a heavy burden lies on him who seek to deprive the relationship of legal origin to prove that no marriage took place. [Para 15] - *Kattukandi Edathil Krishnan* v. *Kattukandi Edathil Valsan* AIR 2022 Supreme Court 2841.

Inference is to be drawn from a particular fact, unless and until such inference is disproved by other facts - Courts are authorised to draw a particular inference from a particular fact, unless and until the truth of such inference is disproved by other facts. The court can, under section 4 of the Evidence Act, raise a presumption for purposes of proof of a fact. It is well settled that a presumption is not in itself evidence but only makes a *prima facie* case for a party for whose benefit it exists. As per English Law, there are three categories of presumptions, namely, (*i*) presumptions of fact or natural presumption; (*ii*) presumption of law (rebuttable and irrebuttable); and (*iii*) mixed presumptions *i.e.*, "presumptions of mixed law and fact" or "presumptions of fact recognised by law". The expression "may presume" and "shall presume" in section 4 of the Evidence Act are also categories of presumptions. Factual presumptions or discretionary presumptions come under the division of "may presume" while legal presumptions or compulsory presumptions come under the division of "shall presume".

"May presume" leaves it to the discretion of the court to make the presumption according to the circumstances of the case but "shall presume" leaves no option with the court, and it is bound to presume the fact as proved until evidence is given to disprove it, for instance, the genuineness of a document purporting to be the Gazette of India. The expression "shall presume" is found in sections 79, 80, 81, 83, 85, 89 and 105 of the Evidence Act. [Para 46] - *Neeraj Dutta* v. *State (Govt. of N.C.T. of Delhi)* AIR 2023 Supreme Court 330.

Unless explanation is supported by proof, presumption created by provision cannot be said to be rebutted - A fact is said to be proved when its existence is directly established or when upon the material brought before it, the Court finds its existence to be so probable that a reasonable man would act on the supposition that it exists. Unless, therefore, the explanation is supported by proof, the presumption created by the provision cannot be said to be rebutted.

One of the modes through which a fact can be proved. But, that is not the only mode envisaged under the Evidence Act. Proof of the fact depends upon the degree of probability of it having existed. The standard required for reaching the supposition is that of a prudent man acting in any important matter concerning him.

As opposed to the expressions "may presume" and "shall presume", the expression conclusive proof is also used in section 4 of the Evidence Act. When the law says that a particular kind of evidence would be conclusive, that fact can be proved either by that evidence or by some other evidence that the court permits or requires. When evidence which is made conclusive is adduced, the court has no option but to hold that the fact exists. For instance, the statement in an order of the court is conclusive of what happened before the presiding officer of the court. Thus, conclusive proof gives an artificial probative effect by the law to certain facts. No evidence is allowed to be produced with a view to combat that effect. When a statute makes certain facts final and conclusive, evidence to disprove such facts is not to be allowed. [Paras 51, 52] - *Neeraj Dutta* v. *State (Govt. of N.C.T. of Delhi)* AIR 2023 Supreme Court 330.

Presumption must be drawn considering other evidence on record - A presumption of fact under section 114(*a*), Evidence Act must be drawn considering other evidence on record and without corroboration from other cogent evidence, it must not be drawn in isolation. [Para 36] - *Manoj Kumar Soni* v. *State of Madhya Pradesh* AIR 2023 Supreme Court 3857.

Presumption as to absence of consent in certain prosecution for rape.

120. In a prosecution for rape under sub-section (2) of section 64 of the Bharatiya Nyaya Sanhita, 2023, where sexual intercourse by the accused is proved and the question is whether it was without the consent of the woman alleged to have been raped and such woman states in her evidence before the Court that she did not Consent, the Court shall presume that she did not consent.

Explanation.—In this section, "sexual intercourse" shall mean any of the acts mentioned in section 63 of the Bharatiya Nyaya Sanhita, 2023.

Corresponding Provision **:** Section 114A of Indian Evidence Act, 1872

CHAPTER VIII

ESTOPPEL

Estoppel.

121. When one person has, by his declaration, act or omission, intentionally caused or permitted another person to believe a thing to be true and to act upon such belief, neither he nor his representative shall be allowed, in any suit or proceeding between himself and such person or his representative, to deny the truth of that thing.

Illustration

A intentionally and falsely leads B to believe that certain land belongs to A, and thereby induces B to buy and pay for it. The land afterwards becomes the property of A, and A seeks to set aside the sale on the ground that, at the time of the sale, he had no title. He must not be allowed to prove his want of title.

Corresponding Provision **:** Section 115 of Indian Evidence Act, 1872

Estoppel of tenant and of licensee of person in possession.

122. No tenant of immovable property, or person claiming through such tenant, shall, during the continuance of the tenancy or any time thereafter, be permitted to deny that the landlord of such tenant had, at the beginning of the tenancy, a title to such immovable property; and no person who came upon any immovable property by the licence of the person in possession thereof shall be permitted to deny that such person had a title to such possession at the time when such licence was given.

Corresponding Provision : Section 116 of Indian Evidence Act, 1872

Estoppel of acceptor of bill of exchange, bailee or licensee.

123. No acceptor of a bill of exchange shall be permitted to deny that the drawer had authority to draw such bill or to endorse it; nor shall any bailee or licensee be permitted to deny that his bailor or licensor had, at the time when the bailment or licence commenced, authority to make such bailment or grant such licence.

Explanation 1.—The acceptor of a bill of exchange may deny that the bill was really drawn by the person by whom it purports to have been drawn.

Explanation 2.—If a bailee delivers the goods bailed to a person other than the bailor, he may prove that such person had a right to them as against the bailor.

Corresponding Provision : Section 117 of Indian Evidence Act, 1872

CHAPTER IX

OF WITNESSES

Who may testify.

124. All persons shall be competent to testify unless the Court considers that they are prevented from understanding the questions put to them, or from giving rational answers to those questions, by tender years, extreme old age, disease, whether of body or mind, or any other cause of the same kind.

Explanation.—A person of unsound mind is not incompetent to testify, unless he is prevented by his unsoundness of mind from understanding the questions put to him and giving rational answers to them.

Corresponding Provision **:** Section 118 of Indian Evidence Act, 1872

COMMENTS

A child witness is competent to depose; Trial Judge should ensure that child is able to understand questions and he is not tutored - Under section 118 of the Evidence Act, 1872 a child witness is competent to depose unless the Court considers that he is prevented from understanding the questions put to him, or from giving rational answers by the reason of his tender age. As regards the administration of oath to a child witness, section 4 of the Oaths Act, 1969 (for short "Oaths Act") is relevant. Under the proviso to sub-section (1) of section 4, it is laid down that in case of a child witness under 12 years of age, unless satisfaction as required by the said proviso is recorded, an oath cannot be administered to the child witness. When age of child witness was 12 years at the time of the recording of evidence, the proviso to section 4 of the Oaths Act will not apply in this case. However, in view of the requirement of section 118 of the Evidence Act, the learned Trial Judge was under a duty to record his opinion that the child is able to understand the questions put to him and that he is able to give rational answers to the questions put to him. The Trial Judge must also record his opinion that the child witness understands the duty of speaking the truth and state why he is of the opinion that the child understands the duty of speaking the truth. It is a well-settled principle that corroboration of the testimony of a child witness is not a rule but a measure of caution and prudence. A child witness of tender age is easily susceptible to tutoring. However, that by itself is no ground to reject the evidence of a child witness. The Court must make careful scrutiny of the evidence of a child witness. The Court must apply its mind to the question whether there is a possibility of the child witness being tutored. Therefore, scrutiny of the evidence of a child witness is required to be made by the Court with care and caution. Before recording evidence of a minor, it is the duty of a Judicial Officer to ask preliminary questions to him with a view to ascertain whether the minor can understand the questions put to him and is in a position to give rational answers. The Judge must be satisfied that the minor is able to understand the questions and respond to them and understands the importance of speaking the truth. Therefore, the role of the Judge who records the evidence is very crucial. He has to make a proper preliminary examination of the minor by putting appropriate questions to ascertain whether the minor is capable of understanding the questions put to him and is able to give rational answers. It is advisable to record the preliminary questions and answers so that the Appellate Court can go into the correctness of the opinion of the Trial Court. [Paras 7, 8 and 9] - *Pradeep* v. *State of Haryana* AIR 2023 Supreme Court 3245.

Evidence of rape victim was found credible - Illustration - The prosecutrix has fully supported the case of the prosecution. She has been consistent right from the very beginning. Nothing has been specifically pointed out why the sole testimony of the prosecutrix should not be believed. Even after thorough cross-examination, she has stood by what she has stated and has fully supported the case of the prosecution. There is no reason to doubt the credibility and/or trustworthiness of the prosecutrix. The submission that no other independent witnesses have been examined and/or supported the case of the prosecution and the conviction on the basis of the sole testimony of the prosecutrix cannot be sustained is concerned, the aforesaid has no substance. [Para 5.1] - *Phool Singh* v. *State of Madhya Pradesh* AIR 2022 Supreme Court 222.

Witness unable to communicate verbally.

125. A witness who is unable to speak may give his evidence in any other manner in which he can make it intelligible, as by writing or by signs; but such writing must be written and the signs made in open Court and evidence so given shall be deemed to be oral evidence:

Provided that if the witness is unable to communicate verbally, the Court shall take the assistance of an interpreter or a special educator in recording the statement, and such statement shall be videographed.

Corresponding Provision : Section 119 of Indian Evidence Act, 1872

Competency of husband and wife as witnesses in certain cases.

126. (1) In all civil proceedings the parties to the suit, and the husband or wife of any party to the suit, shall be competent witnesses.

(2) In criminal proceedings against any person, the husband or wife of such person, respectively, shall be a competent witness.

Corresponding Provision : Section 120 of Indian Evidence Act, 1872

Judges and Magistrates.

127. No Judge or Magistrate shall, except upon the special order of some Court to which he is subordinate, be compelled to answer any question as to his own conduct in Court as such Judge or Magistrate, or as to anything which came to his knowledge in Court as such Judge or Magistrate; but he may be examined as to other matters which occurred in his presence whilst he was so acting.

Illustrations

(*a*) A, on his trial before the Court of Session, says that a deposition was improperly taken by B, the Magistrate. B cannot be compelled to answer questions as to this, except upon the special order of a superior Court.

(*b*) A is accused before the Court of Session of having given false evidence before B, a Magistrate. B cannot be asked what A said, except upon the special order of the superior Court.

(*c*) A is accused before the Court of Session of attempting to murder a police officer whilst on his trial before B, a Sessions Judge. B may be examined as to what occurred.

Corresponding Provision : Section 121 of Indian Evidence Act, 1872

Communications during marriage.

128. No person who is or has been married, shall be compelled to disclose any communication made to him during marriage by any person to whom he is or has been married; nor shall he be permitted to disclose any such communication, unless the person who made it, or his representative in interest, consents, except in suits between married persons, or proceedings in which one married person is prosecuted for any crime committed against the other.

Corresponding Provision **:** Section 122 of Indian Evidence Act, 1872

Evidence as to affairs of State.

129. No one shall be permitted to give any evidence derived from unpublished official records relating to any affairs of State, except with the permission of the officer at the head of the department concerned, who shall give or withhold such permission as he thinks fit.

Corresponding Provision **:** Section 123 of Indian Evidence Act, 1872

Official communications.

130. No public officer shall be compelled to disclose communications made to him in official confidence, when he considers that the public interests would suffer by the disclosure.

Corresponding Provision **:** Section 124 of Indian Evidence Act, 1872

Information as to commission of offences.

131. No Magistrate or police officer shall be compelled to say when he got any information as to the commission of any offence, and no revenue officer shall be compelled to say when he got any information as to the commission of any offence against the public revenue.

Explanation.—"revenue officer" means any officer employed in or about the business of any branch of the public revenue.

Corresponding Provision **:** Section 125 of Indian Evidence Act, 1872

Professional Communications.

132. (1) No advocate, shall at any time be permitted, unless with his client's express consent, to disclose any communication made to him in the course and for the purpose of his service as such advocate, by or on behalf of his client, or to state the contents or condition of any document with which he has become acquainted in the course and for the purpose of his professional service, or to disclose any advice given by him to his client in the course and for the purpose of such service:

Provided that nothing in this section shall protect from disclosure of—

(*a*) any such communication made in furtherance of any illegal purpose;

(*b*) any fact observed by any advocate, in the course of his service as such, showing that any crime or fraud has been committed since the commencement of his service.

Corresponding Provision **:** Section 126 of Indian Evidence Act, 1872

(2) It is immaterial whether the attention of such advocate referred to in the proviso to sub-section (1), was or was not directed to such fact by or on behalf of his client.

Explanation.—The obligation stated in this section continues after the professional service has ceased.

Illustrations

(*a*) A, a client, says to B, an advocate—"I have committed forgery, and I wish you to defend me". As the defence of a man known to be guilty is not a criminal purpose, this communication is protected from disclosure.

(*b*) A, a client, says to B, an advocate—"I wish to obtain possession of property by the use of a forged deed on which I request you to sue". This communication, being made in furtherance of a criminal purpose, is not protected from disclosure.

(*c*) A, being charged with embezzlement, retains B, an advocate, to defend him. In the course of the proceedings, B observes that an entry has been made in A's account book, charging A with the sum said to have been embezzled, which entry was not in the book at the commencement of his professional service. This being a fact observed by B in the course of his service, showing that a fraud has been committed since the commencement of the proceedings, it is not protected from disclosure.

Corresponding Provision **:** Section 126 of Indian Evidence Act, 1872

(3) The provisions of this section shall apply to interpreters, and the clerks or employees of advocates.

Corresponding Provision **:** Section 127 of Indian Evidence Act, 1872

Privilege not waived by volunteering evidence.

133. If any party to a suit gives evidence therein at his own instance or otherwise, he shall not be deemed to have consented thereby to such disclosure as is mentioned in section 132; and, if any party to a suit or proceeding calls any such advocate, as a witness, he shall be deemed to have consented to such disclosure only if he questions such advocate, on matters which, but for such question, he would not be at liberty to disclose.

Corresponding Provision **:** Section 128 of Indian Evidence Act, 1872

Confidential communication with legal advisers.

134. No one shall be compelled to disclose to the Court any confidential communication which has taken place between him and his legal adviser, unless he offers himself as a witness, in which case he may be compelled to disclose any such communications as may appear to the Court necessary to be known in order to explain any evidence which he has given, but no others.

Corresponding Provision **:** Section 129 of Indian Evidence Act, 1872

Production of title-deeds of witness not a party.

135. No witness who is not a party to a suit shall be compelled to produce his title-deeds to any property, or any document in virtue of which he holds any property as pledgee or mortgagee or any document the production of which might tend to criminate him, unless he has agreed in writing to produce them with the person seeking the production of such deeds or some person through whom he claims.

Corresponding Provision **:** Section 130 of Indian Evidence Act, 1872

Production of documents or electronic records which another person, having possession, could refuse to produce.

136. No one shall be compelled to produce documents in his possession or electronic records under his control, which any other person would be entitled to refuse to produce if they were in his possession or control, unless such last-mentioned person consents to their production.

Corresponding Provision **:** Section 131 of Indian Evidence Act, 1872

Witness not excused from answering on ground that answer will criminate.

137. A witness shall not be excused from answering any question as to any matter relevant to the matter in issue in any suit or in any civil or criminal proceeding, upon the ground that the answer to such question will criminate, or may tend directly or indirectly to criminate, such witness, or that it will expose, or tend directly or indirectly to expose, such witness to a penalty or forfeiture of any kind:

Provided that no such answer, which a witness shall be compelled to give, shall subject him to any arrest or prosecution, or be proved against him in any criminal proceeding, except a prosecution forgiving false evidence by such answer.

Corresponding Provision **:** Section 132 of Indian Evidence Act, 1872

Accomplice.

138. An accomplice shall be a competent witness against an accused person; and a conviction is not illegal if it proceeds upon the corroborated testimony of an accomplice.

Corresponding Provision **:** Section 133 of Indian Evidence Act, 1872

Number of witnesses.

139. No particular number of witnesses shall in any case be required for the proof of any fact.

Corresponding Provision **:** Section 134 of Indian Evidence Act, 1872

COMMENTS

It is not necessary to insist upon a plurality of witnesses; evidence of a single reliable witness could lead to a conviction - Section 134 of Indian Evidence Act, 1872, enshrines the well-recognized maxim that evidence has to be weighed and not counted. In other words, it is the quality of evidence that matters and not the quantity. As a sequitur, even in a case of murder, it is not necessary to insist upon a plurality of witnesses and the oral evidence of a single witness, if found to be reliable and trustworthy, could lead to a conviction. [Para 28] - *Munna Lal* v. *State of Uttar Pradesh* AIR 2023 Supreme Court 634.

CHAPTER X

OF EXAMINATION OF WITNESSES

Order of production and examination of witnesses.

140. The order in which witnesses are produced and examined shall be regulated by the law and practice for the time being relating to civil and criminal procedure respectively, and, in the absence of any such law, by the discretion of the Court.

Corresponding Provision **:** Section 135 of Indian Evidence Act, 1872

Judge to decide as to admissibility of evidence.

141. (1) When either party proposes to give evidence of any fact, the Judge may ask the party proposing to give the evidence in what manner the alleged fact, if proved, would be relevant; and the Judge shall admit the evidence if he thinks that the fact, if proved, would be relevant, and not otherwise.

(2) If the fact proposed to be proved is one of which evidence is admissible only upon proof of some other fact, such last mentioned fact must be proved before evidence is given of the fact first mentioned, unless the party undertakes to give proof of such fact, and the Court is satisfied with such undertaking.

(3) If the relevancy of one alleged fact depends upon another alleged fact being first proved, the Judge may, in his discretion, either permit evidence of the first fact to be given before the second fact is proved, or require evidence to be given of the second fact before evidence is given of the first fact.

Illustrations

(*a*) It is proposed to prove a statement about a relevant fact by a person alleged to be dead, which statement is relevant under section 26. The fact that the person is dead must be proved by the person proposing to prove the statement, before evidence is given of the statement.

(*b*) It is proposed to prove, by a copy, the contents of a document said to be lost. The fact that the original is lost must be proved by the person proposing to produce the copy, before the copy is produced.

(*c*) A is accused of receiving stolen property knowing it to have been stolen. It is proposed to prove that he denied the possession of the property. The relevancy of the denial depends on the identity of the property. The Court may, in its discretion, either require the property to be identified before the denial of the possession is proved, or permit the denial of the possession to be proved before the property is identified.

(*d*) It is proposed to prove a fact A which is said to have been the cause or effect of a fact in issue. There are several intermediate facts B, C and D which must be shown to exist before the fact A can be regarded as the cause or effect of the fact in issue. The Court may either permit A to be proved before B, C or D is proved, or may require proof of B, C and D before permitting proof of A.

Corresponding Provision : Section 136 of Indian Evidence Act, 1872

COMMENTS

In assessing eye witness, possibility of their presence at spot and reliability of their evidence are to be established - When the evidence of an injured eye-witness is to be appreciated, the under-noted legal principles enunciated by the Courts are required to be kept in mind : (*a*) The presence of an injured eye-witness at the time and place of the occurrence cannot be doubted unless there are material contradictions in his deposition. (*b*) Unless, it is otherwise established by the evidence, it must be believed that an injured witness would not allow the real culprits to escape and falsely implicate the accused. (*c*) The evidence of injured witness has greater evidentiary value and unless compelling reasons exist, their statements are not to be discarded lightly. (*d*) The evidence of injured witness cannot be doubted on account of some embellishment in natural conduct or minor contradictions. (*e*) If there be any exaggeration or immaterial embellishments in the evidence of an injured witness, then such contradiction, exaggeration or embellishment should be discarded from the evidence of injured, but not the whole evidence. (*f*) The broad substratum of the prosecution version must be taken into consideration and discrepancies which normally creep due to loss of memory with passage of time should be discarded.

In assessing the value of the evidence of the eye witnesses, two principal considerations are whether, in the circumstances of the case, it is possible to believe their presence at the scene of occurrence or in such situations as would make it possible for them to witness the facts deposed to by them and secondly, whether there is anything inherently improbable or unreliable in their evidence. In respect of both these considerations, circumstances either elicited from those witnesses themselves or established by other evidence tending to improbabilise their presence or to discredit the veracity of their statements, will have a bearing upon the value which a Court would attach to their evidence. Although in cases where the plea of the accused is a mere denial, the evidence of the prosecution witnesses has to be examined on its own merits, where the accused raise a definite plea or put forward a positive case which is inconsistent with that of the prosecution, the nature of such plea or case and the probabilities in respect of it will also have to be taken into account while assessing the value of the prosecution evidence. [Paras 26, 27] - *Balu Sudam Khalde* v. *State of Maharashtra* AIR 2023 Supreme Court 1736.

Minor contradictions cannot be a ground to discredit testimony of witnesses - While appreciating the evidence in a criminal trial, only contradictions in material particulars and not minor contradictions can be a ground to discredit the testimony of the witnesses. [Para 17] - *Anuj Singh Alias Ramanuj Singh Alias Seth Singh* v. *State of Bihar* AIR 2022 Supreme Court 2817.

Examination of witnesses.

142. (1) The examination of a witness by the party who calls him shall be called his examination-in-chief.

(2) The examination of a witness by the adverse party shall be called his cross-examination.

(3) The examination of a witness, subsequent to the cross-examination, by the party who called him, shall be called his re-examination.

***Corresponding Provision* :** Section 137 of Indian Evidence Act, 1872

COMMENTS

Answer to suggestion hurled on witness during cross-examination, if incriminates accused, would be binding - During the course of cross-examination with a view to discredit the witness or to establish the defence on preponderance of probabilities suggestions are hurled on the witness but if such suggestions, the answer to those incriminate the accused in any manner then the same would definitely be binding and could be taken into consideration along with other evidence on record in support of the same. However, it would all depend upon the nature of the suggestions and with what idea in mind such suggestions are made to the witness. [Paras 44, 45] - *Balu Sudam Khalde* v. *State of Maharashtra* AIR 2023 Supreme Court 1736.

Suggestions made to witness by defence counsel and reply to such suggestions would definitely form part of evidence and can be relied upon by Court - The suggestion made by the defence counsel to a witness in the cross-examination if found to be incriminating in nature in any manner would definitely bind the accused and the accused cannot get away on the pica that his counsel had no implied authority to make suggestions in the nature of admissions against his client.

Any concession or admission of a fact by a defence counsel would definitely be binding on his client, except the concession on the point of law. As a legal proposition we cannot agree with the submission canvassed on behalf of the appellants that an answer by a witness to a suggestion made by the defence counsel in the cross-examination docs not deserve any value or utility if it incriminates the accused in any manner.

It is a cardinal principle of criminal jurisprudence that the initial burden to establish the case against the accused beyond reasonable doubt rests on the prosecution. It is also an elementary principle of law that the prosecution has to prove its case on its own legs and cannot derive advantage or benefit from the weakness of the defence.

Suggestions by itself are not sufficient to hold the accused guilty if they are incriminating in any manner or are in the form of admission in the absence of any other reliable evidence on record. It is true that a suggestion has no evidentiary value but this proposition of law would not hold good at all times and in a given case during the course of cross-examination the defence counsel may put such a suggestion the answer to which may directly go against the accused.

The principle of law that in a criminal case, a lawyer has no implied authority to make admissions against his client during the progress of the trial, would hold good only in cases where dispensation of proof by the prosecution is not permissible in law.

Suggestions made to the witness by the defence counsel and the reply to such suggestions would definitely form part of the evidence and can be relied upon by the Court along with other evidence on record to determine the guilt of the accused.

The main object of cross-examination is to find out the truth on record and to help the Court in knowing the truth of the case. It is a matter of common experience that many a times the defence lawyers themselves get the discrepancies clarified arising during the cross-examination in one paragraph and getting themselves contradicted in the other paragraph. The line of cross-examination is always on the basis of the defence which the counsel would keep in mind to defend the accused. [Paras 38 to 43] - *Balu Sudam Khalde* v. *State of Maharashtra* AIR 2023 Supreme Court 1736.

Order of examinations.

143. (1) Witnesses shall be first examined-in-chief, then (if the adverse party so desires) cross-examined, then (if the party calling him so desires) re-examined.

(2) The examination-in-chief and cross-examination must relate to relevant facts, but the cross-examination need not be confined to the facts to which the witness testified on his examination-in-chief.

(3) The re-examination shall be directed to the explanation of matters referred to in cross-examination; and, if new matter is, by permission of the Court, introduced in re-examination, the adverse party may further cross-examine upon that matter.

Corresponding Provision **:** Section 138 of Indian Evidence Act, 1872

Cross-examination of person called to produce a document.

144. A person summoned to produce a document does not become a witness by the mere fact that he produces it, and cannot be cross-examined unless and until he is called as a witness.

Corresponding Provision **:** Section 139 of Indian Evidence Act, 1872

Witnesses to character.

145. Witnesses to character may be cross-examined and re-examined.

Corresponding Provision **:** Section 140 of Indian Evidence Act, 1872

Leading questions.

146. (1) Any question suggesting the answer which the person putting it wishes or expects to receive, is called a leading question.

Corresponding Provision **:** Section 141 of Indian Evidence Act, 1872

(2) Leading questions must not, if objected to by the adverse party, be asked in an examination-in-chief, or in a re-examination, except with the permission of the Court.

Corresponding Provision **:** Section 142 of Indian Evidence Act, 1872

(3) The Court shall permit leading questions as to matters which are introductory or undisputed, or which have, in its opinion, been already sufficiently proved.

Corresponding Provision **:** Section 142 of Indian Evidence Act, 1872

(4) Leading questions may be asked in cross-examination.

Corresponding Provision **:** Section 143 of Indian Evidence Act, 1872

Evidence as to matters in writing.

147. Any witness may be asked, while under examination, whether any, contract grant or other disposition of property, as to which he is giving evidence, was not contained in a document, and if he says that it was, or if he is about to make any statement as to the contents of any document, which, in the opinion of the Court, ought to be produced, the adverse party may object to such evidence being given until such document is produced, or until facts have been proved which entitle the party who called the witness to give secondary evidence of it.

Explanation.—A witness may give oral evidence of statements made by other persons about the contents of documents if such statements are in themselves relevant facts.

Illustration

The question is, whether A assaulted B. C deposes that he heard A say to D—"B wrote a letter accusing me of theft, and I will be revenged on him". This statement is relevant, as showing A's motive for the assault, and evidence may be given of it, though no other evidence is given about the letter.

Corresponding Provision **:** Section 144 of Indian Evidence Act, 1872

Cross-examination as to previous statements in writing.

148. A witness may be cross-examined as to previous statements made by him in writing or reduced into writing, and relevant to matters in question, without such writing being shown to him, or being proved; but, if it is intended to contradict him by the writing, his attention must, before the writing can be proved, be called to those parts of it which are to be used for the purpose of contradicting him.

Corresponding Provision **:** Section 145 of Indian Evidence Act, 1872

Questions lawful in cross-examination.

149. When a witness is cross-examined, he may, in addition to the questions hereinbefore referred to, be asked any questions which tend—

(*a*) to test his veracity; or

(*b*) to discover who he is and what is his position in life; or

(*c*) to shake his credit, by injuring his character, although the answer to such questions might tend directly or indirectly to criminate him, or might expose or tend directly or indirectly to expose him to a penalty or forfeiture:

Provided that in a prosecution for an offence under section 64, section 65, section 66, section 67, section 68, section 69, section 70 or section 71 of the Bharatiya Nyaya Sanhita, 2023 or for attempt to commit any such offence, where the question of consent is an issue, it shall not be permissible to adduce evidence or to put questions in the cross-examination of the victim as to the general immoral character, or previous sexual experience, of such victim with any person for proving such consent or the quality of consent.

Corresponding Provision **:** Section 146 of Indian Evidence Act, 1872

When witness to be compelled to answer.

150. If any such question relates to a matter relevant to the suit or proceeding, the provisions of section 137 shall apply thereto.

Corresponding Provision **:** Section 147 of Indian Evidence Act, 1872

Court to decide when question shall be asked and when witness compelled to answer.

151. (1) If any such question relates to a matter not relevant to the suit or proceeding, except in so far as it affects the credit of the witness by injuring his character, the Court shall decide whether or not the witness shall be compelled to answer it, and may, if it thinks fit, warn the witness that he is not obliged to answer it.

(2) In exercising its discretion, the Court shall have regard to the following considerations, namely:—

(*a*) such questions are proper if they are of such a nature that the truth of the imputation conveyed by them would seriously affect the opinion of the Court as to the credibility of the witness on the matter to which he testifies;

(*b*) such questions are improper if the imputation which they convey relates to matters so remote in time, or of such a character, that the truth of the imputation would not affect, or would affect in a slight degree, the opinion of the Court as to the credibility of the witness on the matter to which he testifies;

(*c*) such questions are improper if there is a great disproportion between the importance of the imputation made against the witness's character and the importance of his evidence;

(*d*) the Court may, if it sees fit, draw, from the witness's refusal to answer, the inference that the answer if given would be unfavourable.

Corresponding Provision **:** Section 148 of Indian Evidence Act, 1872

Question not to be asked without reasonable grounds.

152. No such question as is referred to in section 151 ought to be asked, unless the person asking it has reasonable grounds for thinking that the imputation which it conveys is well-founded.

Illustrations

(*a*) An advocate is instructed by another advocate that an important witness is a dacoit. This is a reasonable ground for asking the witness whether he is a dacoit.

(*b*) An advocate is informed by a person in Court that an important witness is a dacoit. The informant, on being questioned by the advocate, gives satisfactory reasons for his statement. This is a reasonable ground for asking the witness whether he is a dacoit.

(*c*) A witness, of whom nothing whatever is known, is asked at random whether he is a dacoit. There are here no reasonable grounds for the question.

(*d*) A witness, of whom nothing whatever is known, being questioned as to his mode of life and means of living, gives unsatisfactory answers. This may be a reasonable ground for asking him if he is a dacoit.

Corresponding Provision **:** Section 149 of Indian Evidence Act, 1872

Procedure of Court in case of question being asked without reasonable grounds.

153. If the Court is of opinion that any such question was asked without reasonable grounds, it may, if it was asked by any advocate, report the circumstances of the case to the High Court or other authority to which such advocate is subject in the exercise of his profession.

Corresponding Provision : Section 150 of Indian Evidence Act, 1872

Indecent and scandalous questions.

154. The Court may forbid any questions or inquiries which it regards as indecent or scandalous, although such questions or inquiries may have some bearing on the questions before the Court, unless they relate to facts in issue, or to matters necessary to be known in order to determine whether or not the facts in issue existed.

Corresponding Provision : Section 151 of Indian Evidence Act, 1872

Questions intended to insult or annoy.

155. The Court shall forbid any question which appears to it to be intended to insult or annoy, or which, though proper in itself, appears to the Court needlessly offensive in form.

Corresponding Provision : Section 152 of Indian Evidence Act, 1872

Exclusion of evidence to contradict answers to questions testing veracity.

156. When a witness has been asked and has answered any question which is relevant to the inquiry only in so far as it tends to shake his credit by injuring his character, no evidence shall be given to contradict him; but, if he answers falsely, he may afterwards be charged with giving false evidence.

Exception 1.—If a witness is asked whether he has been previously convicted of any crime and denies it, evidence may be given of his previous conviction.

Exception 2.—If a witness is asked any question tending to impeach his impartiality, and answers it by denying the facts suggested, he may be contradicted.

Illustrations

(*a*) A claim against an underwriter is resisted on the ground of fraud. The claimant is asked whether, in a former transaction, he had not made a fraudulent claim. He denies it. Evidence is offered to show that he did make such a claim. The evidence is inadmissible.

(*b*) A witness is asked whether he was not dismissed from a situation for dishonesty. He denies it. Evidence is offered to show that he was dismissed for dishonesty. The evidence is not admissible.

(*c*) A affirms that on a certain day he saw B at Goa. A is asked whether he himself was not on that day at Varanasi. He denies it. Evidence is offered to show that A was on that day at Varanasi. The evidence is admissible, not as contradicting A on a fact which affects his credit, but as contradicting the alleged fact that B was seen on the day in question in Goa. In each of these cases, the witness might, if his denial was false, be charged with giving false evidence.

(*d*) A is asked whether his family has not had a blood feud with the family of B against whom he gives evidence. He denies it. He may be contradicted on the ground that the question tends to impeach his impartiality.

***Corresponding Provision* :** Section 153 of Indian Evidence Act, 1872

Question by party to his own witness.

157. (1) The Court may, in its discretion, permit the person who calls a witness to put any question to him which might be put in cross-examination by the adverse party.

(2) Nothing in this section shall disentitle the person so permitted under sub-section (1), to rely on any part of the evidence of such witness.

***Corresponding Provision* :** Section 154 of Indian Evidence Act, 1872

COMMENTS

Even if a witness is treated as "hostile" and is cross-examined, his evidence cannot be written off altogether - Even if a witness is treated as "hostile" and is cross-examined, his evidence cannot be written off altogether but must be considered with due care and circumspection and that part of the testimony which is creditworthy must be considered and acted upon. It is for the judge as a matter of prudence to consider the extent of evidence which is creditworthy for the purpose of proof of the case. In other words, the fact that a witness has been declared "hostile" does not result in an automatic rejection of his evidence. Even, the evidence of a "hostile witness" if it finds corroboration from the facts of the case may be taken into account while judging the guilt of the accused. Thus, there is no legal bar to raise a conviction upon a "hostile witness" testimony if corroborated by other reliable evidence. [Para 67] - *Neeraj Dutta* v. *State (Govt. of N.C.T. of Delhi)* AIR 2023 Supreme Court 330.

Impeaching credit of witness.

158. The credit of a witness may be impeached in the following ways by the adverse party, or, with the consent of the Court, by the party who calls him—

(*a*) by the evidence of persons who testify that they, from their knowledge of the witness, believe him to be unworthy of credit;

(*b*) by proof that the witness has been bribed, or has accepted the offer of a bribe, or has received any other corrupt inducement to give his evidence;

(*c*) by proof of former statements inconsistent with any part of his evidence which is liable to be contradicted.

Explanation.—A witness declaring another witness to be unworthy of credit may not, upon his examination-in-chief, give reasons for his belief, but he may be asked his reasons in cross-examination, and the answers which he gives cannot be contradicted, though, if they are false, he may afterwards be charged with giving false evidence.

Illustrations

(*a*) A sues B for the price of goods sold and delivered to B. C says that he delivered the goods to B. Evidence is offered to show that, on a previous occasion, he said that he had not delivered goods to B. The evidence is admissible.

(*b*) A is accused of the murder of B. C says that B, when dying, declared that A had given B the wound of which he died. Evidence is offered to show that, on a previous occasion, C said that B, when dying, did not declare that A had given B the wound of which he died. The evidence is admissible.

Corresponding Provision : Section 155 of Indian Evidence Act, 1872

COMMENTS

Discrepancies in witness story due to lapse of time is minor - Discrepancies do creep in, when a witness deposes in a natural manner after lapse of some time, and if such discrepancies are comparatively of a minor nature and do not go to the root of the prosecution story, then the same may not be given undue importance. [Para 28] - *Munna Lal* v. *State of Uttar Pradesh* AIR 2023 Supreme Court 634.

Non-examination of investigating Officer is prejudicial but not fatal - Non-examination of the Investigating Officer must result in prejudice to the accused; if no prejudice is caused, mere non-examination would not render the prosecution case fatal. [Para 28] - *Munna Lal* v. *State of Uttar Pradesh* AIR 2023 Supreme Court 634.

Questions tending to corroborate evidence of relevant fact, admissible.

159. When a witness whom it is intended to corroborate gives evidence of any relevant fact, he may be questioned as to any other circumstances which he observed at or near to the time or place at which such relevant fact occurred, if the Court is of opinion that such circumstances, if proved, would corroborate the testimony of the witness as to the relevant fact which he testifies.

Illustration

A, an accomplice, gives an account of a robbery in which he took part. He describes various incidents unconnected with the robbery which occurred on his way to and from the place where it was committed. Independent evidence of these facts may be given in order to corroborate his evidence as to the robbery itself.

Corresponding Provision **:** Section 156 of Indian Evidence Act, 1872

Former statements of witness may be proved to corroborate later testimony as to same fact.

160. In order to corroborate the testimony of a witness, any former statement made by such witness relating to the same fact, at or about the time when the fact took place, or before any authority legally competent to investigate the fact, may be proved.

Corresponding Provision **:** Section 157 of Indian Evidence Act, 1872

What matters may be proved in connection with proved statement relevant under section 26 or 27.

161. Whenever any statement, relevant under section 26 or 27, is proved, all matters may be proved either in order to contradict or to corroborate it, or in order to impeach or confirm the credit of the person by whom it was made, which might have been proved if that person had been called as a witness and had denied upon cross-examination the truth of the matter suggested.

Corresponding Provision **:** Section 158 of Indian Evidence Act, 1872

Refreshing memory.

162. (1) A witness may, while under examination, refresh his memory by referring to any writing made by himself at the time of the transaction concerning which he is questioned, or so soon afterwards that the Court considers it likely that the transaction was at that time fresh in his memory:

Provided that the witness may also refer to any such writing made by any other person, and read by the witness within the time aforesaid, if when he read it, he knew it to be correct.

(2) Whenever a witness may refresh his memory by reference to any document, he may, with the permission of the Court, refer to a copy of such document:

Provided that the Court be satisfied that there is sufficient reason for the non-production of the original:

Provided further that an expert may refresh his memory by reference to professional treatises.

Corresponding Provision **:** Section 159 of Indian Evidence Act, 1872

Testimony to facts stated in document mentioned in section 162.

163. A witness may also testify to facts mentioned in any such document as is mentioned in section 162, although he has no specific recollection of the facts themselves, if he is sure that the facts were correctly recorded in the document.

Illustration

A book-keeper may testify to facts recorded by him in books regularly kept in the course of business, if he knows that the books were correctly kept, although he has forgotten the particular transactions entered.

Corresponding Provision **:** Section 160 of Indian Evidence Act, 1872

Right of adverse party as to writing used to refresh memory.

164. Any writing referred to under the provisions of the two last preceding sections shall be produced and shown to the adverse party if he requires it; such party may, if he pleases, cross-examine the witness thereupon.

Corresponding Provision **:** Section 161 of Indian Evidence Act, 1872

Production of documents.

165. (1) A witness summoned to produce a document shall, if it is in his possession or power, bring it to Court, notwithstanding any objection which there may be to its production or to its admissibility:

Provided that the validity of any such objection shall be decided on by the Court.

(2) The Court, if it sees fit, may inspect the document, unless it refers to matters of State, or take other evidence to enable it to determine on its admissibility.

(3) If for such a purpose it is necessary to cause any document to be translated, the Court may, if it thinks fit, direct the translator to keep the contents secret, unless the document is to be given in evidence and, if the interpreter disobeys such direction, he shall be held to have committed an offence under section 198 of the Bharatiya Nyaya Sanhita, 2023:

Provided that no Court shall require any communication between the Ministers and the President of India to be produced before it.

Corresponding Provision **:** Section 162 of Indian Evidence Act, 1872

Giving, as evidence, of document called for and produced on notice.

166. When a party calls for a document which he has given the other party notice to produce, and such document is produced and inspected by the party calling for its production, he is bound to give it as evidence if the party producing it requires him to do so.

Corresponding Provision **:** Section 163 of Indian Evidence Act, 1872

Using, as evidence, of document production of which was refused on notice.

167. When a party refuses to produce a document which he has had notice to produce, he cannot afterwards use the document as evidence without the consent of the other party or the order of the Court.

Illustration

A sues B on an agreement and gives B notice to produce it. At the trial, A calls for the document and B refuses to produce it. A gives secondary evidence of its contents. B seeks to produce the document itself to contradict the secondary evidence given by A, or in order to show that the agreement is not stamped. He cannot do so.

Corresponding Provision **:** Section 164 of Indian Evidence Act, 1872

Judge's power to put questions or order production.

168. The Judge may, in order to discover or obtain proof of relevant facts, ask any question he considers necessary, in any form, at any time, of any witness, or of the parties about any fact; and may order the production of any document or thing; and neither the parties nor their representatives shall be entitled to make any objection to any such question or order, nor, without the leave of the Court, to cross-examine any witness upon any answer given in reply to any such question:

Provided that the judgment must be based upon facts declared by this Adhiniyam to be relevant, and duly proved:

Provided further that this section shall not authorise any Judge to compel any witness to answer any question, or to produce any document which such witness would be entitled to refuse to answer or produce under sections 127 to 136, both inclusive, if the question were asked or the document were called for by the adverse party; nor shall the Judge ask any question which it would be improper for any other person to ask under section 151 or 152; nor shall he dispense with primary evidence of any document, except in the cases hereinbefore excepted.

Corresponding Provision **:** Section 165 of Indian Evidence Act, 1872

COMMENTS

Trial judge has to participate in trial in order to ascertain truth - Under Section 165 of the Evidence Act, a trial judge has tremendous powers to "ask any question he pleases, in any form, at any time, of any witness, or of the parties about any fact relevant or irrelevant". It is in fact the duty of the Trial Judge to do so if it is felt that some important and crucial question was left from being asked from a witness. The duty of the presiding judge of a criminal trial is not to watch the proceedings as a spectator or a recording machine but he has to participate in the trial by evincing intelligent active interest by putting questions to witnesses in order to ascertain the truth. [Para 11] - *Dinesh Kumar* v. *State of Haryana* AIR 2023 Supreme Court 2795.

CHAPTER XI

OF IMPROPER ADMISSION AND REJECTION OF EVIDENCE

No new trial for improper admission or rejection of evidence.

169. The improper admission or rejection of evidence shall not be ground of itself for a new trial or reversal of any decision in any case, if it shall appear to the Court before which such objection is raised that, independently of the evidence objected to and admitted, there was sufficient evidence to justify the decision, or that, if the rejected evidence had been received, it ought not to have varied the decision.

Corresponding Provision : Section 167 of Indian Evidence Act, 1872

CHAPTER XII

REPEAL AND SAVINGS

Repeal and savings.

170. (1) The Indian Evidence Act, 1872 (1 of 1872) is hereby repealed.

(2) Notwithstanding such repeal, if, immediately before the date on which this Adhiniyam comes into force, there is any application, trial, inquiry, investigation, proceeding or appeal pending, then, such application, trial, inquiry, investigation, proceeding or appeal shall be dealt with under the

provisions of the Indian Evidence Act, 1872 (1 of 1872), as in force immediately before such commencement, as if this Adhiniyam had not come into force.

Corresponding Provision **:** Section 2 of Indian Evidence Act, 1872

SCHEDULE

[*See* section 63(4)(*c*)]

CERTIFICATE

PART A

(To be filled by the Party)

I, ________________(name), son/daughter/spouse of ______________ residing/employed at ____________ ____________________________ do hereby solemnly affirm and sincerely state and submit as follows:—

I have produced electronic record/output of the digital record taken from the following device/digital record source (tick mark):—

Computer/Storage Media	☐	DVR	☐	Mobile	☐
Flash Drive	☐	CD/DVD	☐	Server	☐
Cloud	☐	Other	☐		

Other:______________________________

Make & Model: __________ Colour: ____________

Serial Number: ______________

IMEI/UIN/UID/MAC/CloudID______________(as applicable) and any other relevant information, if any, about the device/digital record ____________________ _________(specify).

The digital device or the digital record source was under the lawful control for regularly creating, storing or processing information for the purposes of carrying out regular activities and during this period, the computer or the communication device was working properly and the relevant information was regularly fed into the computer during the ordinary course of business. If the computer/digital device at any point of time was not working properly or out of operation, then it has not affected the electronic/digital record or its accuracy. The digital device or the source of the digital record is:—

Owned ☐ Maintained ☐

Managed ☐ Operated ☐

by me (select as applicable).

I state that the HASH value/s of the electronic/digital record/s is______________, obtained through the following algorithm:—

☐ SHA1:

☐ SHA256:

☐ MD5:

☐ Other__________(Legally acceptable standard)

(Hash report to be enclosed with the certificate)

(Name and signature)

Date (DD/MM/YYYY):______

Time (IST):__________hours (In 24 hours format)

Place:________________

PART B

(To be filled by the Expert)

I, ________________ (Name), son/daughter/spouse of _______________________ residing/employed at _________________________ do hereby solemnly affirm and sincerely state and submit as follows:—

The produced electronic record/output of the digital record are obtained from the following device/digital record source (tick mark):—

Computer/Storage Media	☐	DVR	☐	Mobile	☐
Flash Drive	☐	CD/DVD	☐	Server	☐
Cloud	☐	Other	☐		

Other: ____________________________________

Make & Model: __________ Colour: ______________

Serial Number: ______________

IMEI/UIN/UID/MAC/CloudID____________________(as applicable) and any other relevant information, if any, about the device/digital record ____ ____________(specify).

I state that the HASH value/s of the electronic/digital record/s is______________, obtained through the following algorithm:—

☐ SHA1:

☐ SHA256:

☐ MD5:

☐ Other__________(Legally acceptable standard)

(Hash report to be enclosed with the certificate)

(Name, designation and signature)

Date (DD/MM/YYYY):________

Time (IST):__________hours (In 24 hours format)

Place:__________________

STATEMENT OF OBJECTS AND REASONS

The Indian Evidence Act, 1872 was enacted in the year 1872 with a view to consolidate the law relating to evidence on which the Court could come to the conclusion about the facts of the case and then pronounce judgment thereupon and it came into force on 1st September, 1872.

2. The experience of seven decades of Indian democracy calls for comprehensive review of our criminal laws including the Indian Evidence Act, 1872 and adopt them in accordance with the contemporary needs and aspirations of the people. The law of evidence (not being substantive or procedural law), falls in the category of "adjective law", that defines the pleading and methodology by which the substantive or procedural laws are operationalised. The existing law does not address the technological advancement undergone in the country during the last few decades.

3. Accordingly, a Bill, namely, the Bharatiya Sakshya Bill, 2023 was introduced in Lok Sabha on 11th August, 2023. The Bill was referred to the Department-related Parliamentary Standing Committee on Home Affairs for its consideration and report. The Committee after deliberations made its recommendations in its report submitted on 10th November, 2023. The recommendations made by the Committee have been considered by the Government and it has been decided to withdraw the Bill pending in Lok Sabha and introduce a new Bill incorporating therein those recommendations made by the Committee that have been accepted by the Government.

4. The proposed legislation, *inter alia,* provides as under:—

(*i*) it provides that "evidence" includes any information given electronically, which would permit appearance of witnesses, accused, experts and victims through electronic means;

(*ii*) it provides for admissibility of an electronic or digital record as evidence having the same legal effect, validity and enforceability as any other document;

(*iii*) it seeks to expand the scope of secondary evidence to include copies made from original by mechanical processes, copies made from or compared with the original, counterparts of documents as against the parties who did not execute them and oral accounts of the contents of a document given by some person who has himself seen it and giving matching hash value of original record will be admissible as proof of evidence in the form of secondary evidence;

(*iv*) it seeks to put limits on the facts which are admissible and its certification as such in the courts. The proposed Bill introduces more precise and uniform rules of practice of courts in dealing with facts and circumstances of the case by means of evidence.

5. The Notes on Clauses explain the various provisions of the Bill.

6. The Bill seeks to achieve the above objectives.

NEW DELHI; AMIT SHAH.

The 9th December, 2023.

NOTES ON CLAUSES

Clause 1 of the Bill seeks to provide for short title, application and commencement.

Clause 2 of the Bill seeks to provide for definition of certain expressions used in the proposed Legislation.

Clause 3 of the Bill relates to evidence given of facts in issue and relevant facts.

It seeks to provide evidence may be given in any suit or proceeding of the existence or non-existence of every fact in issue and of such other facts declared to be relevant, and of no others. It further explains that this clause shall not enable any person to give evidence of fact which he is disentitles to prove relating to Civil Procedure.

Clause 4 of the Bill relates to relevancy of facts forming part of same transaction.

It seeks to provide that facts which, though not in issue, are so connected with a fact in issue or a relevant fact as to form part of the same transaction, are relevant, whether they occurred at the same time and place or at different times and places.

Clause 5 of the Bill relates to facts which are the occasion, cause or effect of facts in issue or relevant facts.

It seeks to provide that facts which are the occasion, cause or effect, immediate or otherwise, of relevant facts, or facts in issue, or which constitute the state of things under which they happened, or which afforded an opportunity for their occurrence or transaction, are relevant.

Clause 6 of the Bill relates to motive, preparation and previous or subsequent conduct.

It seeks to provides that any fact is relevant which shows or constitutes a motive or preparation for any fact in issue or relevant fact.

It is proposed that the conduct of any party, or of any agent to any party, to any suit or proceeding, in reference to such suit or proceeding, or in reference to any fact in issue therein or relevant thereto, and the conduct of any person, an offence against whom is the subject of any proceeding, is relevant, if such conduct influences or is influenced by any fact in issue or relevant fact, and whether it was previous or subsequent thereto. It further explains the expression of the word "conduct".

Clause 7 of the Bill relates to facts necessary to explain or introduce fact in issue or relevant facts.

It seeks to provides that facts necessary to explain or introduce a fact in issue or relevant fact, or which support or rebut an inference suggested by a fact in issue or a relevant fact, or which establish the identity of anything, or person whose identity, is relevant, or fix the time or place at which any fact in issue or relevant fact happened, or which show the relation of parties by whom any such fact was transacted, are relevant insofar as they are necessary for that purpose.

Clause 8 of the Bill relates to things said or done by conspirator in reference to common design.

It seeks to provide that there is reasonable ground to believe that two or more persons have conspired together to commit an offence or an actionable wrong, anything said, done or written by any one of such persons in reference to their common intention, after the time when such intention was first entertained by any one of them, is a relevant fact as against each of the persons believed to be so conspiring, as well for the purpose of proving the existence of the conspiracy as for the purpose of showing that any such person was a party to it.

Clause 9 of the Bill relates to facts not otherwise relevant become relevant.

It seeks to provide that facts not otherwise relevant are relevant that if they are inconsistent with any fact in issue or relevant fact and if by themselves or in connection with other facts they make the existence or non-existence of any fact in issue or relevant fact highly probable or improbable.

Clause 10 of the Bill relates to facts tending to enable Court to determine amount are relevant in suits for damages.

It *inter alia* provides that suits in which damages are claimed, any fact which will enable the Court to determine the amount of damages which ought to be awarded is relevant.

Clause 11 of the Bill relates to facts relevant when right or custom is in question.

It deals with the question of the existence of any right or custom, the facts are relevant, that any transaction by which the right or custom in question was created, claimed, modified, recognised, asserted or denied, or which was inconsistent with its existence and particular instances in which the right or custom was claimed, recognised or exercised, or in which its exercise was disputed, asserted or departed from.

Clause 12 of the Bill relates to facts showing existence of state of mind, or of body of bodily feeling.

It seeks to provide that facts showing the existence of any state of mind such as intention, knowledge, good faith, negligence, rashness, ill-will or goodwill towards any particular person, or showing the existence of any state of body or bodily feeling, are relevant, when the existence of any such state of mind or body or bodily feeling is in issue or relevant.

It further provides in *Explanations* 1 and 2 that the relevant state of mind and previous commission by the accused of an offence is relevant fact.

Clause 13 of the Bill relates to facts bearing on question whether act was accidental or intentional.

It seeks to provide that there is a question whether an act was accidental or intentional, or done with a particular knowledge or intention, the fact that such act formed part of a series of similar occurrences, in each of which the person doing the act was concerned, is relevant.

Clause 14 of the Bill relates to existence of course of business when relevant.

It seeks to provide that there is a question whether a particular act was done, the existence of any course of business, according to which it naturally would have been done, is a relevant fact.

Clause 15 of the Bill defined the term "Admission".

It defined that an admission is a statement, oral or documentary or contained in electronic form, which suggests any inference as to any fact in issue or relevant fact, and which is made by any of the persons, and under the circumstances, hereinafter mentioned.

Clause 16 of the Bill relates to Admission by party to proceeding or his agent.

It *inter alia* provides that the statements made by a party to the proceeding, or by an agent to any such party, whom the Court regards, under the circumstances of the case, as expressly or impliedly authorised by him to make them, are admissions.

It is further proposed that statements made in suits in a representative character, are not admissions, unless they were made while the party making them held that character and further persons who have any proprietary or pecuniary interest in the subject matter of the proceeding, and who make the statement in their character of persons so interested, or persons from whom the parties to the suit have derived their interest in the subject matter of the suit, are admissions, if they are made during the continuance of the interest of the persons making the statements.

Clause 17 of the Bill relates to admissions by persons whose position must be proved as against party to suit.

It seeks to provide that the statements made by persons whose position or liability, it is necessary to prove as against any party to the suit, are admissions, if such statements would be relevant as against such persons in relation to such position or liability in a suit brought by or against them, and if they are made whilst the person making them occupies such position or is subject to such liability.

Clause 18 of the Bill relates to admissions by persons expressly referred to by party to suit.

It deals with the statements made by persons to whom a party to the suit has expressly referred for information in reference to a matter in dispute are admissions.

Clause 19 of the Bill relates to admissibility of proof of admissions against persons making them, and by or on their behalf.

It provides that the admissions are relevant and may be proved as against the person who makes them, or his representative in interest; but they cannot be proved by or on behalf of the person who makes them or by his representative in interest.

It further provides exception in certain cases in which statement of facts in issue or relevant fact by person who is dead or cannot be found. It is also exempted that where an admission may be proved by or on behalf of the person making it when it consists of a statement of the existence of any state of mind or body, relevant or in issue, made at or about the time when such state of mind or body existed, and is accompanied by conduct rendering its falsehood improbable and if it is relevant otherwise than as an admission.

Clause 20 of the Bill deals when an oral admissions as to contents of documents are relevant.

It provides that oral admissions as to the contents of a document are not relevant, unless and until the party proposing to prove them shows that he is entitled to give secondary evidence of the contents of such document under the rules hereinafter contained, or unless the genuineness of a document produced is in question.

Clause 21 of the Bill deals as to admissions in civil cases when relevant.

It provides that in civil cases no admission is relevant, if it is made either upon an express condition that evidence of it is not to be given, or under circumstances from which the Court can infer that the parties agreed together that evidence of it should not be given.

Clause 22 of the Bill relates to confession caused by inducement, threat, coercion or promise, when irrelevant in criminal proceeding.

It provides that confession made by an accused person is irrelevant in a criminal proceeding, have been caused by any inducement, threat, coercion or promise having reference to the charge against the accused person, proceeding from a person in authority and sufficient, in the opinion of the Court, to give the accused person grounds which would appear to him reasonable for supposing that by making it he would gain any advantage or avoid any evil of a temporal nature in reference to the proceedings against him.

Clause 23 of the Bill deals with the confession to police officer.

It explains that no confession made to a police officer shall be proved as against a person accused of any offence, unless it is made in the immediate presence of a Magistrate shall be proved against him.

It further provides in the proviso that when any fact is deposed to as discovered in consequence of information received from a person accused of any offence, in the custody of a police officer, so much of such information, whether it amounts to a confession or not, as relates distinctly to the fact thereby discovered, may be proved.

Clause 24 of the Bill relates to consideration of proved confession affecting person making it and others jointly under trial for same offence.

It provides that when more persons than one are being tried jointly for the same offence, and a confession made by one of such persons affecting himself and some other of such persons is proved, the Court may take into consideration such confession as against such other person as well as against the person who makes such confession. It further explains the term "Offence"; and it also explains that the trial conducted in the absence of an accused or who fails to comply with a proclamation issued under section 84 of the Bharatiya Nagarik Suraksha Sanhita, 2023 is deemed to be a joint trial.

Clause 25 of the Bill deals that admissions not conclusive proof, but may estop.

It provides that admissions are not conclusive proof of the matters admitted but they may operate as estoppels.

Clause 26 of the Bill relates to the cases in which statement of facts in issue or relevant fact by person who is dead or cannot be found, etc., is relevant.

It provides *inter alia* deals with statements, written or verbal, of relevant facts made by a person who is dead, or who cannot be found, or who has become incapable of giving evidence, or whose attendance cannot be procured without an amount of delay or expense which under the circumstances of the case appears to the Court unreasonable, are themselves or relevant facts, in case of statement of a person, resulted in his death; in the ordinary course of business; against the pecuniary or proprietary interest of the person; the opinion of any such person, as to the existence of any public right or custom or matters of public or general interest; the existence of any relationship by blood, marriage or adoption between persons.

Clause 27 of the Bill deals with the relevancy of certain evidence for proving, in subsequent proceeding.

It provides that evidence given by a witness in a judicial proceeding, or before any person authorised by law to take it, is relevant for the purpose of proving, in a subsequent judicial proceeding, the proceeding was between the same parties or their representatives in interest; that the adverse party in the first proceeding had the right and opportunity to cross-examine and the questions in issue were substantially the same in the first as in the second proceeding.

Clause 28 of the Bill relates to entries in books of account when relevant.

It provides that the entries in the books of account, including those maintained in an electronic form, regularly kept in the course of business are relevant whenever they refer to a matter into which the Court has to inquire, but such statements shall not alone be sufficient evidence to charge any person with liability.

Clause 29 of the Bill relates to relevancy of entry in public record or an electronic record made in performance of duty.

It provides that an entry made in any public or other official book, register or record or an electronic record, stating a fact in issue or relevant fact, and made by a public servant in the discharge of his official duty, or by any other person in performance of a duty specially enjoined by the law of the country in which such book, register or record or an electronic record, is kept, is itself a relevant fact.

Clause 30 of the Bill relates to relevancy of statements in maps, charts and plans.

It provides that the Statements of facts in issue or relevant facts, made in published maps or charts generally offered for public sale, or in maps or plans made under the authority ' of the Central Government or any State Government, as to matters usually represented or stated in such maps, charts or plans, are themselves relevant facts.

Clause 31 of the Bill relates to relevancy of statement as to fact of public nature contained in certain Acts or notifications.

It provides that when the Court has to form an opinion as to the existence of any fact of a public nature, any statement of it, made in a recital contained in any Central Act or State Act or in a Central Government or State Government notification appearing in the respective Official Gazette or in any printed paper or in electronic or digital form purporting to be such Gazette, is a relevant fact.

Clause 32 of the Bill relates to relevancy of statements as to any law contained in law books including electronic or digital form.

It provides that when the Court has to form an opinion as to a law of any country, any statement of such law contained in a book purporting to be printed or published including in electronic or digital form under the authority of the Government of such country and to contain any such law, and any report of a ruling of the Courts of such country contained in a book including in electronic or digital form purporting to be a report of such rulings, is relevant.

Clause 33 of the Bill relates to evidence to be given when statement forms part of a conversation, document, electronic record, book or series of letters or papers.

It provides that any statement of which evidence is given forms part of a longer statement, or of a conversation or part of an isolated document, or is contained in a document which forms part of a book, or is contained in part of electronic record or of a connected series of letters or papers, evidence shall be given of so much and no more of the statement, conversation, document, electronic record, book or series of letters or papers as the Court considers necessary in that particular case to the full understanding of the nature and effect of the statement, and of the circumstances under which it was made.

Clause 34 of the Bill relates to previous judgments relevant to bar a second suit or trial.

It provides that the existence of any judgment, order or decree which by law prevents any Court from taking cognizance of a suit or holding a trial, is a relevant fact when the question is whether such Court ought to take cognizance of such suit or to hold such trial.

Clause 35 of the Bill relates to relevancy of certain judgments in exercise of jurisdiction in execution of probate, etc.

It *inter alia* provide relevancy of final judgment, order or decree of a competent Court or Tribunal, in the exercise of probate, matrimonial, admiralty or insolvency jurisdiction, which confers upon or takes away from any person any legal character, or which declares any person to be entitled to any such character, or to be entitled to any specific thing, not as against any specified person but absolutely, is relevant when the existence of any such legal character, or the title of any such person to any such thing, is relevant and the said judgment, order, decree is conclusive proof.

Clause 36 of the Bill relates to relevancy and effect of judgments, orders or decrees, other those mentioned in clause 35.

It provides that Judgments, orders or decrees other than those mentioned in clause 35 are relevant if they relate to matters of a public nature relevant to the enquiry; but such judgments, orders or decrees are not conclusive proof of that which they state.

Clause 37 of the Bill relates to Judgments, orders or decrees, other than those mentioned in clauses 34, 35 and 36 when relevant.

It provides that the judgments or orders or decrees, other than those mentioned in clauses 34, 35 and 36 are irrelevant, unless the existence of such judgment or order or decree is a fact in issue, or is relevant under some other provision of this Adhiniyam.

Clause 38 of the Bill relates to fraud or collusion in obtaining judgment, or incompetency of Court, may be proved.

It provides that any party to a suit or other proceeding may show that any judgment, order or decree which is relevant under clause 34, 35 or 36, and which has been proved by the adverse party, was delivered by a Court not competent to deliver it, or was obtained by fraud or collusion.

Clause 39 of the Bill relates to opinions of experts.

It provides that the Court has to form an opinion of the experts upon a point of foreign law or of science, or art, or any other field, or as to identity of hand-writing or finger impressions are relevant facts and such specially skilled persons are called experts, and matters relating to any information transmitted or stored in any computer resource or any other electronic or digital form, the opinion of the Examiner of Electronic Evidence referred to in section 79A of the Information Technology Act, 2000, is a relevant fact.

Clause 40 of the Bill relates to the facts bearing upon opinions of experts.

It provides that the facts, not otherwise relevant, are relevant if they support or are inconsistent with the opinions of experts, when such opinions are relevant.

Clause 41 of the Bill relates to the opinion as to hand writing and signature, when relevant.

It provides that the Court has to form an opinion as to the person by whom any document was written or signed, the opinion of any person acquainted with the handwriting of the person by whom it is supposed to be written or signed that it was or was not written or signed by that person and electronic signature of any person, is a relevant fact.

It further provides that when the Court has to form an opinion as to the electronic signature of any person, the opinion of the Certifying Authority which has issued the Electronic Signature Certificate is a relevant fact.

It also explains that person is said to be acquainted with the handwriting of another person when he has seen that person to write, or when he has received documents purporting to be written by that person in answer to documents written by himself or under his authority and addressed to that person, or when, in the ordinary course of business, documents purporting to be written by that person have been habitually submitted to him.

Clause 42 of the Bill relates to relevancy of opinion as to existence of general custom or right. It further explains that expression "general custom or right" includes customs or rights common to any considerable class of persons.

It provides that the Court has to form an opinion as to the existence of any general custom or right, the opinions, as to the existence of such custom or right, of persons who would be likely to know of its existence if it existed, are relevant.

Clause 43 of the Bill relates to relevancy of opinion as to usage, tenets, etc.

It provides that the Court has to form an opinion as to the usages and tenets, of any body of men or family, the constitution and governance of any religious or charitable foundation, or the meaning of words or terms used in particular districts or by particular classes of people, the opinions of persons having special means of knowledge thereon, are relevant facts.

Clause 44 of the Bill relates to relevancy of opinion on relationship.

It provides that the Court has to form an opinion as to the relationship of persons on the opinion, expressed by conduct, as to the existence of such relationship, of any person who, as a member of the family or otherwise, has special means of knowledge on the subject, is a relevant fact, provided that such opinion shall not be sufficient to prove a marriage in proceedings under the Divorce Act, 1869, or in prosecutions under sections 82 and 84 of the Bharatiya Nyaya Sanhita, 2023.

Clause 45 of the Bill relates to relevancy of grounds of opinion.

It provides that opinion of any living person is relevant, the grounds on which such opinion is based are also relevant.

Clause 46 of the Bill relates to in civil cases character to prove conduct imputed, irrelevant.

It provides that in civil cases, the fact that the character of any person concerned is such as to render probable or improbable any conduct imputed to him, is irrelevant, except insofar as such character appears from facts otherwise relevant.

Clause 47 of the Bill relates to criminal cases previous good character relevant.

It provides that in criminal proceedings, the fact that the person accused is of a good character, is relevant.

Clause 48 of the Bill relates to the evidence of character or previous sexual experience not relevant in certain cases.

It provides that in a prosecution for an offence under section 64, section 65, section 66, section 67, section 68, section 69, section 70, section 71, section 74, section 75, section 76, section 77 or section 78 of the Bharatiya Nyaya Sanhita, 2023 or for attempt to commit any such offence, where the question of consent is in issue, evidence of the character of the victim or of such person's previous sexual experience with any person shall not be relevant on the issue of such consent or the quality of consent.

Clause 49 of the Bill relates to relevancy of previous bad character not relevant, except in reply.

It provides that in criminal proceedings, the fact that the accused has a bad character, is irrelevant, unless evidence has been given that he has a good character, in which case it becomes relevant.

Clause 50 of the Bill relates to character of any person is such as to affect the amount of damages which he ought to receive, is relevant in civil cases.

It further explains that this clause does not apply to cases in which the bad character of any person is itself a fact in issue and a previous conviction is relevant as evidence of bad character.

Clause 51 of the Bill provides that no fact of which the Court will take judicial notice need to be proved.

Clause 52 of the Bill relates to the facts of which Court shall take judicial notice.

It provides that the Court shall take judicial notice *inter alia,* all laws in force in the territory of India including laws having extra-territorial operation; international treaty, agreement or convention with country or countries by India, or decisions made by India at the international associations or other bodies; the course of proceeding of the Constituent Assembly of India, of Parliament of India and of the State Legislatures; the seals of all Courts and Tribunals.

It further provides that on all matters of public history, literature, science or art, the Court may resort for its aid to appropriate books or documents of reference and if the Court is called upon by any person to take judicial notice of any fact, it may refuse to do so unless and until such person produces any such book or document.

Clause 53 of the Bill relates to the facts admitted need not be proved.

It provides that no fact need be proved in any proceeding which the parties thereto or their agents agree to admit at the hearing, or which, before the hearing, they agree to admit by any writing under their hands, or which by any rule of pleading in force at the time they are deemed to have admitted by their pleadings, subject to the condition that the Court may, in its discretion, require the facts admitted to be proved otherwise than by such admissions.

Clause 54 of the Bill relates to all facts, except the contents of documents may be proved by oral evidence.

Clause 55 of the Bill relates to the oral evidence to be direct.

It provides that Oral evidence shall, in all cases whatever, be direct; if it *inter alia* refers to a fact which could be seen, it must be the evidence of a witness who says he saw it; a fact which could be heard, it must be the evidence of a witness who says he heard it; a fact which could be perceived by any other sense or in any other manner.

Clause 56 of the Bill relates to the contents of documents may be proved either by primary or by secondary evidence.

Clause 57 of the Bill relates to the primary evidence.

It provides that the primary evidence means the document itself produced for the inspection of the Court. It further explains the circumstances under which a document, electronic digital record and video recording is to be treated as primary evidence.

Clause 58 of the Bill relates to the secondary evidence.

It provides that the secondary evidence includes certified copies; copies made from the original by mechanical processes which in themselves ensure the accuracy of the copy, and copies compared with such copies; copies made from or compared with the original; counterparts of documents as against the parties who did not execute them; oral accounts of the contents of a document given by some person who has himself seen it; oral admissions; written admissions and evidence of a person who has examined a document, the original of which consists of numerous accounts or other documents which cannot conveniently be examined in Court, and who is skilled in the examination of such documents.

Clause 59 of the Bill relates to the documents shall be proved by primary evidence except expressly provided otherwise.

Clause 60 of the Bill relates to cases in which secondary evidence may be given of the existence, condition, or contents of a document. It explains that when existence, condition, or contents of a document is admissible.

Clause 61 of the Bill relates to the admissibility of electronic or digital record.

It provides that nothing in the Adhiniyam shall apply to deny the admissibility of an electronic or digital record in the evidence on the ground that it is an electronic or digital record and such record shall have the same legal effect, validity and enforceability as paper records.

Clause 62 of the Bill relates to special provisions as to evidence relating to electronic record.

It provides that the contents of electronic records may be proved in accordance with the provisions of clause 63.

Clause 63 of the Bill relates to admissibility of electronic records.

It provides that any information contained in an electronic record which is printed on paper, stored, recorded or copied in optical or magnetic media or semiconductor memory which is produced by a computer or any communication device or otherwise stored, recorded or copied in any electronic form shall be deemed to be also a document and computer in question and shall be admissible in any proceedings, without further proof or production of the original, as evidence or any contents of the original or of any fact stated therein of which direct evidence would be admissible.

Clause 64 of the Bill relates to rules as to notice to produce.

It provides that the secondary evidence of the contents of the documents, shall not be given unless the party proposing to give such secondary evidence has previously given to the party in whose possession or power the document is, or to his advocate or representative, such notice to produce it as is prescribed by law; and if no notice is prescribed by law, then such notice as the Court considers reasonable under the circumstances of the case, subject to the condition such notice shall not be required in order to render secondary evidence admissible.

Clause 65 of the Bill relates to proof of signature and handwriting of person alleged to have signed or written document produced.

It provides that the document is alleged to be signed or to have been written wholly or in part by any person, the signature or the handwriting of so much of the document as is alleged to be in that person's handwriting must be proved to be in his handwriting.

Clause 66 of the Bill relates to proof as to electronic signature.

It provides that the electronic signature of any subscriber is alleged to have been affixed to an electronic record, such electronic signature is the electronic signature of the subscriber must be proved.

Clause 67 of the Bill relates to proof of execution of document required by law to be attested.

It provides that the document is required by law to be attested, it shall not be used as evidence until one attesting witness at least has been called for the purpose of proving its execution, subject to the call an attesting witness in proof of the execution of any document, not being a will, which has been registered in accordance with the provisions of the Indian Registration Act, 1908, unless its execution by the person by whom it purports to have been executed is specifically denied.

Clause 68 of the Bill relates to proof where no attesting witness found.

It provides that no such attesting witness can be found, it must be proved that the attestation of one attesting witness at least is in his handwriting, and that the signature of the person executing the document is in the handwriting of that person.

Clause 69 of the Bill relates to admission of execution by party to attested document.

It provides that admission of a party to an attested document of its execution by himself shall be sufficient proof of its execution as against him, though it be a document required by law to be attested.

Clause 70 of the Bill relates to the attesting witness denies or does not recollect the execution of the document, its execution may be proved by other evidence.

Clause 71 of the Bill relates to an attested document not required by law to be attested may be proved as if it was unattested.

Clause 72 of the Bill relates to the comparison of signature, writing or seal with others admitted or proved.

It provides to ascertain a signature, writing, or seal admitted or proved to the satisfaction of the Court to have been written or made by that person may be compared with the one which is to be proved, although that signature, writing, or seal has not been produced or proved for any other purpose. It further provides that the Court may direct any person present in Court to write any words or figures for the purpose of enabling the Court to compare the words or figures so written with any words or figures alleged to have been written by such person and applies with any necessary modifications, to finger impressions.

Clause 73 of the Bill relates to proof as to verification of digital signature.

It provides that to ascertain a digital signature is that of the person by whom it purports to have been affixed, the Court may direct the person or the Controller or the Certifying Authority to produce the Digital Signature Certificate and any other person to apply the public key listed in the Digital Signature Certificate and verify the digital signature purported to have been affixed by that person.

Clause 74 of the Bill relates to public and private documents.

It provides public documents includes documents forming the acts, or records of the acts of the sovereign authority; official bodies and tribunals; public officers, legislative, judicial and executive of India or of a foreign country; and public records kept in any State or Union territory of private documents. Except all the above others are private documents.

Clause 75 of the Bill relates to the certified copies of public documents.

It provides that public officer having the custody of a public document shall be called certified copies. It further explains that, any officer who, by the ordinary course of official duty, is authorised to deliver such copies, shall be deemed to have the custody of such documents within the meaning of this clause.

Clause 76 of the Bill relates to the proof of documents by production of certified copies.

It provides that certified copies may be produced in proof of the contents of the public documents or parts of the public documents of which they purport to be copies.

Clause 77 of the Bill relates to the proof of other official documents, *inter alia.* Acts, orders or notifications of the Central Government in any of its Ministries and Departments or of any State Government or any Department of any State Government or Union territory Administration, the proceedings of Parliament or a State Legislature, and proclamations, orders or Regulations issued by the President of India or the Governor of a State or the Administrator or Lieutenant Governor of a Union territory.

Clause 78 of the Bill relates to the presumption as to genuineness of certified copies.

It provides that the Court shall presume to be genuine every document purporting to be a certificate, certified copy or other document, which is by law declared to be admissible as evidence of any particular fact, and which purports to be duly certified by any officer of the Central Government or of a State Government, subject to the document is substantially in the form and purports to be executed in the manner directed by law in that behalf and the Court shall also presume that any officer by whom any such document purports to be signed or certified, held, when he signed it, the official character which he claims in such paper.

Clause 79 of the Bill relates to presumption as to documents produced as record of evidence, etc.

It provides that the any document is produced before any Court, purporting to be a record or memorandum of the evidence, or of any part of the evidence, given by a witness in a judicial proceeding or before any officer authorised by law to take such evidence or to be a statement or confession by any prisoner or accused person, taken in accordance with law, and purporting to be signed by any Judge or Magistrate, or by any such officer as aforesaid, the Court shall presume that the document is genuine; any statements as to the circumstances under which it was taken, purporting to be made by the person signing it, are true; and such evidence, statement or confession was duly taken.

Clause 80 of the Bill relates to presumption as to Gazettes, newspapers, and other documents.

It provides that the Court shall presume the genuineness of every document purporting to be the Official Gazette, or to be a newspaper or journal, and of every document purporting to be a document directed by any law to be kept by any person, if such document is kept substantially in the form required by law and is produced from proper custody.

It further explains that, for the purposes of this clause and clause 92, document is said to be in proper custody if it is in the place in which, and looked after by the person with whom such document is required to be kept; but no custody is improper if it is proved to have had a legitimate origin, or if the circumstances of the particular case are such as to render that origin probable.

Clause 81 of the Bill relates to the presumption as to Gazettes in electronic or digital record.

It provides that the Court shall presume the genuineness of every electronic or digital record purporting to be the Official Gazette, or purporting to be electronic or digital record directed by any law to be kept by any person, if such electronic or digital record is kept substantially in the form required by law and is produced from proper custody.

It further explains that, for the purposes of this clause and clause 93, electronic records are said to be in proper custody if they are in the place in which, and looked after by the person with whom such document is required to be kept; but no custody is improper if it is proved to have had a legitimate origin, or the circumstances of the particular case are such as to render that origin probable.

Clause 82 of the Bill relates to the presumption as to maps or plans made by authority of Government.

It provides that the Court shall presume that maps or plans purporting to be made by the authority of the Central Government or any State Government were so made, and are accurate; but maps or plans made for the purposes of any cause must be proved to be accurate.

Clause 83 of the Bill relates to the presumption as to collections of laws and reports of decisions.

It provides that the Court shall presume the genuineness of, every book purporting to be printed or published under the authority of the Government of any country, and to contain any of the laws of that country, and of every book purporting to contain reports of decisions of the Courts of such country.

Clause 84 of the Bill relates to the presumption as to powers-of-attorney.

It provides that the Court shall presume that every document purporting to be a power-of-attorney, and to have been executed before, and authenticated by, a Notary Public, or any Court, Judge, Magistrate, Indian Consul or Vice-Consul, or representative of the Central Government, was so executed and authenticated.

Clause 85 of the Bill relates to the presumption as to electronic agreements.

It provides that the Court shall presume that every electronic record purporting to be an agreement containing the electronic or digital signature of the parties was so concluded by affixing the electronic or digital signature of the parties.

Clause 86 of the Bill relates to the presumption as to electronic records and electronic signatures.

It provides that any proceeding involving a secure electronic record, the Court shall presume unless contrary is proved, that the secure electronic record has not been altered since the specific point of time to which the secure status relates.

It further provides that the case involving secure electronic signature, the Court shall presume secure electronic signature is affixed by subscriber with the intention of signing or approving the electronic record and nothing in this clause shall create any presumption, relating to authenticity and integrity of the electronic record or any electronic signature.

Clause 87 of the Bill relates to presumption as to Electronic Signature Certificates.

It provides that the information listed in an Electronic Signature Certificate is correct, except for information specified as subscriber information which has not been verified, if the certificate was accepted by the subscriber.

Clause 88 of the Bill relates to presumption as to certified copies of foreign judicial records.

It provides that the Court may presume that any document purporting to be a certified copy of any judicial record of any country beyond India is genuine and accurate, if the document purports to be certified in any manner which is certified by any representative of the Central Government, in or for such country, to be the manner commonly in use in that country for the certification of copies of judicial records.

It further provides that, an officer who, with respect to any territory or place outside India is a Political Agent therefor, as defined in clause *(43)* of section 3 of the General Clauses Act, 1897, shall, for the purposes of this clause, be deemed to be a representative of the Central Government in and for the country comprising that territory or place.

Clause 89 of the Bill relates to presumption as to books, maps and charts.

It provides that the Court may presume that any book to which it may refer for information on matters of public or general interest, and that any published map or chart, the statements of which are relevant facts, and which is produced for its inspection, was written and published by the person, and at the time and place, by whom or at which it purports to have been written or published.

Clause 90 of the Bill relates to presumption as to electronic messages.

It provides that the Court may presume that an electronic message, forwarded by the originator through an electronic mail server to the addressee to whom the message purports to be addressed corresponds with the message as fed into his computer for transmission; but the Court shall not make any presumption as to the person by whom such message was sent.

Clause 91 of the Bill relates to presumption as to due execution of documents not produced.

It provides that the Court shall presume that every document, called for and not produced after notice to produce, was attested, stamped and executed in the manner required by law.

Clause 92 of the Bill relates to presumption as to documents thirty years old.

It provides that any document, purporting or proved to be thirty years old, is produced from any custody which the Court in the particular case considers proper, the Court may presume that the signature and every other part of such document, which purports to be in the handwriting of any particular person, is in that person's handwriting, and, in the case of a document executed or attested, that it was duly executed and attested by the persons by whom it purports to be executed and attested.

It further explains that clause 80 shall also apply to this clause.

Clause 93 of the Bill relates to presumption as to electronic records five years old.

It provides that any electronic record, purporting or proved to be five years old, is produced from any custody which the Court in the particular case considers proper, the Court may presume that the electronic signature which purports to be the electronic signature of any particular person was so affixed by him or any person authorised by him in this behalf.

It further explains that clause 81 shall also apply to this clause.

Clause 94 of the Bill relates to evidence of terms of contracts, grants and other dispositions of property reduced to form of document.

It provides that the terms of a contract, or of a grant, or of any other disposition of property, have been reduced to the form of a document, and in all cases in which any matter is required by law to be reduced to the form of a document, no evidence shall be given in proof of the terms of such contract, grant or other disposition of property, or of such matter, except the document itself, or secondary evidence of its contents in cases in which secondary evidence is admissible under the provisions and with few exceptions.

It further provides in *Exceptions* 1 and 2 that when a public officer is required by law to be appointed in writing, and when it is shown that any particular person has acted as such officer, the writing by which he is appointed need not be proved and Wills admitted to probate in India may be proved by the probate.

It also explains that, this clause applies equally to cases in which the contracts, grants or dispositions of property referred to are contained in one document, and to cases in which they are contained in more documents than one.

Clause 95 of the Bill relates to exclusion of evidence of oral agreement.

It *inter alia* provides that no evidence of any oral agreement or statement shall be admitted, as between the parties to any such instrument or their representatives in interest, for the purpose of contradicting, varying, adding to, or subtracting from the proved evidence.

Clause 96 of the Bill relates to exclusion of evidence to explain or amend ambiguous document.

It provides that the language used in a document is, on its face, ambiguous or defective, evidence may not be given of facts which would show its meaning or supply its defects.

Clause 97 of the Bill relates to exclusion of evidence against application of document to existing facts.

It provides that the language used in a document is plain in itself, and when it applies accurately to existing facts, evidence may not be given to show that it was not meant to apply to such facts.

Clause 98 of the Bill relates to evidence as to document unmeaning in reference to existing facts.

It provides that the language used in a document is plain in itself, but is unmeaning in reference to existing facts, evidence may be given to show that it was used in a peculiar sense.

Clause 99 of the Bill relates to evidence as to application of language which can apply to one only of several persons.

It provides that the facts are such that the language used might have been meant to apply to any one, and could not have been meant to apply to more than one, of several persons or things, evidence may be given of facts which show which of those persons or things it was intended to apply to.

Clause 100 of the Bill relates to evidence as to application of language to one of two sets of facts, to neither of which the whole correctly applies.

It provides that the language used applies partly to one set of existing facts, and partly to another set of existing facts, but the whole of it does not apply correctly to either, evidence may be given to show to which of the two it was meant to apply.

Clause 101 of the Bill relates to evidence as to meaning of illegible characters.

It provides that evidence may be given to show the meaning of illegible or not commonly intelligible characters, of foreign, obsolete, technical, local and regional expressions, of abbreviations and of words used in a peculiar sense.

Clause 102 of the Bill relates to the persons who give evidence of agreement varying terms of document.

It provides that persons who are not parties to a document, or their representatives in interest, may give evidence of any facts tending to show a contemporaneous agreement varying the terms of the document.

Clause 103 of the Bill relates to saving of provisions of Indian Succession Act, 1925 relating to the construction of wills.

Clause 104 of the Bill relates to burden of proof.

It provides that whoever desires any Court to give judgment as to any legal right or liability dependent on the existence of facts which he asserts must prove that those facts exist, and when a person is bound to prove the existence of any fact, it is said that the burden of proof lies on that person.

Clause 105 of the Bill relates to the person with whom burden of proof lies.

It provides that the burden of proof in a suit or proceeding lies on that person who would fail if no evidence at all were given on either side.

Clause 106 of the Bill relates to the burden of proof as to particular fact.

It provides that the burden of proof as to any particular fact lies on that person who wishes the Court to believe in its existence, unless it is provided by any law that the proof of that fact shall lie on any particular person.

Clause 107 of the Bill relates to the burden of proving fact to be proved to make evidence admissible.

It provides that the burden of proving any fact necessary to be proved in order to enable any person to give evidence of any other fact is on the person who wishes to give such evidence.

Clause 108 of the Bill relates to the burden of proving that case of accused comes within exceptions.

It provides that the accused of any offence, the burden of proving the existence of circumstances bringing the case within any of the general exceptions in the

Bharatiya Nyaya Sanhita, 2023 or within any special exception or proviso contained in any other part of the said Sanhita, or in any law defining the offence, is upon him, and the Court shall presume the absence of such circumstances.

Clause 109 of the Bill relates to burden of proving fact especially within knowledge. This clause provides that when any fact is especially within the knowledge of any person, the burden of proving that fact is upon him.

Clause 110 of the Bill relates to burden of proving death of person known to have been alive within thirty years.

It provides that the question is whether a man is alive or dead, and it is shown that he was alive within thirty years, the burden of proving that he is dead is on the person who affirms it.

Clause 111 of the Bill relates to burden of proving that person is alive who has not been heard of for seven years.

It provides that the question is whether that a man is alive or dead, and it is proved that he has not been heard of for seven years by those who would naturally have heard of him if he had been alive, the burden of proving that he is alive is shifted to the person who affirms it.

Clause 112 of the Bill relates to burden of proof as to relationship in the cases of partners, landlord and tenant, principal and agent.

It provides that the persons are partners, landlord and tenant, or principal and agent, and it has been shown that they have been acting as such, the burden of proving that they do not stand, or have ceased to stand, to each other in those relationships respectively, is on the person who affirms it.

Clause 113 of the Bill relates to burden of proof as to ownership.

It provides that when the question is whether any person is owner of anything of which he is shown to be in possession, the burden of proving that he is not the owner is on the person who affirms that he is not the owner.

Clause 114 of the Bill relates to proof of good faith in transactions where one party is in relation of active confidence.

It provides that the question as to the good faith of a transaction between parties, one of whom stands to the other in a position of active confidence, the burden of proving the good faith of the transaction is on the party who is in a position of active confidence.

Clause 115 of the Bill relates to presumption as to certain offences.

It provides that where a person is accused of having committed any offence specified under this clause and it is shown that such person had been at a place in such area at a time when firearms or explosives were used at or from that place to attack or resist the members of any armed forces or the forces charged with the maintenance of public order acting in the discharge of their duties, it shall be presumed, unless the contrary is shown, that such person had committed such offence.

Clause 116 of the Bill relates to birth during marriage, conclusive proof of legitimacy.

It provides that the fact that any person was born during the continuance of a valid marriage between his mother and any man, or within two hundred and eighty days after its dissolution, the mother remaining unmarried, shall be conclusive proof that he is the legitimate child of that man unless it can be shown that the parties to the marriage had no access to each other at any time when he could have been begotten.

Clause 117 of the Bill relates to presumption as to abetment of suicide by a married woman.

It provides that a woman committed suicide had been abetted by her husband or any relative of her husband and it is shown that she had committed suicide within a period of seven years from the date of her marriage and that her husband or such relative of her husband had subjected her to cruelty, the Court may presume, having regard to all the other circumstances of the case, that such suicide had been abetted by her husband or by such relative of her husband.

It further explains that "cruelty" shall have the same meaning as in section 86 of the Bharatiya Nyaya Sanhita, 2023.

Clause 118 of the Bill relates to presumption as to dowry death.

It provides that when the question is whether a person has committed the dowry death of a woman and it is shown that soon before her death, such woman had been subjected by such person to cruelty or harassment for, or in connection with, any demand for dowry, the court shall presume that such person had caused the dowry death, "dowry death" shall have the same.

It further explains that "dowry death" shall have the same meaning as in section 80 of the Bharatiya Nyaya Sanhita, 2023.

Clause 119 of the Bill relates to Court may presume existence of certain facts.

It provides that the Court may presume the existence of any fact which it thinks likely to have happened, regard being had to the common course of natural events, human conduct and public and private business, in their relation to the facts of the particular case.

It further provides that Court shall also have regard to such given facts in considering whether such maxims do or do not apply to the particular case before it.

Clause 120 of the Bill relates to presumption as to absence of consent in certain prosecution for rape.

It provides that the prosecution for rape, under sub-section (2) of section 64 of the Bharatiya Nyaya Sanhita, 2023, where sexual intercourse by the accused is proved and the question is whether it was without the consent of the woman alleged to have been raped and such woman states in her evidence before the court that she did not consent, the court shall presume that she did not consent.

Clause 121 of the Bill relates to Estoppel.

It provides that when one person has, by his declaration, act or omission, intentionally caused or permitted another person to believe a thing to be true and to act upon such belief, neither he nor his representative shall be allowed, in any suit or proceeding between himself and such person or his representative, to deny the truth of that thing.

Clause 122 of the Bill relates to Estoppel of tenants and of licensee of person in possession.

It provides that no tenant of immovable property, or person claiming through such tenant, shall, during the continuance of the tenancy or any time thereafter, be permitted to deny that the landlord of such tenant had, at the beginning of the tenancy, a title to such immovable property; and no person who came upon any immovable property by the licence of the person in possession thereof shall be permitted to deny that such person had a title to such possession at the time when such licence was given.

Clause 123 of the Bill relates to Estoppel of acceptor of bill of exchange, bailee or licensee.

It provides that no acceptor of a bill of exchange shall be permitted the drawer had authority to draw such bill or to endorse it; nor shall any bailee or licensee be permitted to deny that his bailor or licensor had, at the time when the bailment or licence commenced, authority to make such bailment or grant such licence.

It further explains that the acceptor of a bill of exchange may deny that the bill was really drawn by the person by whom it purports to have been drawn, and if a bailee delivers the goods bailed to a person other than the bailor, he may prove that such person had a right to them as against the bailor.

Clause 124 of the Bill relates to the person who may testify.

It provides that all persons shall be competent to testify unless the Court considers that they are prevented from understanding the questions put to them, or from giving rational answers to those questions, by tender years, extreme old age, disease, whether of body or mind, or any other cause of me same kind.

It further explains that A person with unsound mind is not incompetent to testify, unless he is prevented by his unsoundness of mind from understanding the questions put to him and giving rational answers to them.

Clause 125 of the Bill relates to witness unable to communicate verbally.

It provides that a witness who is unable to speak may give his evidence in any other manner in which he can make it intelligible, as by writing or by signs; but such writing must be written and the signs made in open Court and evidence so given shall be deemed to be oral evidence, subject to the assistance of interpreter.

It further provides that if the witness is unable to communicate verbally, the Court shall take the assistance of an interpreter or a special educator in recording the statement, and such statement shall be videographed.

Clause 126 of the Bill relates to competency of husband and wife as witnesses in certain cases.

It provides that in all civil proceedings the parties to the suit, and the husband or wife of any party to the suit, shall be competent witnesses and in criminal proceedings against any person, the husband or wife of such person, respectively, shall be a competent witness.

Clause 127 of the Bill relates to Judges and Magistrates.

It provides that the no Judge or Magistrate shall, except upon the special order of some Court to which he is subordinate, be compelled to answer any questions as to his own conduct in Court as such Judge or Magistrate, or as to anything which came to his knowledge in Court as such Judge or Magistrate; but he may be examined as to other matters which occurred in his presence whilst he was so acting.

Clause 128 of the Bill relates to communications during marriage.

It provides that the no person who is or has been married, shall be compelled to disclose any communication made to him during marriage by any person to whom he is or has been married; nor shall he be permitted to disclose any such communication, unless the person who made it, or his representative in interest, consents, except in suits between married persons, or proceedings in which one married person is prosecuted for any crime committed against the other.

Clause 129 of the Bill relates to evidence as to affairs of State.

It provides that no one shall be permitted to give any evidence derived from unpublished official records relating to any affairs of State, except with the permission of the officer at the head of the department concerned, who shall give or withhold such permission as he thinks fit.

Clause 130 of the Bill relates to the official communications.

It provides mat no public officer shall be compelled to disclose communications made to him in official confidence, when he considers that the public interests would suffer by the disclosure.

Clause 131 of the Bill relates to the information as to commission of offences.

It provides that no Magistrate or police officer shall be compelled to say when he got any information as to the commission of any offence, and no revenue-officer shall be compelled to say when he got any information as to the commission of any offence against the public revenue.

It further explains that "revenue officer" means any officer employed in or about the business of any branch of the public revenue.

Clause 132 of the Bill relates to professional communications.

It provides that no advocate, shall at any time be permitted, unless with his client's express consent, to disclose any communication made to him in the course and for the purpose of his service as such advocate, by or on behalf of his client, or to state the contents or condition of any document with which he has become acquainted in the course and for the purpose of his professional service, or to disclose any advice given by him to his client in the course and for the purpose of such service.

It further provides that nothing in this clause shall protect from disclosure of any such communication made in furtherance of any illegal purpose and any fact observed by any advocate, in the course of his service as such, showing that any crime or fraud has been committed since the commencement of his service.

It also explains that the obligation stated in this clause continues after the professional service has ceased.

Clause 133 of the Bill relates to privilege not waived by volunteering evidence.

It provides that any party to a suit gives evidence therein at his own instance or otherwise, he shall not be deemed to have consented thereby to such disclosure as is mentioned in clause 132; and, if any party to a suit or proceeding calls any such advocate, as a witness, he shall be deemed to have consented to such disclosure only if he questions such advocate, on matters which, but for such question, he would not be at liberty to disclose.

Clause 134 of the Bill relates to confidential communication with legal advisers.

It provides that no one shall be compelled to disclose to the Court any confidential communication which has taken place between him and his legal adviser, unless he offers himself as a witness, in which case he may be compelled to disclose any such communications as may appear to the Court necessary to be known in order to explain any evidence which he has given, but no others.

Clause 135 of the Bill relates to production of title-deeds of witness not a party.

It provides that no witness who is not a party to a suit shall be compelled to produce his title-deeds to any property, or any document in virtue of which he holds any property as pledge or mortgagee or any document the production of which might tend to criminate him, unless he has agreed in writing to produce them with the person seeking the production of such deeds or some person through whom he claims.

Clause 136 of the Bill relates to production of documents or electronic records which another person, having possession, could refuse to produce.

It provides that no one shall be compelled to produce documents in his possession or electronic records under his control, which any other person would be entitled to refuse to produce if they were in his possession or control, unless such last-mentioned person consents to their production.

Clause 137 of the Bill relates to witness not excused from answering on ground that answer will criminate.

It provides that the witness shall not be excused from answering any question as to any matter relevant to the matter in issue in any suit or in any civil or criminal proceeding, upon the ground that the answer to such question will criminate, or may tend directly or indirectly to criminate, such witness, or that it will expose, or tend directly or indirectly to expose, such witness to a penalty or forfeiture of any kind.

It further provides that no such answer, which a witness *shall be compelled to give,* shall subject him to any arrest or prosecution, or be proved against him in any criminal proceeding, except a prosecution forgiving false evidence by such answer.

Clause 138 of the Bill relates to accomplice.

It provides that the accomplice shall be a competent witness against an accused person; and a conviction is not illegal if it proceeds upon the corroborated testimony of an accomplice.

Clause 139 of the Bill relates to number of witnesses.

It provides that no particular number of witnesses shall in any case be required for the proof of any fact.

Clause 140 of the Bill relates to order of production and examination of witnesses.

It provides that the order in which witnesses are produced and examined shall be regulated by the law and practice for the time being relating to civil and criminal procedure respectively, and, in the absence of any such law, by the discretion of the Court.

Clause 141 of the Bill relates to Judge to decide as to admissibility of evidence.

It provides that the Judge shall admit the evidence if he thinks that the fact, if proved, would be relevant, and not otherwise and the fact proposed to be proved is one of which evidence is admissible only upon proof of some other fact, such last mentioned fact must be proved before evidence is given of the fact first mentioned, unless the party undertakes to give proof of such fact, and the Court is satisfied with such undertaking.

It further provides that if the relevancy of one alleged fact depends upon another alleged fact being first proved, the Judge may, in his discretion, either permit evidence of the first fact to be given before the second fact is proved, or require evidence to be given of the second fact before evidence is given of the first fact.

Clause 142 of the Bill relates to examination of witnesses.

It provides that the examination of witness by the party who calls him shall be called his examination-in-chief and the examination of a witness by the adverse party shall be called his cross-examination and subsequent to the cross-examination, by the party who called him, shall be called his re-examination.

Clause 143 of the Bill relates to order of examinations.

It provides that the witnesses shall be first examined-in-chief, then (if the adverse party so desires) cross-examined, then (if the party calling him so desires) re-examined.

The examination-in-chief and cross-examination must relate to relevant facts but the cross-examination need not be confined to the facts to which the witness testified on his examination-in-chief.

It further provides that re-examination shall be directed to the explanation of matters referred to in cross-examination; and, if new matter is, by permission of the Court, introduced in re-examination, the adverse party may further cross-examine upon that matter.

Clause 144 of the Bill relates to cross-examination of person called to produce a document.

It provides that a person summoned to produce a document does not become a witness by the mere fact that he produces it, and cannot be cross-examined unless and until he is called as a witness.

Clause 145 of the Bill relates to witnesses to character may be cross-examined and re-examined.

Clause 146 of the Bill relates to leading questions.

It provides that any question suggesting the answer which the person putting it wishes or expects to receive, is called a leading question and leading questions must not, if objected to by the adverse party, be asked in an examination-in-chief, or in a re-examination, except with the permission of the Court.

It further provides that the Court shall permit leading questions as to matters which are introductory or undisputed, or which have, in its opinion, been already sufficiently proved and leading questions may be asked in cross-examination.

Clause 147 of the Bill relates to evidence as to matters in writing.

It provides that any witness may be asked, while under examination, whether any contract, grant or other disposition of property, as to which he is giving evidence, was not contained in a document, and if he says that it was, or if he is about to make any statement as to the contents of any document, which, in the opinion of the Court, ought to be produced, the adverse party may object to such evidence being given until such document is produced, or until facts have been proved which entitle the party who called the witness to give secondary evidence of it.

It further explains that a witness may give oral evidence of statements made by other persons about the contents of documents if such statements are in themselves relevant facts.

Clause 148 of the Bill relates to cross-examination as to previous statements in writing.

It provides that a witness may be cross-examined as to previous statements made by him in writing or reduced into writing, and relevant to matters in question, without such writing being shown to him, or being proved; but, if it is intended to contradict him by the writing, his attention must, before the writing can be proved, be called to those parts of it which are to be used for the purpose of contradicting him.

Clause 149 of the Bill relates to questions lawful in cross-examinations.

It provides for testing the veracity of the witness during cross-examination and to discover who he is and what is his position in life or to shake his credit by injuring his character although the answer to such questions might tend directly or indirectly to criminate him, or might expose or tend directly or indirectly to expose him to a penalty or forfeiture.

It further provides that under given circumstances it shall not be permissible to, adduce evidence or to put questions in the cross-examination of the victim as to the general immoral character, or previous sexual experience, of such victim with any person for proving such consent or the quality of consent.

Clause 150 of the Bill relates to circumstances when witness to compel to answer.

It is proposed that if any such question relates to a matter relevant to the suit or proceeding, the provisions of clause 137 shall apply thereto.

Clause 151 of the Bill relates to the Court to decide when question shall be asked and when witness compelled to answer and in exercising its discretion, the Court shall have regard to the considerations provided under this clause.

Clause 152 of the Bill relates to question not to be asked without reasonable grounds.

It is proposed to provides that no such question as is referred to in clause 151 ought to be asked, unless the person asking it has reasonable grounds for thinking that the imputation which it conveys is well-founded.

Clause 153 of the Bill relates to procedure of Court in case of question being asked without reasonable grounds.

It provides that the Court is of opinion that any question was asked without reasonable grounds, it may, if it was asked by any advocate, report the circumstances of the case to the High Court or Other authority to which such advocate, is subject in the exercise of his profession.

Clause 154 of the Bill relates to indecent and scandalous questions.

It provides that the Court may forbid any questions or inquiries which it regards as indecent or scandalous, although such questions or inquiries may have some bearing on the questions before the Court, unless they relate to facts in issue, or to matters necessary to be known in order to determine whether or not the facts in issue existed.

Clause 155 of the Bill relates to questions intended to insult or annoy.

It provides that the Court shall forbid any question which appears to it to be intended to insult or annoy, or which, though proper in itself, appears to the Court needlessly offensive inform.

Clause 156 of the Bill relates to exclusion of evidence to contradict answers to questions testing veracity.

It is proposed to provide that when a witness has been asked and has answered any question which is relevant to the inquiry only insofar as it tends to shake his credit by injuring his character, no evidence shall be given to contradict him; but, if he answers falsely, he may afterwards be charged with giving false evidence.

It further provides that if a witness is asked whether he has been previously convicted of any crime and denies it, evidence may be given of his previous conviction and if a witness is asked any question tending to impeach his impartiality, and answers it by denying the facts suggested, he may be contradicted.

Clause 157 of the Bill relates to question by party to his own witness.

It provides that the Court may, in its discretion, permit the person who calls a witness to put any questions to him which might be put in cross-examination by the adverse party.

It further provides that nothing in this clause shall disentitle the person so permitted under sub-clause (*1*), to rely on any part of the evidence of such witness.

Clause 158 of the Bill relates to impeaching credit of witness.

It provides that how the credit of a witness may be impeached in by the adverse party or with the consent of the Court.

It further explains that a witness declaring another witness to be unworthy of credit may not, upon his examination-in-chief, give reasons for his belief, but he may be asked his reasons in cross-examination, and the answers which he gives cannot be contradicted, though, if they are false, he may afterwards be charged with giving false evidence.

Clause 159 of the Bill relates to questions tending to corroborate evidence of relevant fact, admissible.

It provides that a witness whom it is intended to corroborate gives evidence of any relevant fact, he may be questioned as to any other circumstances which he observed at or near to the time or place at which such relevant fact occurred, if the Court is of opinion that such circumstances, if proved, would corroborate the testimony of the witness as to the relevant fact which he testifies.

Clause 160 of the Bill relates to former statements of witness may be proved to corroborate later testimony as to same fact.

It provides that in order to corroborate the testimony of a witness, any former statement made by such witness relating to the same fact, at or about the time when the fact took place, or before any authority legally competent to investigate the fact, may be proved.

Clause 161 of the Bill relates to matters may be proved in connection with proved statement relevant under clause 26 or 27.

It is proposed that whenever any statement, relevant under clause 26 or 27, is proved, all matters may be proved either in order to contradict or to corroborate it, or in order to impeach or confirm the credit of the person by whom it was made, which might have been proved if that person had been called as a witness and had denied upon cross-examination the truth of the matter suggested.

Clause 162 of the Bill relates to refreshing memory of the witness.

It provides that a witness may, while under examination, refresh his memory by referring to any writing made by himself at the time of the transaction concerning which he is questioned, or so soon afterwards that the Court considers it likely that the transaction was at that time fresh in his memory and further a witness may refresh his memory by reference to any document, he may, with the permission of the Court, refer to a copy of document.

It further provides that the Court be satisfied that there is sufficient reason for the non-production of the original and an expert may refresh his memory by reference to professional treatises.

Clause 163 of the Bill relates to testimony to facts stated in document mentioned in clause 162.

It provides that a witness may also testify to facts mentioned in any such document as is mentioned in clause 162, although he has no specific recollection of the facts themselves, if he is sure that the facts were correctly recorded in the document.

Clause 164 of the Bill relates to right of adverse party as to writing used to refresh memory.

It provides that any writing referred to under the provisions of the two last preceding clauses shall be produced and shown to the adverse party if he requires it; such party may, if he pleases, cross-examine the witness thereupon.

Clause 165 of the Bill relates to production of documents.

It provides that a witness summoned to produce a document in possession or power, bring it Court notwithstanding any objection which there may be to its production or to its admissibility.

It further provides that the Court, if it sees fit, may inspect the document, unless it refers to matters of State, or take other evidence to enable it to determine on its admissibility and if for such a purpose it is necessary to cause any document to be translated, the Court may, if it thinks fit, direct the translator to keep the contents secret, unless the document is to be given in evidence and, if the interpreter disobeys such direction, he shall be held to have committed an offence under section 198 of the Bharatiya Nyaya Sanhita, 2023.

It also provides that no Court shall require any communication between the Ministers and the President of India to be produced before it.

Clause 166 of the Bill relates to giving, as evidence, of document called for and produced on notice.

It provides that when a party calls for a document which he has given the other party notice to produce, and such document is produced and inspected by the party calling for its production, he is bound to give it as evidence if the party producing it requires him to do so.

Clause 167 of the Bill relates to using, as evidence, of document production of which was refused on notice.

It provides that when a party refuses to produce a document which he has had notice to produce, he cannot afterwards use the document as evidence without the consent of the other party or the order of the Court.

Clause 168 of the Bill relates to Judge's power to put questions or order production.

It provides that the Judge may, in order to discover or obtain proof of relevant facts, ask any question he considers necessary, in any form, at any time, of any witness, or of the parties about any fact; and may order the production of any document or thing; and neither the parties nor their representatives shall be entitled to make any objection to any such question or order, nor, without the leave of the Court, to cross-examine any witness upon any answer given in reply to any such question.

It further provides that the judgment must be based upon facts declared by this Adhiniyam to be relevant, and duly proved and this clause shall not authorise any Judge to compel any witness to answer any question, or to produce any document which such witness would be entitled to refuse to answer or produce under given circumstances.

Clause 169 of the Bill relates to no new trial for improper admission or rejection of evidence.

It provides that the improper admission or rejection of evidence shall not be ground of itself for a new trial or reversal of any decision in any case, if it shall appear to the Court before which such objection is raised that, independently of the evidence objected to and admitted, there was sufficient evidence to justify the decision, or that, if the rejected evidence had been received, it ought not to have varied the decision.

Clause 170 of the Bill relates to repeal and savings.

It provides that notwithstanding such repeal, if, immediately before the date on which this Adhiniyam comes into force, there is any application, trial, inquiry, investigation, proceeding or appeal pending, then, such application, trial, inquiry, investigation, proceeding or appeal shall be dealt with under the provisions of the Indian Evidence Act, 1872, as in force immediately before such commencement, as if this Adhiniyam had not come into force.

248TH REPORT ON BHARATIYA SAKSHYA BILL, 2023 - PARLIAMENTARY STANDING COMMITTEE ON HOME AFFAIRS - OBSERVATIONS/ RECOMMENDATIONS - AT A GLANCE

The Committee takes note of the efforts of the Ministry of Home Affairs and the Ministry of Law & Justice in undertaking the mammoth task of drafting new legislations in an attempt to have comprehensive criminal laws. The extensive consultations and threadbare discussions undertaken in the drafting process have been reflected in the Bills that have imbibed Indian thought process and the Indian soul. A comprehensive review of India's legal system was the need of the hour to bring it on par with the contemporary aspirations of the people. Having taken a citizen-centric approach, these Bills serve as a reassurance to the Indian citizens. The Committee appreciates the combined efforts of the Ministries in reviewing 3,200 suggestions and thereby drafting comprehensive amendments to the Indian Penal Code, 1860, Code of Criminal Procedure, 1973 and the Indian Evidence Act, 1872.

(Para 2.7)

CLAUSE 1 - Short title, application and commencement

The Committee notes the wording of Article 348 of the Constitution of India which says that language to be used in the Supreme Court and in the High Courts, as well as for acts, bills and other legal documents shall be in English language. The Committee finds that as the text of the Bill is in English, it does not violate the provisions of Article 348 of the Constitution. The Committee is satisfied with the response of the Ministry and holds that the name given to the proposed legislation is not in violation of Article 348 of the Constitution of India.

(Para 4.2.2)

The Committee takes note of the submission of stakeholders and is of the opinion that the addition of the words "in the Official Gazette" in this clause will make the provision in tune with similar provisions in all other legislations. The Committee, therefore, recommends that the words "in the Official Gazette" may be inserted after the word "notification" in this clause.

(Para 4.2.5)

CLAUSE 2 - Definitions

The Committee deliberated at length regarding the inclusion of the words "any information" in the definition of evidence. The Committee opines that inclusion of "any information" along with "statement" in the same line may cause complications in its interpretation. The Committee, therefore, recommends that the words "any information" may be deleted in this clause to avoid such complications.

(Para 4.3.2)

CLAUSE 3 - Evidence may be given of facts in issue and relevant facts

The Committee examined the text of this clause along with the corresponding section of the Indian Evidence Act, 1872 and it observes that the particular reference made in illustration (*b*) pertains to the "Code of Civil Procedure" and not the Bharatiya Nagarik Suraksha Sanhita, 2023. The Committee, therefore, recommends that "the Bharatiya Nagarik Suraksha Sanhita, 2023" in illustration (*b*) may be replaced with "Code of Civil Procedure".

(Para 4.4.2)

CLAUSE 26 - Cases in which statement of facts in issue or relevant fact by person who is dead or cannot be found, etc., is relevant

The Committee examined in detail the submission made before the Committee and it observes that the parallel section of clause 26 in the Indian Evidence Act, 1872 *i.e.*, section 32 has no mention of "facts in issue" and only uses "relevant facts". The Committee also notes that "facts in issue" and "relevant facts" have a distinct connotation in judicial parlance and cannot be used interchangeably. The Committee opines that the use of "facts in issue" in this particular clause is erroneous. The Committee, therefore, recommends the Ministry to delete the words "facts in issue" in this clause.

(Para 4.5.3)

CLAUSE 48 - Evidence of character or previous sexual experience not relevant in certain cases

The Committee analysed the text of the clause and notes that section 376A of the Indian Penal Code, 1860 corresponds with section 66 of the Bharatiya Nyaya Sanhita, 2023. Further, section 53A of the Indian Evidence Act, 1872 corresponds with section 48 of the Bharatiya Sakshya Bill, 2023. Upon undertaking a comparative analysis of the two corresponding sections, the Committee observes that section 376A of the IPC which was referred to in section 53A of the IEA has been omitted from section 48 of the BSB. The Committee is of the opinion that "section 66" of the BNS should also be included in the offences referred to in this clause. The Committee, therefore, recommends that "section 66" is inserted after "section 65" to cover all the corresponding offences referred to in the BNS.

(Para 4.6.1)

The Committee further observes that the term "Bharatiya Nagarik Suraksha Sanhita, 2023" used in clause 48 of the Bill is incongruous since the offences referred under this clause are provided in the Bharatiya Nyaya Sanhita, 2023. The Committee, therefore, recommends that the words "the Bharatiya Nagarik Suraksha Sanhita, 2023" in clause 48 be replaced with "the Bharatiya Nyaya Sanhita, 2023" as it has been erroneously mentioned.

(Para 4.6.2)

CLAUSE 57 - Primary evidence

The Committee is of the opinion that safeguarding the authenticity and integrity of electronic and digital records acquired during the course of investigation is crucial due to the fact that such evidences are prone to tampering. The Committee takes into account the suggestion submitted before the Committee and recommends that a provision may be inserted to mandate that all electronic and digital records acquired as evidence during the course of investigation, are securely handled and processed through proper chain of custody. Appropriate provision in this regard may be made in the Bharatiya Nagarik Suraksha Sanhita, 2023.

(Para 4.7.2)

CLAUSE 62 - Special provisions as to evidence relating to electronic record

The Committee notes that "section 59" of the Bill relates to the documents to be proved by primary evidence while "section 63" of the Bill relates to admissibility of electronic records. The Committee agrees with the submission of stakeholders and observes that the appropriate reference in this clause should be "section 63". The Committee, therefore, recommends that "section 59" may be replaced with "section 63" to rectify error in cross-referencing.

(Para 4.8.2)

CLAUSE 77 - Proof of other official documents

The Committee observes that the sentence construction of this clause is incomplete as the word "officer" and the words "the legal custody" in fourth line are not appropriately connected. The Committee recommends that the word "having" may be inserted after the word "officer" to make the sentence grammatically correct.

(Para 4.9.1)

CLAUSE 138 - Accomplice

The Committee undertook a nuanced analysis of clause 138 and it observes that the original text of section 133, which is the corresponding section to this clause in the Indian Evidence Act, 1872 has been retained in this clause. However, a closer scrutiny of clause 138 and cross-analysing it with illustration (*b*) to clause 119(1) highlights evident contradiction between the two clauses which has not been rectified in the IEA. Clause 138 considers an accomplice as a competent witness against an accused person and uncorroborated testimony of an accomplice is made admissible in conviction. However, illustration (*b*) to clause 119(1) states otherwise and treats uncorroborated testimony of an accomplice as unworthy of credit. The Committee is of the opinion that such contradictions between clauses in the Bill may jeopardise efficacy of the Bill in its application. The Committee, therefore, recommends that suitable amendments in clause 138 may be made.

(Para 4.10.3)

CLAUSE 168 - Judge's power to put questions or order production

The Committee recommends that the word "Act" in the first proviso may be replaced with "Adhiniyam" as is already used in preceding portions of the Bill.

(Para 4.11.1)

SCHEDULE

CERTIFICATE

The Committee observes that the certificate in Part A of the schedule does not conform to the requirements prescribed in sub-clause (2) of clause 63. The Committee opines that such shortcomings may jeopardise the authenticity, reliability and integrity of the electronic and digital records submitted as evidence in the court of law and will be susceptible to tampering during handling of evidence. The Committee, therefore, recommends that the certificate in Part A may be amended to meet the requirements prescribed in clause 63, sub-clause (2)(*a*) to sub-clause (2)(*d*).

(Para 4.12.1)

The Committee also undertook a detailed examination of the text of each clause and noted that the Bill contains some cross-referencing errors. The Committee, therefore, recommends the Ministry to rectify such errors.

(Para 4.13)

The Committee agrees with the remaining clauses of the Bill without any changes. The Committee strongly believes that the changes brought in the Bill would reflect the growing importance of digital evidence and the need for a more comprehensive legal framework in line with 21st century technological advancements and societal changes.

(Para 4.14)

SPEECH OF HONOURABLE MINISTER OF HOME AFFAIRS AND MINISTER OF COOPERATION (SHRI AMIT SHAH) IN LOK SABHA ON 20-12-2023

I have taken initiatives in this historic House to bring about a paradigm shift in the three laws that are almost 150 years old and govern our criminal justice system in order to address the concerns of the people who care for Indianness, the Indian Constitution and the people of India. The Indian Penal Code, 1860 has been replaced by The Bharatiya Nyaya Sanhita, 2023, The Criminal Procedure Code, 1898 has been replaced by The Bharatiya Nagarik Suraksha Sanhita, 2023 and The Indian Evidence Act, 1872 has been replaced by the Bharatiya Sakshya Bill, 2023. Through this epochal change, an attempt has been made to add soul to our criminal justice system. Earlier on, there were laws with a centralised idea of awarding punishment and now victim-centric justice is going to evolve. Ease of Justice should be implemented through simple, consistent, transparent and accountable procedures. There will be fair, time-bound evidence-based speedy trials for enforcement, this is going to reduce the burden on courts and prisons and the conviction ratio is also going to increase. We have strengthened the prosecution on the basis of forensic science in the investigation and have made it mandatory to record the rape victim through audio-video recording. After the passing of this law, there will be a single type of justice system in the entire country and equality in the justice system. Accountability of the police has been fixed in many cases. Now it has been decided that information about arrested persons will have to be kept at every police station and a police officer will have to be made responsible for it. Right to compensation for loss has been given and zero FIR has been introduced. Now the court cannot withdraw any case without the permission of the victim and without hearing it, merely at the behest of the state. The responsibility of the police has been fixed to inform the victim about the progress of the investigation within 90 days. For the first time, we have completely abolished section 124 (A) of treason. Now, just by committing rape, all the sections of POCSO will be invoked through this Nyaya Sanhita and the culprit will be punished. In consensual rape cases, we have increased the existing age limit of 15 years to 18 years. Organised crime has also been defined for the first time. There was no special law for this. We have brought a new provision against mob lynching. We have made a provision to send the rape victim's report directly to the police station and court within seven days. There was no time limit for the charge sheet earlier. Now you cannot keep the charge sheet pending after 180 days, we have made this provision. The time limit as to when the proceedings will start before the Magistrate has also been fixed. We have made compulsory provision of video recording in all three evidence, search and seizure. Under this Bill, in order to improve the quality of investigation, so that investigation may be carried out using the scientific method and aiming at a 90 per cent conviction rate, we have made a provision that in all the crimes in which the punishment is more than seven years, the FSL team's visit has been made compulsory. We have come up with a new witness protection scheme. Every State will have to declare it. Thus, I can simply assure you that in the event of its implementation in all the Police Stations located across the length and breadth of the country, our judicial system shall turn out to be an ultra-modern judicial system in the world. We have made a whole host of provisions to this end. Under ICJS the integration of Forensic Science University, Police Stations, Department of Home Affairs, and Offices of the Public Prosecutor, Prisons and Courts under one umbrella through the application of Software and making them accessible online is in its last leg. This will be of huge relief for those citizens seeking justice and the delivery of justice shall be fast. Smart phones, Laptops, Messages, Websites and locational evidence have been brought within the definition of evidence. The accused, experts, and victims have been permitted their appearance before the court through electronic media and the entire procedure for the admissibility of electronic or digital records and its enforcement has been provided in the Bills. There has not been a definition of terrorism in the Code of Criminal Procedure so far which would allow the perpetrators to adopt the escape route. All such routes have since been done away with through this legislation. This Bill provides for the safety of those women who intend to hide the identity of the persons involved for the reasons of false promises of getting hitched. From now onwards, no one can escape the law. I want to assure the House on this count. As far as the devolution of powers to the police personnel is concerned, we have curtailed their powers also. On several counts, we have made enough provisions to keep a vigil on their functioning. We have tried to include a slew of provisions in the Bills to effect check and balance on their powers. I hold the firm conviction that all the three Bills viz. the Bharatiya Nyaya Sanhita, Bharatiya Nagarik Suraksha Sanhita and Bharatiya Sakshya Sanhita shall be evolving ones with elbow room for encapsulating the upcoming technology over at least a hundred years down the line and enough provisions to this effect figure in the Bills. Bharat is going to be a unique country to incorporate Forensic Science in law with so much severity and firmness. These are going to be entirely Indianised versions of laws by doing away with all the footprints hitherto in existence and of course, in a way, overtly indicative of the British colonial System and serving as reminders of our subjection during the British period. The spirit of our constitution is of doing justice to all and the Indian concept is founded on the award of punishment and dispensation of justice. Given that spirit, these laws are being made. I do seek the blessings of all the Hon'ble. Members and urge them to extend their support for the passage of the Bills.

The Bill, as amended, was passed.

APPENDIX

PROVISIONS OF OTHER ACTS REFERRED TO IN BHARATIYA SAKSHYA ADHINIYAM, 2023

INFORMATION TECHNOLOGY ACT, 2000

CHAPTER XIIA

EXAMINER OF ELECTRONIC EVIDENCE

Central Government to notify Examiner of Electronic Evidence.

79A. The Central Government may, for the purposes of providing expert opinion on electronic form evidence before any court or other authority specify, by notification in the Official Gazette, any Department, body or agency of the Central Government or a State Government as an Examiner of Electronic Evidence.

Explanation.—For the purposes of this section, "electronic form evidence" means any information of probative value that is either stored or transmitted in electronic form and includes computer evidence, digital audio, digital video, cell phones, digital fax machines.

GENERAL CLAUSES ACT, 1897

Definitions.

3. In this Act, and in all Central Acts and Regulations made after the commencement of this Act, unless there is anything repugnant in the subject or context—

** ** **

(*43*) "Political Agent" shall mean,—

(*a*) in relation to any territory outside India, the Principal Officer, by whatever name called, representing the Central Government in such territory; and

(*b*) in relation to any territory within India to which the Act or Regulation containing the expression does not extend, any officer appointed by the Central Government to exercise all or any of the powers of a Political Agent under that Act or Regulation;

** ** **

SUBJECT INDEX

Burden of proof